MW00528380

DIASPORIC BLACKNESS

DIASPORIC BLACKNESS

The Life and Times of
ARTURO ALFONSO
SCHOMBURG

Vanessa K. Valdés

Cover photograph by James Latimer Allen, ca. 1920s
Book design by Steve Kress

Published by State University of New York Press, Albany

© 2017 State University of New York

All rights reserved

Printed in the United States of America

No part of this book may be used or reproduced in any manner whatsoever
without written permission. No part of this book may be stored in a retrieval
system or transmitted in any form or by any means including electronic, elec-
trostatic, magnetic tape, mechanical, photocopying, recording, or otherwise
without the prior permission in writing of the publisher.

For information, contact State University of New York Press, Albany, NY
www.sunypress.edu

Production, Ryan Morris
Marketing, Fran Keneston

Library of Congress Cataloging-in-Publication Data

Names: Valdés, Vanessa Kimberly, author.
Title: Diasporic blackness : the life and times of Arturo Alfonso Schomburg /
   Vanessa K. Valdés.
Description: Albany, NY : State University of New York Press, [2017] | Includes
   bibliographical references.
Identifiers: LCCN 2016031412 (print) | LCCN 2017000321 (ebook) | ISBN
   9781438465135 (hardcover : alk. paper) | ISBN 9781438465159 (ebook) | ISBN
   9781438465142 (paperback : alk. paper)
Subjects: LCSH: Schomburg, Arthur Alfonso, 1874-1938. | African American
   historians—Biography. | Historians—United States—Biography. | African
   American book collectors—Biography. | Book collectors—Biography. | Puerto
   Ricans—United States—Biography. | African Americans—Relations with
   Hispanic Americans. | African Americans—Intellectual life—20th century. |
   African Americans—Race identity. | Puerto Ricans—Ethnic identity. |
   Caribbean Area—Intellectual life—20th century.
Classification: LCC E185.97.S36 V35 2017 (print) | LCC E185.97.S36 (ebook)
   | DDC 002.075092 [B]—dc23
LC record available at https://lccn.loc.gov/2016031412

10 9 8 7 6 5 4 3 2 1

For Arturo Alfonso Schomburg,
Robert Valdés Jr.,
and all men like them,
men who make more of themselves
than their circumstances dictate
and who defy categorization

CONTENTS

ILLUSTRATIONS

ACKNOWLEDGMENTS

I THANK GOD for the completion of this project, as well as all of His accompanying angels and saints. To my ancestors and orishas who accompany me, love me and protect me, and who guide all of my projects, I offer my highest praise and gratitude. To my parents, Iris Delia y Robert, who inspire me, always, and to my Madrina and best friend, Gina Bonilla, infinite thanks for your love and patience with me. Thank you to Leroy Martin Bess, Mercedes Robles, Ana Martinez, and Iya Dawn Amma McKen for all of your love and support through the years.

To the City College of New York, I thank you for the sabbatical year that allowed me to complete this project; I thank my friends, loved ones, and colleagues who understood and respected this much-needed time away.

I thank Doris Cintrón, interim dean of the Humanities and Arts Division of The City College of New York, for her support of this manuscript and its needed images; Moe Liu D'Albero, director of budget and operations in the Humanities and Arts Division of The City College of New York, and Thomas Lisanti, manager of Permissions and Reproduction Services of the New York Public Library. I thank Leo Peralta of the Humanities and Arts division for his technical assistance.

To Mary Yearwood, curator of the Photography and Print Division of the Schomburg Center for Research in Black Culture, thank you for your time and for guiding me in the joys of archival research. To her staff, including Michael Mery, Anthony Toussaint, and Linden Anderson for your assistance over the months as well.

To Steven G. Fullwood, curator of the Manuscripts and Rare Books Division of the Schomburg Center, thank you for your support and assistance from our first conversation.

To Chantel Clark, curator of Special Collections of the John Hope and Aurelia E. Franklin Library of Fisk University and inheritor of Schomburg's collection there, thank you for your candor about the nature of the archive, as well as your support of this project.

To the following scholars, whose work inspired me and carried this project to completion, my immeasurable gratitude: Elinor Des Verney Sinnette, Flor Piñeiro de Rivera, Lisa Sánchez González, Miriam Jiménez Román, Juan Flores, Antonio López, Jesse Hoffnung-Garskof, Camara Dia Holloway, Nicole Fleetwood, Shawn Michelle Smith, Mark Anthony Neal, Ifeoma Kiddoe Nwankwo, Ileana M. Rodríguez-Silva, Jossianna Arroyo, Virginia Sánchez Korrol, Edna Acosta-Belén, Nancy Raquel Mirabal, Sharifa Rhodes-Pitts, Lorrin Thomas, Silvio Torres-Saillant, Kevin Meeham, William Luis, Michelle Ann Stephens, Amy Kaplan, Hazel V. Carby, Victoria Núñez and Victoria Ortiz.

To Beth Bouloukos, thank you for your support of this project, and to the anonymous readers of this manuscript who offered insightful suggestions that demonstrated their support of this study. I thank Rafael Chaiken for his assistance with the digital files of the photographs included here. I thank Ryan Morris, Senior Production Editor, Alan V. Hewat, copyeditor, and Fran Keneston, Director of Marketing and Publicity, for their contributions to the production of this book.

I wish to acknowledge the following archives, without which the completion of this study would not have been possible: the Schomburg Center for Research in Black Culture of the New York Public Library; Yale University Library Manuscripts and Archives; Columbia University Rare Books and Manuscripts Library; the Center for Puerto Rican Studies / el Centro de Estudios Puertorriqueños (Centro) of Hunter College and the City University of New York; and the Special Collections of the John Hope and Aurelia E. Franklin Library of Fisk University.

To the Dark Room Collective, whose intellectual exchange and humor has motivated me to push further and deeper, thank you.

A los pueblos de Vega Baja y Manatí, Puerto Rico: desde ahí vienen mis antepasados y ahí todavía puedo encontrar miembros de las familias Valdés y Colón; ofrezco este estudio humildemente. Luz a todos ustedes que andan conmigo, acompañándome en este camino, y a todos sus descendientes. Pido su bendición.

To the Nuyorican community, thank you for your inspiration, always.

To children of the diaspora, speaking in tongues distinct from those spoken by our ancestors, living in spaces unimagined by our predecessors, thriving in ways inconceivable to them.

Thank you to the students of the City College of New York, past and present, who motivate me on a daily basis.

Support for this project was provided by a PSC-CUNY Award, jointly funded by the Professional Staff Congress and the City University of New York.

The portrait of Arturo Schomburg, as he appears in *Negro: An Anthology* (1934), edited by Nancy Cunard, is from the Manuscripts, Archives, and Rare Books Division, Schomburg Center for Research in Black Culture, the New York Public Library, Astor, Lenox and Tilden Foundations. All of the other portraits are from images found in the Photographs and Prints Division, Schomburg Center for Research in Black Culture, the New York Public Library, Astor, Lenox and Tilden Foundations.

INTRODUCTION

————◆————

THE SILENCE AND THE MEANING OF IT ALL

Imagine a boy living in the city of his birth and not knowing who was the most noted native painter! It is true the fact was recorded on a marble tablet duly inscribed and placed on the wall of a building where it could easily be read. However, the inhabitants of San Juan knew but little of the man thus honored. The white Spaniards who knew, spoke not of the man's antecedents. A conspiracy of silence had been handed down through many decades and like a veil covered the canvases of this talented Puerto Rican. Today we understand the silence and know the meaning of it all.

—ARTHUR SCHOMBURG, "José Campeche 1752–1809"

PUBLISHED IN 1934 in *Mission Fields at Home*, a journal published by the Sisters of the Blessed Sacrament, Arthur Schomburg (as his name appeared then) provides for his audience perhaps one of the earliest sketches about black Puerto Rican painter José Campeche written in English. With the subtitle "A Puerto Rican Negro Painter," Schomburg explicitly reveals that for him, there was no contradiction between national identification and race; one could be both Puerto Rican and black, as Campeche was, as he himself was. Schomburg exemplifies and fully inhabits a subjectivity that today has come to be identified as Afro-Latino, a man who is simultaneously of African and Hispanic heritage.[1] An analysis of Schomburg's life should not establish his as the exclusive Afro-Latinx experience to the exclusion of other lived experiences, particularly when considering those of women who shared his racial and ethnic heritage. Such an examination, however, is useful in attempting to understand the complexities of populations of African descent who arrive in the United States speaking the Spanish language, taking into consideration the specificities of historical context. Within this first paragraph of the chronicle that would introduce this eighteenth-century painter for many in his

1

audience, Schomburg makes a distinction in race, highlighting how "white Spaniards" deliberately concealed Campeche's African heritage, all the while celebrating his accomplishments. Schomburg's employment of the descriptor "white" acts not simply as a modification of the noun "Spaniard" but also as an act of emphasis: here he conveys to his audience that whiteness and white supremacy could be found on the Iberian peninsula and its former colonies. White supremacist thought is one that is invested in the maintenance of power for those who believe themselves to be of strictly European descent, irrespective of the fiction of homogenous whiteness on the European continent, and involves, among other actions, a deliberate absenting of achievements and accomplishments done by those deemed as "Other." Within the context of the Americas, the descendants of Africans, whether their progenitors had been enslaved or free, have been the primary targets of such systematic erasure. Hence, Schomburg's assertion, "Today we understand the silence and know the meaning of it all."[2] His response to the methodical expurgation of all evidence of black achievement was to gather documentation to the contrary, scouring bookstores for discarded texts written by and about men and women of African heritage, writing about such triumphs in brief newspaper and magazine articles as well as in essays shared within research societies and in published bibliographies, speaking publicly about such deeds, organizing lectures and exhibitions, and assembling the cultural products of these populations (pamphlets, books, art, music, and the like), crossing national and linguistic boundaries to include texts printed not only in English language but also others, such as French and Spanish.

Arturo Alfonso Schomburg is an innovative and pioneering figure of early-twentieth-century New York City, as a book collector and archivist; well known for those activities, he was also an autodidact, a prominent Freemason, a writer, and an institution builder. While many are aware that there is a library named after him in Harlem, they often have no idea about the man himself. They pause when learning that he was a black man, born and reared primarily in the Hispanic Caribbean, with some time during his adolescence spent in the Danish West Indies. Outside of specialists, most are unaware of his years-long involvement with the cause of Antillean liberation in the late nineteenth century, an activity that brought him in close contact with prominent Cuban and Puerto Rican intellectuals such as José Martí and Eugenio María de Hostos. Later, his collection served as an invaluable resource for such important scholars and writers as W. E. B. Du Bois, Carter G. Woodson, Alain L. Locke, James Weldon Johnson, Zora Neale Hurston, Langston Hughes, Eric Walrond, and Claude McKay, particularly during the years that encompassed the Harlem Renaissance and the New Negro Movement.

Himself the child to which he made reference in the Campeche sketch, Schomburg was born in San Juan, Puerto Rico, in 1874, one year after the abolition of slavery in the Spanish colony, to parents of Puerto Rican, German, and Danish West Indian heritage.[3] He migrated to New York City in 1891 at the age of seventeen, almost immediately becoming involved with the liberation cause of the Antillean colonies, joining the Partido Revolucionario Cubano (Cuban Revolutionary Party), as well as co-founding Las Dos Antillas (The Two Antilles) in 1892. Both groups disbanded after the conclusion of the Spanish-American War in 1898, with the United States annexing Puerto Rico and establishing a military government in its new protectorate of Cuba (which gained self-rule four years later, in 1902). While active in the fight for the independence of these Spanish colonies, Schomburg was also initiated into the Prince Hall Masons, eventually rising to become the Grand Secretary of the Prince Hall Grand Lodge of the State of New York in 1918. In 1911, he co-founded and served as secretary-treasurer of the Negro Society for Historical Research, an organization formed with the explicit mission of combating contemporary racial prejudice by finding documents attesting to the breadth of knowledge of Africans and their descendants in the United States. From 1920 until 1928, he served as president of the American Negro Academy of Washington D.C., an organization founded in 1897 and whose previous presidents included W. E. B. Du Bois. This institution, the "first major Black American learned society,"[4] was committed to the collection and dissemination of overlooked historical texts demonstrating the intellect of men of the African Diaspora. All of these organizations grappled explicitly with definitions of blackness, masculinity, citizenship, and nation; he engaged with these multiple discourses throughout his life, and his interpretation of said notions offers an assessment of Afro-Latinx subjectivity in the late nineteenth and early twentieth centuries in the United States and its commonwealth, Puerto Rico, and in so doing, sheds light on current formulations of this subjectivity in the present historical moment. This study explores not only Schomburg's thoughts on these subjects, as per his writings, but also his responses, as per his collecting, assembling, writing, and speaking, to the cultural milieu in which he lived. All of these activities are grounded in his identity as a man of African descent from a Spanish-speaking country, as an Afro-Latino.

Following the purchase of his private collection in 1926 by the Carnegie Corporation for the New York Public Library for $10,000, Schomburg used some of the funds to travel to Europe for several months, recovering documents from one of Spain's most prominent archives, the Archivo de las Indias, among others, and revealing the presence of men and women of African descent in the

Spanish-speaking Americas and the Iberian peninsula prior to the English establishment of Jamestown in 1619. He also salvaged the life stories of African-descended scholars, writers, artists, and church officials living in the sixteenth, seventeenth, and eighteenth centuries in the Americas and in Europe. In subsequent years, he continued to play an active role in the growth and direction of his collection as the chairman of the committee charged to oversee its management; he also persisted in donating books, prints, and other works, often without compensation for those contributions. From 1931 to 1932, he served as curator of the Negro Collection of the library at Fisk University, then as now one of the leading historically black colleges in the country. In Nashville, Tennessee, he worked alongside groundbreaking sociologists Charles S. Johnson and E. Franklin Frazier, men whose studies continue to be cited as foundational in the disciplines of African American studies and sociology as a whole. There at Fisk he established a collection that replicated what he had accomplished in New York by incorporating works about blacks both here in the United States as well as throughout the Americas and Europe. He returned to New York in 1932, serving as curator of his own collection within the 135th Street Branch Library (which would later become the Schomburg Center) until his death in 1938.

Throughout his life, in all of the circles in which he traveled, Schomburg remained Afro-Latino; that is, he actively thought of himself as such, as a black man born in Puerto Rico. He actively laid claim to the richness of the histories and cultures of the Spanish-speaking world. We see this in the books he collected, the articles he wrote, and the translations he provided from Spanish to English and vice versa. While this subject position has existed for millennia, dating back to peoples of African descent migrating to and living on the Iberian Peninsula, it has only attracted scholarly attention in the Western Hemisphere in the last few decades, influenced to a great extent by the U.S. civil rights movement. Schomburg not only took pride in his African heritage, in his blackness; more to the point, he took pleasure in it, reveled in it. Racial pride is characteristic of the first decades of the twentieth century: in the United States the aftermath of an aborted Reconstruction left hundreds of thousands of men and women fleeing the South, leaving behind the domestic terrorism of the Ku Klux Klan, and moving to the industrial North and Midwest in search for employment opportunities. In an era dominated by a politics of respectability, whereby an individual's personal comportment was thought to be a reflection of the larger group, Schomburg ascended the social ladder within the English-speaking black communities of New York City, becoming a much-admired figure. He achieved this primarily through his involvement with the Freemasons. He was initiated in 1892 in a lodge in Brooklyn that was predominantly Afro-Cuban named Sol de Cuba and affiliated with the Prince Hall Masons; more than twenty years later, he and his brothers petitioned that the lodge change the name to Prince Hall Lodge No. 38, reflecting the demographic shift in lodge membership.[5] Again, Schomburg did not abandon his heritage, taking it upon himself to translate official documents of the once mono-lingual Spanish lodge for his English-speaking brothers. He therefore served as a link for his fraternal organization, a conduit through which distinct contingencies learned about each other. This is a role that repeated in other realms of his life.

This study is long in the making. As a young woman growing up in New York City, I learned of the existence of the Schomburg Center for Research in Black Culture as a place to find research with everything having to deal with the global black experience. In college I learned that Mr. Schomburg was Puerto Rican; this was a critical moment, occurring in the same span of time when I began question-ing how my family had conceived of itself as simply Puerto Rican. In spite of the variety in skin tones of relatives, including within my immediate family, there were no qualifiers to a national identification with this island in the Caribbean. Schomburg's migration would be emblematic of that larger one which would occur primarily in the 1940s, 1950s, and 1960s, as hundreds of thousands would descend on the isle of Manhattan, as well as cities of the Northeast, rarely returning to the land of their birth. (The current historical moment is seeing a similar migratory wave to the mainland from the island, as tens of thousands leave Puerto Rico annually due to economic constraints, many of them moving to Florida.) Schomburg's negotiation first with the small Spanish-speaking communities in the greater New York City area and shortly thereafter with the larger African diasporic communities coming from the West Indies and the U.S. South meant a continuing engagement with how he defined himself. As readers, we can chart this process with how he names himself, as he goes from "Arturo Alfonso Schomburg" to "Arthur Schomburg" to "A. A. Schomburg," then returning to the name of his birth in his final years.

Seemingly lost when we speak about Schomburg are the many lives he lived, the many incarnations of this one life; instead, scholars often focus on one sole aspect: bibliophile and archivist of the Harlem Renaissance, friend to some of the most illustrious members of this artistic movement. Interestingly, this represents only a fraction of his existence. For the first third, he lived for the most part on a Spanish colony and then migrated to the metropolis on the mainland that was one of the centers of the independence movement to liberate that island (the other being Tampa, Florida). In the next two-thirds, he ascended the social ladder by becoming deeply involved with prominent institutions of the African American community, namely the Freemasons, as well as several of the historical societies

tasked with recovering a negated history of black excellence. In addition, he successfully established and curated not one but two collections of thousands of volumes
of books, pamphlets, and art, both of which serve as a testament to the diversity of
the global black experience. Again, in his public life, his African heritage is unques-
tioned; his Spanish-speaking heritage, for the most part, is overlooked and ignored.[6]

There is but one full-length study about Schomburg's life: Elinor Des Verney
Sinnette's *Arthur Alfonso Schomburg: Black Bibliophile and Collector* (1989); this
analysis references Dr. Sinnette as Schomburg's biographer. In addition to this
groundbreaking work, literary critic Lisa Sánchez González has written an article
about Schomburg, naming him a "Transamerican Intellectual," as well as has dedicated a chapter to him in her 2001 study *Boricua Literature: A Literary History of
the Puerto Rican Diaspora*, where she compares him to his contemporary and
fellow Puerto Rican William Carlos Williams. Finally, historian Jesse
Hoffnung-Garskof has written two indispensable articles about the historical times
in which Schomburg lived in his "The Migrations of Arturo Schomburg: On Being
Antillano, Negro, and Puerto Rican in New York 1891–1938" (2001) and "The
World of Arturo Alfonso Schomburg" (2010).

Diasporic Blackness complements these works by examining to a greater degree
each phase of Schomburg's life, from Puerto Rican revolutionary to institution
builder, from writer to collector and archivist. In addition, this work analyzes
Schomburg's portraits to take into consideration how his visual representation is
also a field in which he demonstrates resistance to dominant narratives about
blackness and about black men specifically.

Scholars over the years have debated his identity, often choosing to dissect it
so as to make sense of his interest in black history. Though everyone in his lifetime knew he had been born in Puerto Rico, and had been raised there, with some
time spent during his adolescence in St. Croix, people simply did not know how
to relate this to his later interests. There exists a story that as a child, either a school-
mate or a teacher commented in a classroom setting that black people had no
history; this censure of an entire race of people sparked a lifelong mission to dis-
prove this statement.[7] For some, emphasizing his years in the islands of St. Croix
and St. Thomas and indeed his family's connection to these islands allows them
to make sense of his passion for black history, given the history of migration from
the West Indian islands to the United States.[8] Winston James argues this point,
first in his 1996 article "Afro-Puerto Rican Radicalism in the United States:
Reflections on the Political Trajectories of Arturo Schomburg and Jesús Colón,"
and later in his 1998 book *Holding aloft the Banner of Ethiopia: Caribbean Radicalism
in Early Twentieth-Century America*. After a comparative historical overview of

the Hispanic Caribbean, James writes that Schomburg was exceptional as a "Puerto Rican black nationalist," for the following reasons: his mother was a foreigner, a "black migrant worker from St. Croix"; his paternal line, with which he apparently had no connection, had "strong northern European, Iberian roots"; that he was reared in the Virgin Islands with maternal relatives; and that he was, unlike the majority of the Puerto Rican community, Episcopalian rather than Roman Catholic.[9] For James, then, Schomburg's profile meant that he had a natural affinity for the African American community. In addition, there is the sense that a common language, English, more easily facilitated relationships, as did a common racial component. He overlooks Schomburg's deep connections to Puerto Rico; for this reason, the history of peoples of African descent on that island, official discourses regarding blackness there, and Schomburg's substantial involvement with the Antillean independence efforts of the late nineteenth century are the subject of the first chapter of this study.

When writing or talking about peoples of African descent in the Western Hemisphere, often the Spanish-speaking countries are left out of the equation. In the aftermath of the U.S. civil rights movement, academics in the United States began to produce scholarly works about Afro-Hispanic literature, history, and culture, recovering and promoting the cultural production of writers from the eighteenth, nineteenth, and twentieth centuries.[10] This study does not emphasize his time spent in what were the Danish West Indian islands of St. Thomas and St. Croix, nor does it examine a Caribbean subjectivity, though his undoubtedly is.[11] Rather, it accentuates his *afrolatinidad* specifically because in all of his activities—as a book collector, writer, and translator—he always highlights the Hispanic (i.e. Spanish-speaking) world, including Spain, the Hispanic Caribbean, and Central and South America.

ANXIETIES AND MISCONCEPTIONS ABOUT SCHOMBURG

In an essay offering his reflections on the multiplicities of identity, Silvio Torres-Saillant observes: "People of mixed ancestries seem to encounter the most difficulty since regimes of racial identity have often depended on the rule of homogeneity, the presumption that we have one root, not many, that, counterintuitive as it may sound, to claim more than one origin is to be less."[12] In the case of Arturo Schomburg, contemporaries and, indeed, scholars who have written after his death demonstrate an untenable apprehension when addressing him. One can attribute this anxiety not only to his biological origins but also to his unique standing within the spaces he inhabited. For most of his life, for example, this autodidact with little formal education beyond the secondary level was surrounded by, and interacted with, university-educated men, some of whom had gone on to earn doctorates and other advanced degrees. At the 135th Street Branch Library, the American Negro Academy, the Negro Society for Historical Research, Fisk University, at his numerous lectures throughout the country, Schomburg worked with scholars and academics with no hesitation; his curiosity granted him the ability to see beyond disciplinary boundaries, thereby allowing for more genuine learning. At one point in his later years, he proposed taking courses in library science on the master's level, only for the necessity of the formal acquisition of this certification to be questioned by his recommender, who knew him to be fluent in the realities of the field; his proposal was summarily rejected.[13]

Nevertheless, it is evident that Schomburg himself was considered a transgressive figure in his lifetime, one who threatened fixed notions not only of identity but also of a certain way of thinking that dictated there was only one way for things to be done and for people to exist. In his study of Afro-Cubans in the United States, Antonio López includes a commentary about Schomburg made by Afro-Cuban journalist Gustavo Urrutia, editor of "Ideales de una Raza" (Ideals of a Race), a column that appeared in the Cuban newspaper *El Diario de la Marina* in 1936. Schomburg had contacted Urrutia, who was in Cuba, relating how he had preserved the pages of Urrutia's column and praising him for writing about blacks from a decidedly Afro-Hispanic perspective. Urrutia in turn printed the letter in his page and then bemoaned the loss of heritage by men and women of the Hispanic Caribbean who move to the United States. López notes:

> Urrutia's attitude to Schomburg's writing—that is, to his letter-writing in English, [is] an Afro-Latino textual condition that…confirms the fear of an English-language taint. Urrutia tells readers that "Mr. Arthur Schomburg…hardly remembered Spanish" (*apenas recordaba el castellano*), and he emphasizes the point by remarking, just before quoting "the translation of this letter," that it has arrived "written in English," a "detail that urges us to push forward with the reconquest."[14]

For Urrutia, Schomburg's supposed loss of Spanish signaled that he had been swallowed whole by the imperial project of the United States; this was all the more distressing given that he had identified Schomburg to his readers as an *afroborinqueño* (an Afro-Boricua, or Puerto Rican of African heritage).[15] There is a sense, then, that as a black man of Puerto Rico, he should have resisted more forcefully José Martí's nightmarish monster by, at the very least, maintaining his Spanish.[16]

This sense of disloyalty is noted in many writings about Schomburg from the Puerto Rican perspective. In her incredibly important study *Puerto Rican Citizen: History and Political Identity in Twentieth Century New York City* (2010), Lorrin Thomas writes about Schomburg:

> Arturo Schomburg, who would become the most famous of these early Puerto Rican New Yorkers as a bibliophile and collector of a world-class library of Africana, took a different approach to navigating the city's racial landscape. After migrating to New York in 1891, Schomburg "crossed over" to the African American community that he married into in the early twentieth century, and lived the rest of his life largely separate from his compatriots.[17]

While it is important that she recognizes that his collection was one of "Africana," and not just focused on the African American experience, nevertheless, the implication is that, because he dared to live outside of (so far) officially recognized Puerto Rican enclaves in New York, he turned his back on his community.[18] There is an implication that Schomburg is a traitor who betrayed his people, rather than exploring the reasons why a phenotypically black man of Puerto Rican heritage would live with others who shared a similar physical appearance. In fact, Schomburg may have been representative of a certain segment of the Afro-Latinx migrant population in New York City: as Hoffnung-Garskof points out, the men of Sol de Cuba lodge in late-nineteenth-century Brooklyn more often than not married African American women, and those who were unmarried lived in spaces normally reserved for blacks. He writes: "These men seem to have found the space for independent social organizing through an alliance with African American organizations in the United States to be a welcome alternative to the ways color constrained their membership in the Cuban community."[19] They did not, then, leave their Spanish-Caribbean communities behind; rather, they found acceptance and ease of living in already existing African diasporic spaces.

Later in her study, Thomas writes: "The Puerto Rican bibliophile, collector, and historian Arturo Schomburg's actual 'migration' into New York's African American community, where he lived until his death in 1938, was an unusual if not unique embrace of African American identity; most Puerto Ricans struggled to define a place in the city somewhere between white and Black" (90). Here she tries to put a more positive spin on Schomburg's life, but again, her assertion that his physical movement marked a simultaneous embrace of African American identity and rejection of Puerto Rican identity suggests a duplicity in his dealings with the community of his birth. It also insinuates that he lived a life that was defiant in that it resisted strict adherence to ethnic identification; from a Puerto Rican perspective, he was daring precisely because of his dealings with the other African diasporic communities in New York City.

This perception of Schomburg as a polarizing figure is clear more than a half-century following his death; Flor Piñeiro de Rivera, the editor of the sole published collection of his writings, at times takes on a defensive stance in her introduction of him, almost apologizing for his life's work while making the case for his recognition to her presumably Puerto Rican audience (the collection was published in San Juan by the Centro de Estudios Avanzados de Puerto Rico y El Caribe in both English and Spanish). She writes that the conclusion of the Spanish-American War meant a change in Schomburg's priorities: "A la libertad antillana dedicó sus años mozos; a la libertad afroamericana consagrará el resto de su vida[20] [He who had dedicated his youth to the Antillean fight for freedom now devoted the rest of his life to the fight for freedom for the Afro-American.]"[21] She immediately reassures her audience that this did not mean the abandonment of the land of his birth: "Schomburg se trasladó a vivir en un vecindario negro, pero siguió interesado en la comunidad puertorriqueña[22] [Schomburg moved his residence to a black neighborhood but kept his concern for the Puerto Rican community]."[23] In fact, Schomburg demonstrated throughout his life that one can maintain numerous interests and passions, the majority of which had to do with the African diaspora as a whole, rather than just the populations that lived within the boundaries of the United States.

Nevertheless, Piñeiro de Rivera's tone becomes overly obsequious at moments in her portrait: "Schomburg dominaba el idioma español; de hecho, mejor que el inglés[24] [Schomburg mastered the Spanish language: in fact, he commanded its use better than English]."[25] One wonders how he could have avoided becoming skilled at the language spoken on the island where he was born and where he spent most of his childhood; admittedly, he spent some time in St. Croix as an adolescent, and most likely was introduced to English before migrating to the mainland at seventeen years of age; nevertheless, given that he lived in Cangrejos, the free black community of what is now Santurce, Puerto Rico, he could not have avoided speaking, learning, and being educated in the language of the Spanish colony in which he lived for the great part of the first seventeen years of his life.[26] Still, one sees a sense of national pride here, as his mastery of the Spanish language is meant to convey to her audience a mark of authenticity. She continues:

Así como Schomburg ama la lengua española, ama también la cultura hispánica y los pueblos hispanos. Por su condición de puertorriqueño y su dominio del idioma español, Schomburg se encomendó a sí mismo la misión de descubrir y difundir las contribuciones afrocaribeñas y afrohispanas a la civilización. No obstante, él no se limitó a esto sino que expandió su visión hasta alcanzar la dimensión universal de la experiencia negra.[27]

[Schomburg loved the Hispanic culture and the Hispanic nations as much as he loved the Spanish language. His identity as a Puerto Rican and his mastery of the Spanish language moved him to commit himself to the mission of discovering and making known the Afro-Caribbean and Afro-Hispanic contributions to civilization. His identity as a Black man took him even beyond this and expanded his vision to grasp the universal dimension of the Black experience.][28]

This passage reveals the difficulty, for some, in conceptualizing Afro-Latinx subjectivity; given that it defies how *latinidad* has been conceived historically, there is a temptation to bifurcate one's existence, so that an identification with one's nationality is perceived to be separate and distinct from one's racial and ethnic one. Her language here is stilted, evoking parts of a machine that don't quite gel together; nonetheless, this study coincides with the core of her statement, namely, that Schomburg's Afro-Latino subjectivity, his conception of himself as a diasporic man, granted him access to multiple spheres. Contrary to assertions that he abandoned his people, Schomburg augments the definition of the word *people* so that it included men and women across the African diaspora, including lands where they spoke Spanish.

This study argues that a reassessment of Schomburg and his life assists in unsettling the dominant historiography of Puerto Ricans in New York. Indeed, for several decades now, the leading figures of this narrative have been Bernardo Vega and Jesús Colón, two migrants, the first "white," the other of African descent, who migrated from Puerto Rico to New York in 1916 and 1917 respectively. Both Vega and Colón would recall the early years of the Puerto Rican *colonia* in written publications, Vega with his memoir and Colón with his newspaper columns.[29] By the time of their arrival, Schomburg had already lived in New York for almost two and half decades. All three of these men worked alongside tobacco workers in their youth, either on the island or in New York City. All three went on to become activists, in their own distinct ways; the erasure of Schomburg from mainland Puerto Rican historical narratives appears to stem primarily from his decision to live and thrive within English-speaking black communities.

Schomburg is but one person whose presence has been overlooked in renderings of the mainland Puerto Rican community in the last decades of the nineteenth century and the first ones of the twentieth: certainly, the role of Puerto Rican women of all ethnic heritages has been woefully understudied, in spite of the groundbreaking work of Virginia Sánchez Korrol, Edna Acosta-Belén, Félix V. Matos-Rodríguez, and Lisa Sánchez González. Two women who challenge the masculinist bent of this historiography are Luisa Capetillo and Pura Belpré. Born in 1879, five years after Schomburg, in Arecibo, Puerto Rico, Capetillo was raised by two autodidacts who ensured that their only child, though working-class, was well versed in the literature of the European masters.[30] Like Schomburg, Vega, and Colón, Capetillo worked with the *tabaqueros,* serving as a *lectora* (reader) in an Arecibo factory, and was active in organizing the workers.[31] She contributed to working-class and anarchist newspapers and magazines beginning in 1904 and went on to publish three books: *Ensayos libertarios* (1907); *La humanidad del futuro* (1910); and *Mi opinión* (1911), the latter of which is "considered the first feminist treatise in Puerto Rico and one of the very first in Latin America and the Caribbean."[32] Capetillo was exiled to New York in 1911, and after a year, moved on to Ybor City and Tampa, Florida, where she would live until 1915. Thereafter, she moved to Havana, Cuba, then moved back to Puerto Rico; after three years, she returned to New York, living there from 1919 until 1920, when she once again returned to the island of her youth, dying in 1922. Although never explicit about race in her writings, Capetillo challenged contemporary restrictions on womanhood, instead advocating for equality for women politically, economically, and socially. Commenting on her last publication, Matos Rodríguez writes: "In *Mi opinión*, Capetillo makes a case for the need to change radically all structures of social and economic domination so women could be truly liberated."[33]

Pura Belpré also called for radical change, though in her case, she advocated for children, particularly those born to Puerto Rican parents who had migrated to New York City and who therefore spoke both English and Spanish; these young charges, often from lower-income households, found in Belpré and the libraries in which she worked committed support to them as learners in the years prior to the establishment of bilingual education.[34] Born in Cidra, Puerto Rico, in 1902 to Puerto Rican parents of discernible African heritage, Belpré would travel to New York in 1920 to attend the wedding of an older sister; she would remain there for the rest of her life. Beginning in 1921, she worked at the 135th Street Branch Library for eight years, alongside Arturo Schomburg, after Ernestine Rose, the librarian of the branch, noticed a growing Spanish-speaking population in the area.[35] During these years Belpré would go on to become the first certified Puerto Rican librarian in the New York Public Library system. In an article examining the Puerto Rican presence in Harlem during the Harlem Renaissance, Victoria Núñez notes that there has been little attempt to connect the experiences of Schomburg and Belpré, despite their shared time at this branch, an extraordinary omission given the presence of two Afro-Latinxs in notable positions.[36] Nevertheless, Belpré's dedication to bilingual learners (as made evident in lectures maintained in her papers, which are stored at the Center of Puerto Rican Studies in New York) as well as to the maintenance of folktales of the island of her birth both in her oral presentations and in the books that she published have secured for Belpré a legacy in the field of children's literature: Latinx authors and illustrators whose works "best portray, affirm and celebrate Latino cultural experience" are granted the Pura Belpé Award by the American Library Association in an annual celebration.[37] Alongside Schomburg's, the stories of these women offer a hint at the rich breadth of narratives of Puerto Rican communities from the mainland awaiting recovery in local archives. There remains a great deal of work to be done in comprehending the complexities of this population.

Returning to the subject at hand, misgivings about Schomburg were very much present in his time and were held by his contemporaries, even by those who were close to him. In his study on the American Negro Academy, Alfred A. Moss Jr. includes a letter from October 1922 from John Edward Bruce, who was one of Schomburg's mentors. Born into slavery, Bruce was an autodidact who became a highly regarded journalist, creating such newspapers as the *Chronicle of New York* and the Yonkers *Weekly Standard*.[38] Together he and Schomburg co-founded the Negro Society for Historical Research in 1911, and Bruce served as one of two of Schomburg's recommenders for his admittance to the American Negro Academy in 1914. Schomburg's biographer Elinor Des Verney Sinnette characterizes the relationship between Schomburg and Bruce as that of a father and son.[39] Schomburg's second recommender for this academy was John Wesley Cromwell, newspaper editor, bibliophile, and another father figure to Schomburg; Cromwell, in fact, was the recipient of Bruce's 1922 letter.[40] Schomburg had been elected president of the American Negro Academy in December of 1920, with Cromwell serving as his secretary; still, these paternal figures who held deep affection for Schomburg believed a replacement should be sought for the position. Bruce wrote: "Our half-breed brethren have dual minds and they are not to be expected to think Black as did Alexander Crummell [founder of the ANA]. The head of the Academy should be a *seasoned* well equiped [*sic*] mentally Black scholar soaked from his toes to the outer surfaces of his caput in the ideas and ideals which grew the American Negro Academy" (italics in the original).[41] Sinnette calls attention to Bruce's pan-Africanist ideals, stating that he was explicitly a Race Man, "preaching and writing a doctrine of racial pride and solidarity while passionately advocating that Blacks obtain the best education possible, including a knowledge of their history."[42] More than two decades into their relationship, then, after Schomburg has written and spoken publicly and extensively about the African diaspora, has collected books by and about men and women of African descent for a number of organizations, including the Negro Society for Historical Research, of which Bruce was president, Schomburg's dedication and passion for the race were still susceptible to dismissal based on his biological origins.

Lisa Sánchez González counsels students of Schomburg's legacy wisely when she writes: "Like many (if not the majority) of the Americas' racialized, subaltern communities, Schomburg's intransigent transnational identifications followed the organic course of his lived experience."[43] While her use of "intransigent" may remind us of hegemonic definitions of identity that insist on one clear, defining identification, here she employs it as a means of expressing that Schomburg himself did not deny any part of his identity as an Afro-Latino, though he did not, of course, utilize that nomenclature. She continues:

> As a diasporic intellectual…Schomburg's imagined communities matched his historical displacement (vis-à-vis San Juan, the Antilles, Brooklyn, Africa, Latin America, Spain, and even Germany), and making sense of this displacement required not only documentation (his primary research) but also interruptions of the very concept of nationalist subjectivity so common to even more progressive academic discourses, then and now.[44]

Analyses of Schomburg's life and his life's work, therefore, necessarily call for an understanding of the particularities of his multiple identities.

AFRO-LATINX SUBJECTIVITY

"Afro-Latinx" itself is a construction that conveys that *lo africano*, the African element, is a modification of *latinidad* itself; on a very basic level, *latinidad*, then, continues to be constructed, read, thought of, conflated with whiteness. White supremacist thought dictates that whiteness, that which is conflated specifically with Eurocentrism, remains unmatched in all realms. In a Hispanic context (using the colonial modifier deliberately), whiteness has been stretched to accommodate "impure," uncomfortable, and inconvenient facts, such as the millennia-long encounters with human beings from the African continent, who themselves are all categorized as black despite their own diversity. The construction of *afrolatinidad* remains unsatisfying and inadequate because it does not yet convey that Africanness was constitutive of the Latinx in the Western Hemisphere. This also speaks to the continued renewal and redefining of "Latinx," a signifier whose signification remains in development, in both English and Spanish.

Whereas "Latinx" used to refer solely to inhabitants of the United States whose family members at some point spoke Spanish, in this the second decade of the twenty-first century, the term is becoming inclusive of all Spanish-speaking peoples, irrespective of national origin. "Latinx," then, may be succeeding where "black" hasn't yet, in that in popular parlance, the usage of "black" continues to imply, and as Carole Boyce Davies writes, to be collusive with, U.S. hegemony.[45] At the core of Afro-Latinx scholarship is an attempt at highlighting the overlooked, ignored, and often maligned presence of peoples of African descent; it is also almost always a call for the redefining of *latinidad*. The expansion of the use of "Latinx" as a term is promising; however, it necessarily must include, not only recognize or acknowledge but fully incorporate, the African and the indigenous. Until then, we will continue to qualify the term with the use of the prefix, inadequate though it may be.[46]

In their groundbreaking anthology, *The Afro-Latin@ Reader: History and Culture in the United States* (2010), Miriam Jiménez Román and Juan Flores dispel misgivings about the term, defining it as "people of African descent in Mexico, Central and South America, and the Spanish-speaking Caribbean, and by extension those of African descent in the United States whose origins are in Latin America and the Caribbean."[47] In their estimation, the categorization of this subject position is one that serves as a marker of resistance: "Just as in Latin America, where the prefix Afro has been critical in challenging homogenizing effects of national and regional constructs, so in the United States the term 'Afro-Latin@' has surfaced as a way to signal racial, cultural, and socioeconomic contradictions

within the overly vague idea of 'Latin@.'"[48] For them, then, "Afro-Latin@" is a signifier of difference, one that calls attention to material and distinct inequalities
within the imagined community that is the Latinx community, both within the
borders of the United States and in fact, throughout the Americas.[49]

In addition to a marker of divergence, they bring to light an impulse of social
justice that occurs when the word is used: "In addition to reinforcing those ever-ac-
tive transnational ties, the Afro-Latin@ concept calls attention to the anti-Black
racism within the Latin@ communities themselves."[50] *Afrolatinidad*, then, is a
subjectivity that recognizes, acknowledges, and celebrates multiplicity, calling
attention to difference within communities, whereby Blackness has historically
been marginalized in the name of calls for national and regional unity. Jiménez
Román and Flores make the point that this marginalization has occurred throughout the hemisphere, including during interactions with black English-speaking
communities in the United States: "It is also a standing challenge to the African
American and English-language monopoly over Blackness in the U.S. context,
with obvious implications at a hemispheric level."[51] This is not to dismiss very real
alliances made with other African diasporic communities in the United States,
including that of the English-speaking populations. Still, as a marker of difference,
"Afro-Latin@," denotes distinction from and serves as a challenge to all communities perceived as homogeneous; diasporic in construction, this formulation
ignores national boundaries, emphasizing instead a population brought together
by means of shared cultural traits as well as shared histories of discrimination.
"Shared" should not, however, imply "unchanging"; as critic Stuart Hall reminds
us, there is great value in exploring those deep issues of difference alongside those
of similarity, which places emphasis on the dynamic state that is identity formation.[52]

For his part, Antonio López defines *afrolatinidad* in terms of overlap, as racialized discourses of identity simultaneously and concomitantly affect men and
women of African descent whose heritage can be traced to Latin America and the
Caribbean. He writes:

> Central to afrolatinidad is the social difference that Blackness makes
> in the United States: how an Anglo white supremacy determines the
> life chances of Afro-Latinas/os hailed as Black and how a Latino white
> supremacy reproduces the colonial and postcolonial Latin American
> privileging of *blanco* over *negro* and *mulato* (mixed-race) identities,
> now on behalf of white Latinas/os who may themselves face Anglo
> forms of racializing discrimination.[53]

Critical to this formulation is the geographic specificity of it, as *afrolatinidad,* for López, is applicable to life in the United States. In the rest of the Americas, the construction of subjectivities reflecting African heritage has been slowly moving away from a national identification to a more open-ended, that is to say, diasporic one, so that one hears the use of the term *afrodescendiente,* for example. Within the United States, the rise of populations of Latin American and Caribbean heritage has meant the consolidation of various national identities, resulting in the creation of the "Latinx."[54] Afro-Latinxs therefore have to contend with racialized systems of thought not only of their own countries but also, simultaneously, those of the United States. As López argues, there is a "mutual instantiation of Afro-Latino, African American, and white-Latino identities in the context of hemispheric logics of white-supremacist, colonial domination: whether one is white enough or the right kind of white, or less Black or the right kind of Black, to receive or be denied rights and advantages, based on how one speaks (or does not) in English, Spanish, or both."[55]

Implicit in both of these conceptualizations of Afro-Latinx subjectivity is a recognition of a performance of race that is distinct from constructs based on national identity. As Nicole Fleetwood notes, "The words *performance* and *performing* in academic studies are popular metaphors and strategies especially in studies of gendered and racialized embodiment. Performance has been used as interventionist strategies to shake loose subject formation from fixed notions of identity categories."[56] Both race and national identities are admittedly social constructs, ones that are often defended vehemently in the face of perceived threats to agreed-upon definitions of these notions. In Schomburg's case, he seemingly does not "perform" either his blackness or his Puerto Ricanness to the satisfaction of others. When referencing him, there is the idea that he betrayed or abandoned his Puerto Rican compatriots in favor of a perceived monolithic African American community. For some members of the heterogeneous black communities of African Americans and West Indians in New York, he was someone who came with "knowledge of an area relatively new to them, the Spanish-speaking Caribbean."[57] As Claude McKay posited after his death: "Perhaps a psychologist might have been interested in plumbing him to discover whether the Spanish-European or the African-West Indian was uppermost in his character."[58] Schomburg resisted the impulse to divide his identity in this way, instead embracing his many facets. In the face of attempts to make sense of different aspects of his identity in relation to distinct geographic regions, Schomburg continued his myriad professional roles, always keeping in focus the goal of recovering and promoting the histories of the African diaspora.

The element of the performative in conjunction with the expression of racial and ethnic identity introduces a conversation about that which is recognizable as such. Writing about black expressive culture, E. Patrick Johnson observes:

> [It] has, until recently, been illegible and unintelligible to the undiscerning eyes and ears, and perhaps minds, of some scholars. The subjugated knowledge embedded within black expressive culture, therefore, is not always ameliorated by those who lack the cultural capital to read it or who are altogether disinterested in these forms.[59]

Johnson's observation about the role of "undiscerning eyes and ears" is key: the history of the United States has demonstrated that, historically, ethnic identity has been subsumed within racial identity once those racial categories have been established. "Latinx" as a category has posed a challenge to this construction precisely because it is an ethnic identifier that must necessarily recognize its own multiracial and multinational composition. Blackness, already marginalized within Hispanic contexts, has the opportunity to come to the fore within the United States context; the possibility of the actualization of this potential is at times dependent on the legibility or illegibility of the individual as Afro-Latinx, that is, if the person is read as *both* black *and* Hispanic.

In his 2013 study *Looking for Leroy: Illegible Black Masculinities*, Mark Anthony Neal also engages with this question of recognizability; his project highlights the troubling aspects of the construction of black masculinity in the United States. Aiming to problematize the formulas that allow for the flattening of black masculinity as a subject position, Neal examines figures such as Luther Vandross and Jay-Z in order to emphasize "the radical potential of rendering 'legible' black male bodies—those bodies that are all too real to us—illegible, while simultaneously rendering so-called illegible black male bodies—those black male bodies we can't believe are real—legible."[60] In the case of Arturo Schomburg, his physical appearance made him legible as a man of African descent, while his ethnic identity or, rather, his insistence in claiming and honoring his ethnic identity through his collecting, his writings, and his professional activities, nullified this legibility, or at least qualified it, for some. While his physical appearance may have made him legible as visibly of African descent to his contemporaries, perhaps even his sound, a voice that may have carried resonances of his Caribbean youth, may have complicated that perception, rendering him illegible for some. Afro-Latinx subjectivity, then, is constructed in response to shifting circumstances that influence whether one's blackness *and* one's *latinidad,* both, concurrently, are decipherable to members of the surrounding communities.

DIASPORA

Like many black subjects, Arturo Schomburg is a diasporic being, carrying within him not only narratives of his own migration but also that of his family. His paternal heritage is Puerto Rican, by way of Germany, his father's family having been on the island since the first decades of the nineteenth century; his mother's family originates in what would become the U.S. Virgin Islands, in St. Croix.[61] A discussion about diaspora is therefore not only apropos given his passion as a collector in the global black experience but also in light of his own multiplicities. In the introduction of their study on black performance theory, Thomas F. DeFrantz and Anita Gonzalez observe: "Diaspora is continual; it is the unfolding of experience into a visual, aural, kinesthetic culture of performance. Like skin, it is porous and permeable, flexible and self-repairing, finely spun and fragile. And like skin on a body, diaspora palpably protects us. We wrap ourselves in its possibilities, and they remind us of impossible connectivities."[62] While they are admittedly writing about the connections that link black performances around the world, nevertheless they offer insight into conceptualizations of diaspora itself. Rather than disparate groupings of people that may share a distant genetic connection but still organize their identities around conceptions of the nation-state, for example, their notion of diaspora is something that is much more intimate. Unlike the rigidity of fixed boundaries, diaspora transcends limitation and restraint; it is inherently transgressive, offering an infinite source of potential.

DeFrantz and Gonzalez also offer: "Diaspora also serves as a process of unification. It brings together collective experiences around particular issues, forces, or social movements. Like all alliances, it is strategic."[63] Schomburg never explicitly uses the word *diaspora* in his work, and yet his organizing principle of bringing together artifacts that testify to the achievements and successes of men and women of African descent around the world is clearly established with the goal of combating international white supremacist thought that Africans and their descendants are primitive beings without a history. His work directly confronts a train of thought that preceded the Enlightenment but that gained currency with Hegel and other philosophers of the eighteenth century.

In his study *In Search of the Black Fantastic: Politics and Popular Culture in the Post–Civil Rights Era* (2008), Richard Iton takes the conversation about diaspora one step farther, stating clearly: "Accordingly, beyond doubtful, we might assert that for nonwhites—and for all others, *nous sommes tous des sans-papiers*—nationality is not only doubtful and improbable but indeed impossible and, furthermore, that these impossibilities themselves might be seen as desirable and appealing."[64] Once again, the allure of framing one's identity around a diasporic consciousness is brought to the fore, as the alternative has, in Iton's mind, proven untenable for people not only of African descent but for all who reside outside of whiteness. He proposes that we think of diaspora as an

> anaformative impulse, in other words, that which resists hierarchy, hegemony, and administration....This would require a politics not reducible to the language of citizenship and governance, and, accordingly, allergic to the sensibilities underlying the national (and, to some extent, the inter*national* and trans*national* to the degree that they depend on or re-inscribe the nation-state). Moreover, it would mean being suspicious of homeland narratives and indeed any authenticating geographies that demand fixity, hierarchy, and hegemony. Conceiving of diaspora as anaform, we are encouraged, then, to put (all) space into play.[65]

The call for a diasporic understanding of the world, then, is one that threatens to upend political ontologies grounded in nineteenth-century renderings of the modern nation-state. It is a novel inscription of power, so that systems of domination that currently stand could no longer function. With his formulation, Iton identifies the underlying menace of appeals of "home"; with the creation of the modern nation, inhabitants of lands, certainly men and women of African descent, have often been manipulated to betray their own best interests in order to further the cause of the nation.

Iton's understanding of diaspora also jeopardizes what he calls the "circulation and primacy of national Blacknesses"; as per this formulation, all understandings of the world, including hegemonic measurements of authentic racial identity, could possibly cease to exist. In his collecting, indeed in all of his activities, Schomburg was not restricted or confined to a simple single rendering of his identity; his personal correspondence reveals his attempts at gathering articles of knowledge from black populations found throughout the world, rather than sources written in one national language or from one particular geographic region. Schomburg is born and raised in the Caribbean, a site that engenders multiple interpretations of the world due to the numerous peoples, languages, cultures that live there; more specifically, he is born into an imperial schema that was in its last throes of existence.[66] He witnessed firsthand societal changes in the island of his birth, as he came into the world a year after the abolition of slavery; he therefore saw the manner in which a formerly enslaved segment of the population grappled with the social, economic, and political ramifications of independence. While his mother Maria Josefa was a free woman of the Danish West Indies, where slavery had been abolished a quarter of a century earlier, she was also a migrant laborer who had left family behind in order to settle in Puerto Rico. Schomburg from an early age understood the very real workings of the migratory diasporic existence.

Brent Hayes Edwards explores differing aspects of diaspora in a series of writings throughout his career; in an article about Langston Hughes he reminds us: "There is never a first diaspora: there is never an originary, single dispersion of a single people, but instead a complex historical overlay of a variety of kinds of population movement, narrated and valuated in different ways and to different ends."[67] Like Iton, Edwards does away with the origin narrative, substituting it instead with one that emphasizes being in the midst of movement. Not the beginning or the end, but rather, the middle, the in-process, the ongoing and unending. Edwards calls attention to the innate promise of diaspora when he asks "whether diaspora can be said to involve not only a relation to deprivation and dispossession, but also a particular link to possibility and potential."[68] Whereas a focus on origin almost necessarily summons a discourse of loss and destabilization, here he proposes an alternate perspective, one that compels a dynamic rendering of movement and migration. In this way, Edwards recalls Stuart Hall's formulation of cultural identity, in relation to diaspora, as one that "is a matter of 'becoming' as well as of 'being.'"[69]

The ongoing process that is the cultivation of one's identity in relation to a group irrespective of national identification does not necessarily mean an instantaneous harmony based on perceptions of shared biological characteristics. On the contrary, as Edwards writes in his influential study, *The Practice of Diaspora: Literature, Translation, and the Rise of Black Internationalism* (2003), the employment of *diaspora* as a theoretical framework "forces us to articulate discourses of cultural and political linkage only through and across difference in full view of the risks of that endeavor."[70] Rather than argue that Schomburg's blackness was one that was fully embraced without obstruction during his lifetime, this study emphasizes instead his differences, both perceived and existent, in order to highlight some of the mechanisms at play in the construction of Afro-Latinx subjectivity.

This subject position is one that is the most apt for this migrant of African descent of the Hispanic Caribbean who arrives on the mainland in the last decade

of the nineteenth century. In her study on nineteenth-century texts and their rev-
elations about disparate notions of identity by peoples of African descent in the
United States, Cuba, and the British West Indies, Ifeoma Kiddoe Nwankwo reminds
the reader how the impact of the Haitian Revolution forced these men and women
to define themselves in relation to the state. In the face of widespread fear on the
part of colonizers that armed rebellion was a very real possibility, Africans and
their descendants, enslaved and free, were obligated to clarify for themselves their
affiliation with that event and, to a greater extent, with the societies in which they
lived. Nwankwo writes:

> Race, nation, and humanity were three major referents through which
> individuals defined themselves and others in their world (the Atlantic
> world), but only one of the three referents was allowed people of African
> descent—race. Consequently, this population essentially had to prior-
> itize, and choose which of the parameters denied them they most wished
> to challenge, and by extension which referent they most want to have
> the right to claim.[71]

Nwankwo's assertion that both a national and, on a more fundamental level, human
subjectivity, were denied peoples of African descent is important to remember
when contextualizing Schomburg in his historical period. As we will see in the
first chapter of this study, the islands where he spent his childhood were politically incapable of offering a national subjectivity as all remained integral parts of
European imperial projects, Puerto Rico as part of the waning Spanish empire
and St. Croix and St. Thomas of the Danish one at the time of his birth. Considerations
of postabolition Danish West Indies remain outside the scope of this project;
however, postabolition Puerto Rico will be studied, given that he was born in 1874,
four years after the 1870 Moret Law freeing enslaved children born in 1868 as well
as enslaved men and women over the age of sixty, and one year after the Abolition
Law of 1873, which freed the remaining enslaved population on the island. This,
even though, as Virginia Sánchez-Korrol writes, "[b]y law, all others were forced
to work an additional three years as indemnity to their owners."[72] In his late teens
and early twenties, having already migrated to the United States, Schomburg played
an integral role in the fight for independence of the island of his birth; his relationship with said island, and the uneasy integration of its population of African
descent in the insular imaginary during its transition from a Spanish colony to
an unincorporated territory of the United States, is the subject of chapter 1. From
the perspective of this study, Schomburg is emblematically Afro-Latinx; as Lisa

Sánchez González writes: "Schomburg's legacy posits a challenge to reconfigure transamerican subjectivity in a dynamic and highly politicized assessment of cultural history."[73]

TRANSLATION

In *The Practice of Diaspora*, Brent Hayes Edwards makes the point that it is unfeasible to write about diaspora without simultaneously addressing questions of translation, given that peoples of African descent speak languages other than English.[74] Though Schomburg was surrounded by other men and women of the Hispanic Caribbean throughout his life, scholarship written on him has sometimes given the impression that he was the sole representative of the region. Undoubtedly, there are some circles, such as the American Negro Academy, where he was in the distinct minority; additionally, there are instances in which Schomburg took on greater responsibilities due to his proficiency in the languages of Spanish and French, such as his role of translator within his Masonic lodge. In his professional life, he had been named head of the foreign division of the mailing department at Bankers Trust and therefore had greater opportunity to communicate with friends and colleagues internationally.[75] The role of translation in general, and of the translator in particular, then, is one of critical importance in this study.

To this end, I follow Vera M. Kutzinski, who writes of translation as a combination of "the act of moving oneself (*translatio*) with that of leading or carrying someone or something across some sort of divide (*traductio*)."[76] For Kutzinski, and Brent Hayes Edwards, translation does not mean a simple and direct identification of equivalent words and concepts in two languages; instead, both scholars emphasize that there are some ideas, some notions that escape facile rendition. While Hayes Edwards offers as a model of translation (and more broadly, of diaspora itself) one that puts emphasis on difference, Kutzinski instead puts forth the idea of languages that meet without combination or fusion of some kind, a praxis that is "at once performative and transformative."[77] For her, there exists at times the impulse to reduce cultural difference, an instinct that is to be resisted in scholarship if we are to grasp how people truly thought and lived. This study, then, emphasizes Schomburg's multiplicity, resisting the urge to flatten his experiences in honor of the range of roles he took on throughout his life.

Diasporic Blackness is an examination of the life's work of Arturo Alfonso Schomburg through the lens of Afro-Latinx subjectivity, with the aim of highlighting how this identity position assists us in understanding this current historical moment. The first chapter, "'*Patria y Libertad*': Schomburg and Puerto Rico," reveals that contrary to charges by of some of his countrymen that he abandoned the group to which he was born, an examination of Schomburg's work demonstrates an active and sustained interaction with his intellectual Puerto Rican and Cuban forefathers throughout his lifetime. After brief biographical sketches of important figures from both countries, the chapter moves to an analysis of discourses of blackness present in late-nineteenth-century postabolition Puerto Rico. The attention of the chapter next turns to his contributions to the Antillean war effort and his interaction with discourses of independence created in the mainland, in New York City. It ends with a reflection on the political state of Puerto Rico and its own continued troubling relationship with blackness and its population of African descent.

The second chapter, "The Diasporic Race Man as Institution Builder," examines the concept of the "Race Man" before analyzing the institutions to which Schomburg dedicated his life, namely the Prince Hall Masons, the American Negro Academy, and the Negro Society of Historical Research. While these organizations are, at first glance, homogeneously African American, this review argues that these spaces were ethnically diverse in their time, given that they included members from throughout the African diaspora. Nevertheless, Schomburg's involvement meant a commitment to the further diversification of these spaces, thereby ensuring the inclusion of men of African descent from Latin America.

After establishing Schomburg's articles in the *crónica* tradition, the following chapter, "Afro-Latinx Chronicles: Schomburg's Writings," brings to light several of the objectives of these publications. Indeed, his writings reveal not only an awareness of ongoing sociological and anthropological hemispheric debates about race, blackness, and Africanness (as represented by the work of Franz Boas, Melville Herskovitz, and Gilberto Freyre), but also provide responses to those discussions. For Schomburg, it was imperative to feature the contributions of Afro-Latinxs in the articles he published in such important African American periodicals as the NAACP's *Crisis* and the National Urban League's *Opportunity* so as to broaden predominantly Anglophone definitions of blackness to include Spanish-speaking populations. In several of these chronicles, he highlights the contributions of Afro-Hispanic Catholics, thereby implicitly offering his take on contemporary debates about primitivism. He also brings attention to war heroes, revolutionaries of the Hispanic Caribbean whose bloodshed was indicative of their commitment to the formation of their respective nations; Schomburg did this so as to provide for his English-speaking audience not only examples of valor but also an attendant history that revealed that black peoples throughout the hemisphere had fought in the militaries of their countries in an effort to create more inclusive nations.

The fourth chapter, "'Witness for the Future': Schomburg and His Archives," sees a discussion of archival theory and reveals how Schomburg's, like other ethnic archives, turns these formulations on their heads. Whereas archives are generally conceived to be vaults, mausoleums that withhold knowledge from the general populace under the guise of protecting those items deemed highly valued, often by the state or a private corporate entity, Schomburg's collections reveal a democratic impulse. Both the Schomburg Collection of the 135th Street Branch (later the Schomburg Center for Research in Black Culture) and to a lesser extent, the Negro Collection of Fisk University, were (and remain to this day) liberatory spaces whereby students, scholars, writers, artists, and the general public alike were motivated to learn about the African diaspora and the contributions of men and women of this heritage throughout the world. In many ways ahead of his time, Schomburg's vision was all-encompassing: his collections reflect his desire to emphasize the influence of people of African descent internationally, rather than solely in the Western Hemisphere; this vision was limited only by the vagaries of contemporary funding sources, whose focus instead was on the local population.

"'Furtive as He Looks': The Visual Representation of Schomburg" considers Schomburg in the small corpus of portraits of him that exist. After an overview of the history of photography in the late nineteenth and early twentieth centuries, and a consideration of the impact of this medium for black men and women in the United States, the chapter examines his portraits. Racialized as a black body, Schomburg eludes "capture" by the onlooker in many of his portraits by not looking at the camera, or even (often times) in the direction of the camera. When he does look, he challenges the viewer, resisting a gaze that dares to assume ontological knowledge of him through the photographic medium. In this way, he defies a presumed imperative that dictates that he should be "knowable" to the viewer, forcing them to instead recognize his humanity in all of its complexity.

The conclusion, "The Dynamics of Afro-Latinx Subjectivity," underscores Schomburg's commitment to blackness and black people. From his life's work, we glimpse the complexities of Afro-Latinx subjectivity. It is indeed one that encompasses migrations and displacements, one that is exposed to suspicion from peoples whose identities are more firmly entrenched in fixed definitions and affiliations to a specific aspect of race or nation, and yet one that nevertheless perseveres and is growing in use in the current moment. For the duration of his life, in both the private and public sphere, Schomburg served as a translator, literally and metaphorically; for Schomburg, the recognition of the existence and histories of black people speaking all different languages, including the overlooked Spanish-speaking population, was paramount to his life's project. In all the spaces that he inhabited, he pushed for greater diversity; for him, there was no threat in heterogeneity, his life being one of multiplicity. Unity could better be achieved through acknowledgment of all the lives of peoples of African descent; in his estimation, learning of the excellence of colonized peoples of African descent was an indispensable implement in the fight against white supremacy.

Earl Lewis evokes to great effect an image of waves of peoples from different spaces that come together and interact with each other in his article "To Turn as on a Pivot: Writing African Americans into a History of Overlapping Diasporas." After an extensive and comprehensive overview of the historiography of African Americans published in the *American Historical Review*, he lays out new possible areas of inquiry, all of which focus on what he names "multipositionality," a term that recognizes the complexity of identity formation. Lewis writes: "If we are to take race seriously, we must begin in earnest to theorize and historicize how racial identity informs individual identity and how identity formation in turn informs racial construction....Few of us, after all, acknowledge the number of selves competing for recognition at any given moment."[78] Instead of understanding constructions of racialized selves in a vacuum, he calls for the inclusion of all the different elements of time and space that are in play. He concludes his article with a discussion of Arturo Alfonso Schomburg; Lewis states, quite pointedly, about Schomburg: "The history of how Arturo became Arthur and yet remained Arturo is the challenge for the next generation of scholars."[79] This study is but one response.

"PATRIA Y LIBERTAD"
Schomburg and Puerto Rico

The works of José Julián Acosta and Salvador Brau have been my first inspiration to a further and intense study of the Negro in America.

—ARTURO SCHOMBURG, letter to Richard Pattee, dated February 3, 1937

IN A LETTER WRITTEN IN 1937 to Richard Pattee, professor of Latin
American history at the University of Puerto Rico, Schomburg identifies his intellectual forefathers in the study of peoples of African descent as white Puerto Rican
abolitionist, politician, historian, and a former teacher of his, José Julián Acosta,
and white Puerto Rican journalist, poet, and historian Salvador Brau. Each man
played a vibrant role in Puerto Rico's political sphere at the end of the nineteenth
and first decades of the twentieth century. This chapter explores Arturo Schomburg's
intellectual genealogy; it looks at the men who influenced his development as a
thinker, writer, historian, and archivist. Contrary to charges that he abandoned
the group to which he was born, made by members of the Puerto Rican community and scholars of that history, an examination of Schomburg's life's work reveals
an active interaction with his intellectual Puerto Rican and Cuban forefathers
throughout his life. For many of them, the liberation of enslaved men and women
of African descent was central to their aspirations of creating independent nations.

A consideration of these figures is imperative to understanding the complex
man that Schomburg came to be; indeed, a standard feature of biographical
sketches of influential men and women is a recreation of their own inspirations.
Schomburg's early years have been chiefly characterized by what remains unknown
to this date, and the revolutionary period of his life has received scant critical
attention from scholars either in Puerto Rico or on the mainland United States.[1]

Identifying Schomburg within a strictly Anglophone tradition, and treating his parentage and upbringing as negligible, ignores his raison d'être, namely, broadening and complicating contemporary notions of blackness so as to better learn and appreciate all that peoples of African descent have accomplished since the beginning of recorded history. Understanding the late-nineteenth-century Hispanic Caribbean in the aftermath of the Haitian Revolution and the islands' struggles for freedom, both in terms of ending slavery as well as in terms of the establishment of independent nations, provides a deeper comprehension of this man of African descent. Indeed, for this Afro-Latino, whose own passion for the recovery and assemblage of documents attesting to black excellence necessarily included works from the Spanish-speaking world, from the Iberian Peninsula to its former colonies in the Americas, this period is fertile ground for comprehending the breadth and scope of his later activities.

PORTRAITS OF A REVOLUTION

The last decades of the nineteenth century were a time of upheaval for the two remaining Spanish colonies in the Caribbean, as creole elites created divergent visions for the futures of Puerto Rico and Cuba.[2] Eighteen sixty-eight saw simultaneous uprisings, the Grito de Lares in Puerto Rico and the Grito de Yara in Cuba; while the former was suppressed within days, the latter sparked the Ten Years' War, a conflict that ended in a stalemate, with Cuba still a colony and slavery remaining the social, political, and economic foundation of that society. Whereas the majority of Cuban revolutionaries both on the island and in exile labored for complete independence by the last decades of the nineteenth century, Puerto Rico's political scene was more complicated, with divisions present both within the leadership on the island itself as well as in the New York exile community.[3]

The question of the independence of Puerto Rico in the nineteenth century cannot be discussed without an understanding about the abolition of slavery on the island. Latin American historiography has, to a great extent, pushed to the margins of their inquiries the presence of African peoples and their descendants. In light of the Haitian Revolution, fear of similar occurrences dominated the hemisphere, leading to widespread terrorizing of peoples of African descent, enslaved and free. This was particularly striking in the Hispanic Caribbean, to which landowners, free blacks, and enslaved men and women had fled during the uprising in Saint Domingue.[4] In its aftermath, the sugar industry in Cuba expanded exponentially, as the island became the primary producer of sugar in the hemisphere; Puerto Rico, which had previously been an island mainly used for defense of the region during the eighteenth century, also saw considerable expansion in its sugar industry and consequently in the population of enslaved African laborers during the nineteenth century.[5]

The reality of slavery was also central to Puerto Rican independence efforts; there were rebellions and uprisings throughout the island, as the enslaved fought for their own freedom.[6] Eighteen forty-eight saw the abolition of slavery in the French Caribbean colonies of Guadeloupe and Martinique and a slave rebellion in nearby St. Croix, leading to the passage of the Bando contra la raza africana in Puerto Rico. This decree made no distinction in color (mulatto or black) or legal status (slave or free); anyone who harmed a white person, or who even made a threat against one, was subject to imprisonment, if not mutilation or death.[7] While this decree was revoked within months, its passage speaks to the widespread repression of individual liberties on the island.[8]

Revolutionary fervor therefore marked the decade of the 1860s in the Hispanic Caribbean and its exile communities in the United States. Eighteen sixty-eight saw the Liberal Revolution whereby Queen Isabella II of Spain was deposed on September 17, as well as the uprisings in Puerto Rico, the Grito de Lares, which took place on September 23, and in Cuba, the Grito de Yara, which began on October 10. While conservative factions existed in Puerto Rico, liberalism would be the prevailing political ideology. Writing about the effect of liberalism on Afro-Latin Americans in the nineteenth century, George Reid Andrews observes: "The explicitly egalitarian rhetoric of liberalism—which invoked the concepts of civic equality, political democracy, and the rights of citizenship—touched a powerful chord with these longtime victims of colonial absolutism and social hierarchy."[9] Liberalism therefore created distinct visions of the future of the nation, which were affected by factors such as race, class, and gender.

During the next two decades, there developed two strains of liberal thought regarding the future of Puerto Rico: the Asimilistas desired that the island be declared a province of Spain, its inhabitants sharing the same rights as their peninsular counterparts along with the establishment of institutions that would recognize the specificities of Puerto Rico, while the Autonomistas called for decentralization, with control of the island's economic affairs left in the hands of Puerto Ricans themselves.[10] The latter group would eventually succeed, as the Spanish Crown did grant autonomy to Puerto Rico in 1897; the Carta Autonómica was signed November 25, 1897, with the new Puerto Rican government under the Autonomous Charter installed in February 1898. Two weeks into that month, on February 15, the U.S.S. *Maine* exploded in Havana Harbor, prompting the United States to enter the Cuban insurrection against Spain, which had been ongoing since 1895. It is for this reason that for many Latin Americanists, "Spanish-American War" is a misnomer that erases the fact that it was a war being waged by Cuba for independence; instead, they offer the term "Spanish-Cuban-American War."[11] By the summer of 1898, both islands, along with the Philippines and Guam, had been ceded to the United States, thereby signaling the end of the Spanish Empire.

It is notable that neither group of Liberal politicians called for the complete independence of Puerto Rico; separatism was a characteristic of the exile communities on the mainland, not on the island itself. As Harold J. Lidin writes, "They were liberals, not radicals, and their victory came after much patient insistence that they were faithful to Spain."[12] In her study on the regulation of race and sexuality in Puerto Rico in the decades between 1870 and 1920, Eileen J. Suárez Findlay writes how a tactic used by these lawmakers in their negotiations with the Spanish Crown was to highlight their preference for peace, thereby distinguishing themselves from surrounding islands: "Social conflict had always remained at a minimum, particularly when compared with Haiti and its slave-led revolution, or Cuba, where the struggle to end slavery and gain independence from Spain had exploded in a bloody, decade-long war....Puerto Rico would advance through legislative change, not rebellion, they insisted."[13] In concordance with this point, Ileana M. Rodríguez-Silva writes: "At a moment in which most imperial politicians equated blackness with instability and destruction, particularly in the Caribbean, Puerto Rican liberals sought to represent themselves and the island population as white and hence harmonious and stable."[14] Upon the transfer of power from Spain to the United States, these legislators only slightly shifted their message, assuring the new colonizer that they would not seek independence but instead were eager to be a part of the United States.

Key to the assurances offered by the Liberal leadership to U.S. politicians, as they had to their Spanish counterparts, was the manner in which the abolition of slavery had been managed in the 1860s and 1870s. Puerto Rico avoided the bloodshed of Haiti, Cuba, and the United States itself in its quest to end slavery.[15] Instead, two laws were passed regarding this effort: first, the Law of Partial Abolition, the 1870 Moret Law, whereby the state purchased children born between 1868 and 1870 and vowed to compensate their owners. This legislation also emancipated those enslaved men and women who were over the age of sixty.[16] This latter statute of the law was mostly symbolic, as there were very few enslaved human beings who reached this age.[17] Still, approximately ten thousand persons were freed under the Moret Law; three years later saw the passage of the Abolition Law, which liberated the remaining 31,000 enslaved humans. The state once again vowed payment to the landholders as well as stipulated obligatory labor of three years (contratación) for the newly freed, the *libertos*.[18] In this way, insular politicians were able to later claim that they had kept the Puerto Rican family intact.

The metaphor of the great Puerto Rican family (la gran familia puertorriqueña) is one whose origins are in this historical moment of the late nineteenth century, when the liberation of the small segment of the population that had been enslaved left lawmakers facing the task of integrating them into society, thereby creating a cohesive nation. As Suárez Findlay writes, "To replace the brutality of slavery and the *libreta* labor regime, they posited a benevolent but hierarchical paternalism as the glue which would hold society together under Liberal leadership and which would effectively mold a pliable workforce."[19] Social harmony was a guarantee, then, provided that everyone knew their place within a highly regimented hierarchy and respected said order. The exile communities in New York and Florida did no such thing, instead seeking to destroy such stratification in order to create a region defined by freedom and equality for all.

PUERTO RICAN REVOLUTIONARIES: BETANCES, HOSTOS, RODRÍGUEZ DE TIÓ

Dr. Ramón Emeterio Betances, Eugenio María de Hostos, and Lola Rodríguez de Tió lay the spiritual foundation for the Puerto Rican nation and for a broader Caribbean nation, and so are esteemed throughout the region and its diaspora; exiled by Spanish authorities, all were prolific writers who were deeply involved in the fight for the independence of the lands of the Hispanic Caribbean in order to create a coalition of these nations.[20] Cuba being the largest landmass of the Greater Antilles, the establishment of its sovereignty as a liberated nation would serve to secure the Antillean Confederation.[21] Betances and Hostos died shortly after the United States intervention in 1898, and while Betances's remains were repatriated (he had spent a good part of his life in France), Hostos instructed that he wished to be buried on the island only when Puerto Rico was free; he is buried in the Dominican Republic.[22] Rodríguez de Tió lived into the third decade of the twentieth century; having moved to Cuba a year after the conclusion of the war, she lived and died there, and is buried in Colón Cemetery in Havana.

Dr. Ramón Emeterio Betances
(Cabo Rojo, PR, 1827–Neuilly-sur-Seine, Île-de-France, 1898)

¡Unámonos! Amémonos! Formemos todos un solo pueblo....Las Antillas
para los antillanos.

[Let us unite! Let us love! Together we will form one people....The Antilles
for the Antilleans.]

—RAMÓN EMETERIO BETANCES, *Las Antillas para los antillanos*

Known as *El Padre de la Patria* (The Father of the Nation), Dr. Ramón Emeterio
Betances is a renowned figure in Puerto Rican history. Born into the middle class
in Mayagüez in 1839 to a Dominican father of African descent and a creole mother,
he earned his medical degree in Paris.[23] During a cholera outbreak that affected the
city of his birth, he served the enslaved and freed population of African descent.
Shortly thereafter he co-founded a secret society that was dedicated to the following three goals: the abolition of slavery, the purchase of newborns who were enslaved
so as to grant them their freedom, and the independence of the island.[24] His actions
were an affront to Spanish colonial authorities and he was soon exiled because of
them.[25] Expulsion from the island for Betances meant living in Paris (1858–59); the
Dominican Republic (1861–62); New York (1867); St. Thomas (1868–69); New York
(1869–70); Haiti (1870); and finally, Paris. Despite his deportation, he remained
active in revolutionary causes across the Caribbean region throughout his life, and
developed relationships with those who were also committed to liberation for these
countries, including General Gregorio Luperón of the Dominican Republic; Hostos;
the Afro-Cuban Antonio Maceo (the subject of a biographical chronicle by
Schomburg), leader of the revolutionary forces in Cuba; and José Martí.

In November 1867, Betances published "Los Diez Mandamientos del Hombre
Libre" ("The Ten Commandments of a Free Man"), which were: (1) abolition of
black slavery; (2) right to vote the budget; (3) freedom of religion; (4) freedom of
speech; (5) freedom of commerce; (6) freedom of the press; (7) right to bear
weapons; (8) freedom of assembly; (9) inviolability of the citizen; (10) right to
elect one's own authorities.[26] While for a U.S. audience, several of these items are
resonant of their Constitution, these were considered universal inalienable rights,
not reserved for one particular nation. Striking is Betances's prioritization of the
end of slavery; as the first commandment, it made patently clear his dedication
to the end of this economic system. At the conclusion of the document, which is
set up as a contract between Spain and Puerto Rico (with the ten "commandments"

presented as conditions of the contract), he writes: "Así seremos españoles, Si no, NO. Si no, Puertorriqueños, ¡PACIENCIA! Os juro que seréis libres [That way (if Spain fulfills all of these conditions) we will be Spaniards. If not, NO. If not, Puerto Ricans, Patience! I vow to you that you will be free!]"[27] Extraordinary is the idea that the colony has the right to negotiate with the Mother Country, and that, in this case, Betances communicates how Spain must fulfill these conditions in order for its colony to continue being a part of the empire. While the legal and juridical status of the island revealed it to already be a part of Spain, for all intents and purposes Betances inverts the power dynamic, utilizing a voice that conveys that Spain desires to be a part of Puerto Rico, and not the converse. Additionally, these ten conditions present Puerto Rico as if the entire populace of the island were in agreement, as if they were speaking in one voice. He conveniently ignored the diversity of opinions that have marked the Puerto Rican nation, both then and into the present day.

Betances's commitment to armed insurrection for the liberation of the island of his birth was demonstrated by his leadership of the Grito de Lares; though he was not physically present, he had co-founded the Comité Revolucionario de Puerto Rico in the Dominican Republic in January 1868, which served as the planning committee for the uprising. (He circulated his commandments among the revolutionaries.) Though the rebellion was quickly suppressed by Spanish troops, nevertheless it is cited as the first manifestation of Puerto Rican nationalism and to this day is commemorated by those who are remain staunch supporters of Puerto Rican independence.[28]

For the remaining thirty years of his life, Betances was intimately involved with insurrection efforts, raising funds, writing essays and articles, giving speeches, all for the goal of a free Antilles. Gordon K. Lewis writes: "He is the declared opponent of reformers and annexationists alike because both of them assume that Puerto Rico can be spiritually free while politically related to an outside society."[29] For Betances, such a compromise would be an abomination unto itself, the equivalent of consenting to lesser forms of freedom. Though there is no evidence of this, Schomburg's biographer Elinor Des Verney Sinnette speculates that Schomburg may have learned of Betances in his youth, when Betances was exiled in St. Thomas and when Schomburg was also supposedly on the island.[30] She writes: "Perhaps Betances' messages so fired his youthful enthusiasm that Arturo never tired of hearing what was happening in the revolutionary movement.... [I]t was the Puerto Rican independence struggle that became uppermost among young Schomburg's interests."[31] Sinnette's conjecture is revealing in that it demonstrates a desire to understand how the man who would play a central role in the collection and preservation of African diasporic history, how this person could also be the dedicated young man who committed so much of his time and energy to a cause that seemingly had little to do with these later ambitions. In addition to his position as a Mason (the significance of which is the subject of the next chapter), Betances, in the words of Jossianna Arroyo, "truly embodies a Circum-Atlantic diasporic identity."[32] His passion and dedication to the liberation of the Caribbean and the creation of an Antillean Confederation, one that included all of the islands of the Greater Antilles, including Haiti, provided a model of Afro-Latinx subjectivity for Schomburg and other future scholars and students of black history.[33]

Eugenio María de Hostos
(Mayagüez, PR, 1839–Santo Domingo, DR, 1903)

Cuando hablamos de contienda de raza estamos muy distantes de las sombrías privaciones de aquellos que temen la repetición del drama social de Haití; ésa es una repetición imposible. Lo posible es que la ineptitud o las pasiones de la población predominante utilicen como instrumento de reacción o de anarquía el fraccionamiento de la sociedad en dos razas contradictorias, y reproduzcan los hechos de reconstitución que se observan después de la guerra de abolición en los Estados de la Unión Americana que fueron esclavistas.

[When we speak of a race war we are far from the dismal losses of those who fear a repetition of the social drama of Haiti; that is an impossible recurrence. What is possible is that the ineptitude or the passions of the prevailing population use the division of society into two contradictory races as an implement of reaction or of anarchy, and they reproduce the events of reconstruction that we observe after the war of emancipation in the slaveholding States of the American Union.]

—HOSTOS, "El problema de Cuba" ("The Problem of Cuba")

In the year of Arturo Schomburg's birth, 1874, Eugenio María de Hostos wrote an article that directly confronted the fears that many held regarding revolution in the Antillean nations. "The Problem of Cuba" was published in *El Mundo Nuevo / América Ilustrada*, a biweekly publication published in New York between 1871 and 1875 that was one of the major periodicals written in Spanish.[34] As Kirsten Silva Gruesz writes: "*El Mundo Nuevo* encouraged its readers to align themselves along multiple lines of affiliation: as residents or citizens of the United States who took pride in their cultural Hispanism, or as members of a far-flung transnational community of progressive, elite Spanish Americans—with the political valence of that term left deliberately vague."[35] Notably, the newspaper was founded by

Ernest Piñeyro, who was active in the efforts to end Spanish colonialism and who left Cuba at the beginning of the Ten Years War.[36] Hostos directed his comments, therefore, not only to a Spanish-language audience but, more importantly, to one that included members of the white Cuban upper class, such as Piñeyro himself, who feared the increased participation of Afro-Cubans in the war as soldiers as much as, or perhaps more than, they did their Spanish colonizers. Indeed, the Spanish would conjure the violence of the Haitian Revolution as a means by which to terrorize their colonies, much as did all of the slaveholding societies in the Western Hemisphere.[37] The Spanish utilized this apprehension as a strategy to disarm, literally and figuratively, insurgent troops.[38]

In the midst of his article about Cuba, then, Hostos attempts to reassure his audience by unequivocally stating that no such occurrence could happen in Puerto Rico. Instead, he cites the ongoing Reconstruction project in the United States, whereby there were efforts to legislate equality for all in the eyes of the law, as the humanity of the newly emancipated was recognized in order to integrate this population into the Union. Hostos's allusion to the United States was notable because the United States, like Cuba, had a sizeable population of peoples of African descent; Hostos makes clear that it is possible to successfully bring these populaces together under the guise of a nation.

Indeed, from his perspective, the inhabitants of the remaining Spanish colonies shared one defining characteristic as subjects of the Mother Country; later in the article, he writes: "Nacemos muertos....Esclavos blancos que sabían explotar o cantar su esclavitud; esclavos negros que la sufrían y la lloraban; dominadores hambrientos que necesitaban de ella para retirarse ahítos; ésa es la sociedad de Puerto Rico y Cuba [We are born dead....White slaves who knew how to exploit or sing about their slavery; black slaves who suffered slavery and cried; starving oppressors who needed slavery in order to retire, full; that is the society of Puerto Rico and Cuba]."[39] For Hostos, who employs slavery as a metaphor for political oppression, there is no difference between those of African or European descent on these islands, as they are all subject to the whims of an insatiably corrupt system that benefits no one other than the Spanish Empire itself.

In the nineteenth century, the name Eugenio María de Hostos was known throughout the Spanish-speaking world. One of the first sociologists in the region, he traveled extensively: in Spain for his studies as a young man, then later to New York, where he joined the fight for Antillean independence. Like Betances, Hostos sought the creation of an Antillean Confederation that would unite the Spanish-speaking islands of the Greater Antilles as a political unit. In order to raise awareness and find possible alliances to support the call for revolution,

Hostos traveled for four years, from 1870 to 1874, to a number of South American countries, including Colombia, Peru, Chile, Argentina, and Brazil. In addition to his passion for Puerto Rico and Cuba, Hostos devoted himself to the Dominican Republic; he established a close friendship with General Gregorio Luperón, who led the Dominican insurgency against the Spanish in the 1860s and who would go on to serve as vice president and later president of the country.[40]

Hostos previewed his efforts to unify the nations of the Hispanic Caribbean in his novel *La peregrinación de Bayoán* (1863), where, in a coda, he tells his audience that his protagonist, Bayoán, represents Puerto Rico; Marién, his love interest, represents Cuba; and Guarionex, Marién's father, represents the Dominican Republic. Schomburg would later use "Guarionex" as his pen name in both his concise contributions to Martí's newspaper *Patria* and in his Masonic writings, which is a focus of the third chapter in this study.[41] At Luperón's invitation, Hostos reformed the educational system of the Dominican Republic, establishing schools and advocating for the education of both boys and girls. As Angel Villarini Jusino and Carlos Antonio Torre emphasize, for Hostos, "[d]omination, more than anything, is oppression of the human mind. An oppressed individual's existence resides in underdeveloped thinking. Neocolonial education becomes an instrument of domination in the measure in which it produces a sick mind devoid of conscience, truth, freedom, or justice."[42] Hostos's recognition of the role of the educational system in the perpetuation of ideological discourse is a principle that will echo in one of Schomburg's most famous pieces, his 1913 speech to the Teachers' Summer Class at the Cheyney Institute in Pennsylvania, titled "Racial Integrity: A Plea for the Establishment of a Chair of Negro History in Our Schools and Colleges."

Lola Rodríguez de Tió
(San Germán, PR, 1843–Havana, Cuba, 1924)

Cuba y Puerto Rico son / de un pájaro las dos alas, / reciben flores o balas / sobre el mismo corazón…Cuba and Puerto Rico are / two wings of one bird. / They receive blows or bullets / in the same heart…

—RODRÍGUEZ DE TIÓ, "A Cuba"; translation in Acosta-Belén (2005)

Schomburg historiography, which for this writer includes Schomburg's own publications, is decidedly male-centered (that is, there is a notable absence of women, seemingly in his professional life and work), and so while there is discussion of Betances and Hostos in the same breath as Schomburg, there is little mention of Lola Rodríguez de Tió outside of *independentista* circles and the work of contemporary Puerto Rican feminist scholars such as Virginia Sánchez Korrol and Edna Acosta-Belén. While her name may be little known, Rodríguez de Tió's writings, particularly her poetry, were vital to the Antillean liberation struggle. In 1868, inspired by El Grito de Lares, she wrote the verses of "La Borinqueña," where she urges her compatriots to awaken from their slumber, as the moment for the fight has arrived; the poem was soon put to music and continues to be sung. Rodríguez de Tió's "La Borinqueña" is the anthem of the Puerto Rican independence movement. It is not, however, the national anthem of the island: those lyrics were composed by Manuel Fernández Juncos thirty-five years later. Her poem "A Cuba" provides one of the most widely-known images of the relationship between Puerto Rico and Cuba that survives to this day. Rodríguez de Tió and her husband were exiled from the island from 1877–80 (when they lived in Venezuela); 1889–95 (when they lived in Havana); and 1895–99 (when they lived in New York City). Like Schomburg, Rodríguez de Tió joined the revolutionary activities in New York; she served as an officer in the Club Hermanas de Ríus Rivera, the women's club of the Puerto Rican Section of the Cuban Revolutionary Party, for example.[43] This club, like the others, was charged primarily with fundraising for the war effort in Cuba. Following the conclusion of the 1898 War, Rodríguez de Tió lived the rest of her life in Cuba, working for the Ministry of Education, until her death in 1924; though she visited Puerto Rico only sporadically, she remained committed to its independence.[44]

Historian Félix Ojeda Reyes honors these men and woman as "peregrinos de la libertad," "pilgrims of freedom" in his book of the same name.[45] Each of them fought not only for the independence of their home country, but also for the independence of both Cuba and Puerto Rico. All of them favored the creation of an Antillean Confederation that would include all of the islands of the Greater Antilles—Cuba, Hispaniola, and Puerto Rico. Jossianna Arroyo demonstrates how in Betances's configuration, Haiti played a key role in this union, whereas Hostos thought this nation, while it had an acknowledged legacy of successful revolution, should have no part in the political configuration of the confederation, bowing to the antiblack sentiment that has steered the hemispheric approach to Haiti.[46] Nevertheless, in Betances, Hostos, and Rodríguez de Tió, Schomburg had models of exiles whose writings revealed a deep passion for the independence of the Hispanic Caribbean islands as well as offered a vision of a more holistic Caribbean; with Betances in particular, an Afro-Latino who was deeply invested in the liberation and union of black peoples throughout the Caribbean, Schomburg found an exemplar of African diasporic thought.

CUBAN COMPATRIOTS: SERRA AND MARTÍ

The revolutionary activities in New York toward the end of the nineteenth century brought together exiles from both of the remaining colonies of the Spanish empire; Cuban and Puerto Rican men and women shared the passionate belief that Spain's expulsion from the Caribbean was necessary for the progress of their island nations, and this would only be accomplished through armed insurrection. Thus, they collaborated in all things: fundraising for weapons and supplies, planning, writing newspaper articles, preparing pamphlets, educating one another, all with the single goal of a free Caribbean, where they would enjoy the same rights as all liberal and democratic nations. Schomburg was in the midst of these efforts in New York; he met and worked members of the Cuban community, two of whom were to figure prominently in their countries: Rafael Serra and José Martí. While Serra is the lesser known of the two, he played a critical role, co-founding several revolutionary clubs as well as the Partido Revolucionario Cubano, alongside Martí. He also established a school that provided free classes to members of these communities, many of whom were working-class and of African descent. A depiction of the Antillean revolutionary movement of the late nineteenth century would be incomplete without reference to José Martí, who was its acknowledged core. In his relationship with Afro-Cubans in general and with Serra in particular, as well as in his writings on race, Martí demonstrated his commitment to a free Cuba that was inclusive of all of its inhabitants.

Rafael Serra y Montalvo
(Havana, Cuba, 1858–Havana, Cuba, 1909)

Revolucionar es remover, destruir y cambiar de una vez un sistema por otro que en nada se parezca al sistema caído. Cuando á un sistema solo se le quita ó añade, quedando siempre su base original, entonces no se evoluciona: y los cubanos, como principio de salvación y de progreso, tenemos que revolucionar.

[To revolutionize is to remove, destroy, and change once and for all one system for another that does not resemble in any way the fallen one. When one only removes or adds to a system, leaving its original base intact, it doesn't evolve: and the Cuban people, in the name of salvation and of progress, we need to revolutionize.]

—RAFAEL SERRA, "Hay que pensar" ("One Has to Think")

Published first in his newspaper *La Doctrina de Martí* and later in his collection *Ensayos políticos* (1899), Rafael Serra here makes clear the necessity for the complete destruction and the construction of new social structures through revolution; reminiscent of Audre Lorde's admonition that the "master's tools will never dismantle the master's house,"[47] Serra underscores that the amendment of existing structures will inevitably lead to the replication of those structures, irrespective of intent to the contrary. After the 1898 war and the establishment of the Cuban Republic in 1902, Serra witnessed the infiltration of white supremacist thought in the creation of a new Cuba that systematically excluded Afro-Cuban civic participation; in his writings, which included articles and essays, in the newspapers he created, and in the schools he founded, Serra personally took on the task of creating a more educated populace of African descent who would be able to contribute to their nation in new ways, ones that would allow for both its progress and its salvation.

Serra was one of the two men to whom Schomburg presented himself upon his arrival in New York, the other being Flor Baerga.[48] An Afro-Cuban and an autodidact, Serra was a *tabaquero* and activist whose dedication to the independence of both islands was notable, as was his commitment to the education of men and women of African descent. Born free in Havana, Serra founded a free school, *Armonía*, and a newspaper of the same name in 1879 while living in Matanzas, at the age of twenty-one; his goal for this mutual aid society was the "modeling of citizen consciousness."[49] Within a year, he was exiled to New York, where he lived until the turn of the century. There he co-founded a number of organizations that supported the Antillean insurgency, including Los Independientes (a revolutionary club), the Partido Revolucionario Cubano (Martí's political party) and Las Dos Antillas; Schomburg was a member of the latter two and, and in the case of Las Dos Antillas, served as secretary.[50] In 1890, Serra founded La Liga, which was modeled after the Directorio Central de las Sociedades de la Raza de Color, an Afro-Cuban association founded three years earlier in Cuba with the explicit goal of establishing the "moral and material well-being of the raza de color through the promotion of formal education and 'better habits.'"[51]

Writing about Serra's organization, Aline Helg observes, "The society of La Liga brought together working-class Cubans and Puerto Ricans of African descent living in New York and provided them with general education, a propaganda against Spanish colonialism, and family entertainment."[52] Despite challenges, including the racism of white Cuban exiles, with Martí's support Serra was able to open a similar organization in Tampa for Afro-Cubans there in 1892.[53] Martí himself taught at La Liga, and was named head supervisor and honorary president; it was at this time that his nickname of "Maestro" began to circulate.[54] Serra's passion for the education of peoples of African descent was connected to his ideas of the responsibilities of citizens; Alejandra Bronfman observes, "His was a liberal notion of citizenship, premised on equality but also on a sense that citizens had obligations that could be met only if they began their civic lives with adequate education and preparation."[55] A lingering legacy of racism and enslavement had been the woeful state of educational systems for peoples of African descent on the island, free or enslaved. Serra's schools and newspapers therefore provided an alternative to racist declarations that peoples of African descent could not reach the intellectual capacity of those of European descent. Again, we see an emphasis on education as fundamental for the decolonization of the mind, a theme Schomburg would take up in his own work.

After Martí's death, Serra founded the newspaper *La Doctrina de Martí*, which stood as an important and necessary corrective to those who had willfully misinterpreted Martí's efforts to create a Cuban nation that was inclusive of everyone. Naming Serra's paper as "the most influential of the numerous newspapers that advanced Martí's thought," Gerald E. Poyo writes: "During its existence *La Doctrina* reminded Cubans of Martí's broader nationalist ideals that included creating a republic based on social justice, mutual respect among the social classes, and racial harmony."[56] Serra launched this newspaper in New York in 1896, where it was published with regularity until 1898; this was only one of the several periodicals of which he was in charge.[57] He then published *La Doctrina* in Cuba, to which he returned after the conclusion of the war. In the first decade of the twentieth century, he was elected to the legislative body twice, in 1904 and 1909; in 1907, he published a collection of essays, *Para blancos y negros. Ensayos politicos, sociales y económicos.* The title of the compendium is an indication of the stratification of Cuban society in the first decades of the twentieth century, when Cuban nationalist rhetoric had encouraged racial fraternity by attempting to silence and marginalize the population of African descent. Until his death in 1909, Serra continued to write explicitly about civil rights and social justice issues in language that reflected his liberal beliefs: as Bronfman writes, "his model for equal citizenship was based…on the reality of a conscience that was moral, virtuous, and educated."[58] Citizenship, then had nothing to do with race but instead with the inherent equality of one's soul.[59]

José Martí
(Havana, Cuba, 1853–Dos Ríos, Cuba, 1895)

No hay odio de razas, porque no hay razas....El alma emana, igual y eterna, de los cuerpos diversos en forma y en color. Peca contra la Humanidad el que fomente y propague la oposición y el odio de las razas.

[There is no racial hatred because there is no such thing as race....The soul, equal and eternal, emanates from bodies diverse in form and color. He who foments and spreads opposition and hatred of the races sins against Humanity.]

—JOSÉ MARTÍ, "Nuestra America"("Our America")

José Martí always stated that the republic would have been impossible without the brawn and muscle of all races.

—ARTHUR SCHOMBURG, "General Antonio Maceo"

In his portrait of the Afro-Cuban general Antonio Maceo,[60] Schomburg references José Martí in four instances, each of which honors the man known as "El Apostól de la Revolución," (the Apostle of the Revolution) for his dedication to his beloved homeland. Father of the Cuban nation, Martí's renown is such that he is claimed by all sides of the political spectrum within a Cuban context, from Fidel Castro himself to Castro's most virulent critics. Martí is the sole figure that unites his *patria,* both on the island and in its diaspora. For the greater American audience, English-, Spanish-, Portuguese-, French-, and Dutch-speaking, Martí is held in great esteem for his utopian visions for the island of his birth and his foresight regarding U.S. imperial ambitions throughout the hemisphere. Finally, his essays, articles, and chronicles (*crónicas*) are matched by his creative output, his poems and novels, as Martí is also known as one of the fathers of Latin American Modernismo, a literary movement that heralded the development of a distinctly Latin American literature, as opposed to one that had been considered derivative of European models on the world stage. For all of these reasons, Martí has garnered an expansive amount of scholarly attention since his death in battle in 1895.

While Martí is almost universally revered (as one critic calls him, the "towering figure of Cuban history"),[61] for Schomburg, Martí is a man he knew personally, as he himself writes in an article that appeared in the NAACP's *The Crisis*.[62] Twenty-one years his senior, Martí, who had arrived in New York in 1880, served as a mentor to the young migrant, as he was to many in the exile communities, Puerto Rican and Cuban alike. As Bernardo Vega notes in his memoirs, for members of the working classes (mostly artisans and tobacco workers), Martí harkened back to the era of Hostos himself, as both were intellectuals who called for armed conflict in order to establish sovereignty for these islands.[63]

By the time of his arrival in the United States, Martí had already worked as a journalist; he continued producing articles and essays that appeared in newspapers throughout the Americas, writing in both English and Spanish.[64] Though he traveled incessantly—he was also a highly acclaimed orator, and so gave speeches during fundraisers in support for the revolutionary movement—Martí lived in New York for fifteen years, until his return to Cuba in 1895. In his study introducing Martí, Oscar Montero writes: "While living in the United States, Martí witnessed the progressive unraveling of the promise of emancipation for all."[65] His vision of a new Cuban republic was one that would be inclusive of all of its inhabitants, rather than one that sanctioned and enforced the marginalization of any segment of the population, particularly those of African descent.[66]

Founder of the Partido Revolucionario Cubano (Cuban Revolutionary Party) in 1892 and of the party's newspaper *Patria*, Martí wrote in the first issue of the newspaper that the party's main goal was "'winning the independence of Cuba and lending direct support to the struggle to free Puerto Rico.'"[67] In an editorial accompanying the publication of the party platform, he writes: "'The birth of this newspaper rests on the determination and resources of independent Cubans and Puerto Ricans in New York who are committed to contribute, unfailingly and tirelessly, to the organization of the free men of Cuba and Puerto Rico as is made necessary by the conditions prevailing on the Islands and their future constitution as republics.'"[68] Martí's inclusion of Puerto Rico in the fight for freedom was one that both drew from the activist work of Betances and Hostos and was also a pragmatic decision: given Puerto Rico's geographic proximity to Cuba, Puerto Rico was the site where Spanish troops were stationed before fighting the insurgencies. Appealing to an emerging Puerto Rican nationalism had the potential of disrupting military operations before they commenced.

Martí's vision of a free Caribbean was one that depended on equality for all, irrespective of difference. "Nuestra America" ("Our America") is perhaps his most widely reproduced essay; published originally in January 1891 in both New York and Mexico City, Martí warns his audience about the expansionist ambitions of the United States in the rest of the Americas. It is in the last paragraph that this, one of his most famous statements, appears. His dismissal of the construct of race in favor of an assessment of human beings that centers on the fundamental equality of the soul is one that has been interpreted to mean that Martí advocated a nationalism that ignored racial difference, which is far from true. Instead, Martí believed in freedom for all men and women, black and white; Montero observes:

"True freedom is inseparable from respect for all of those bodies, not just some of them, and only those nations that could transform this simple fact into a guiding vision would survive and prosper."[69]

In an essay published in a collection focused on "Nuestra America," Ada Ferrer provides the historical context of Martí's article; she makes the point that by the 1890s Spanish authorities and creole elites "had long linked the preservation of social order in Cuba with the maintenance of colonial rule. Pointing to the numerical predominance of the nonwhite population and the economic significance of slavery, they argued for the necessity of maintaining a colonial bond with Spain. To challenge that bond, they said, was to imperil life and property."[70] While both Puerto Rico and Cuba were under Spanish dominion, Cuba had a much more significant population of Africans and their descendants, and, as Ferrer reveals, "colonial discourse had constructed [the categories of race and nation] as irreconcilable for almost a century."[71] During the Ten Years War, the revolutionary troops included large numbers of enslaved and freed men of African descent; this was the period in which terms such as "black Cuban" and "citizens of color" entered the lexicon, as revolutionaries made a discursive intervention by uniting race and national identity.[72] Employing the fear tactic that blacks would be taking over the country should the revolutionaries win, the Spanish managed to sow discord within the ranks of the rebels by speaking explicitly about race. Ferrer records: "In the region of Camagüey, for example, approximately 95 percent of the original insurgent forces had surrendered by the third year of the rebellion," many admitting to the fear of conquest by blacks.[73]

This apprehension was one that Spain successfully employed for the subsequent two decades, through the Ten Years War (1868–1878) as well as the Guerra Chiquita of 1879–80, where Spanish troops successfully defeated the insurgency. By the 1890s, some in the revolutionary leadership had developed a new tactic: "If opponents of independence spoke of race—of racial slavery, of the island's racial composition, and of race war—then to defeat those opponents, independence activists would have to strip race of its ideological hold. They would have to silence the issue of race."[74] Martí's emphasis on an all-encompassing nationalism has been appropriated by various constituencies, some of whom have used his vision to justify policies that marginalized those who clamored for true equality before the law.[75] Rafael Serra was only one critic and politician who continued to call attention to the structural inequalities within the nation itself.

Two years after the publication of "Nuestra America," there appeared his most famous essay on race itself, simply titled "Mi raza." In a frequently cited passage, he writes: "Cubano es más que blanco, más que mulato, más que negro. En los campos de batalla, muriendo por Cuba, han subido juntas por los aires las almas de los blancos y de los negros [Cuban is more than white, more than *mulato,* more than black. On the battlefields, the souls of both whites and blacks have both risen, dying for Cuba together]."[76] Once again returning to the theme of souls, Martí focuses on those who died together during previous insurgency efforts: the revolutionary armies during the Ten Years War as well as the Guerra Chiquita were composed of men of both European and African descent, united in a common vision. For Martí, a compartmentalization of a nation by race means division, and as Oscar Montero observes, "To insist on differences between people in order to separate them is to violate the republic, to do violence to the public trust. Martí believed that to violate the rights of one individual was to violate the rights of all. In brief, that was his definition of freedom. Freedom for one person at the expense of another was no freedom at all."[77] It was toward this dream of a unified and integrated nation to which Martí appealed in his writings and speeches.[78]

Martí's death in 1895 had a devastating impact in the exile communities; Jesse Hoffnung-Garskof highlights how, in the only instance in which he makes an appearance in the minutes he recorded as secretary at an October 1895 revolutionary gathering in New York, Schomburg called for a moment of recognition for their fallen leader. Hoffnung-Garskof observes: "Perhaps it was an innocent salute to a nationalist hero. But in the context of the divided Partido Cubano Revolucionario, it was likely an attempt to link the symbol of the fallen martyr to the radical politics of class and race that so permeated the oratory of the evening."[79] Martí had successfully created alliances across gender, race, and class; the fragility of his organization became apparent as struggles for power came to pass almost immediately after his death.

Nevertheless, the revolutionary activity in support of Antillean independence of exiled men and women of African descent at the end of the nineteenth century reveals the extent to which they were invested in the creation of their nations. The United States intervention in what had been a Cuban war for independence, the third in three decades, conclusively changed the political status of the islands. Whereas Puerto Rico would go on to become a U.S. colony, the Cuban Republic was declared in 1902; and while Puerto Rico saw the election of one man of African descent to office, Dr. José Celso Barbosa, Cuba saw more representatives, including Martín Morúa Delgado and Rafael Serra himself.[80] As he did not turn his back on the island of his youth later in life, neither did Schomburg forget the legacy of his Cuban comrades, as they would feature prominently in his writings in African American publications (a subject explored at length in the third chapter of the present study).

SCHOMBURG'S SCHOLARLY INFLUENCES

While the above-mentioned men and woman undoubtedly shaped Schomburg's life and pursuits, he names two men as having sparked his interest in black history: José Julián Acosta and Salvador Brau. Both men were historians: as a young man studying on scholarship in Spain, Acosta had edited an edition of Fray Iñigo Abbad y Lasierra's history of Puerto Rico.[81] This text, originally published in 1788, remains cited as a foundational text in the historiography of the island. For his part, Brau would be named the official historian of Puerto Rico, writing texts that are also considered critical in the discipline. These were two men who demonstrated the significant importance of the construction of narrative in the establishment of a nation.

José Julián Acosta
(San Juan, PR, 1825–San Juan, PR, 1891)

Con la abolición inmediata puede haber, sin duda alguna, inconvenientes y quebrantos, pero son siempre pequeños, y, por su naturaleza, esencialmente pasajeros.

[With immediate abolition there may be, without a doubt, objections and losses, but these are always, by their nature, small and essentially fleeting.]

—SEGUNDO RUIZ BELVIS, JOSÉ JULIÁN ACOSTA, FRANCISCO MARIANO QUIÑONES,
Proyecto para la abolición de la esclavitud en Puerto Rico (Project for the Abolition of Slavery in Puerto Rico)

The Junta Informativa de Ultramar was a committee of delegates from Puerto Rico and Cuba who met in Madrid with the Ministerio de Ultramar (Overseas Ministry) during the final months of 1866 and into 1867 to discuss possible reforms with Spanish officials. From Puerto Rico, the delegates were conservative Manuel Zeno Correa and liberals Segundo Ruiz Belvis, Francisco Mariano Quiñones, and José Julián Acosta. While their conservative counterpart called for a gradual abolition with compensation for landowners, Ruiz Belvis, Quiñones, and Acosta presented a plan for immediate abolition of slavery on the island, with or without compensation. Though the plan was defeated by the junta, nevertheless it established the idea that the question of slavery and its termination could be treated separately in Puerto Rico than it was in Cuba, given the latter's greater dependence on enslaved labor.[82] Representative of liberal politicians, these men were intent on distinguishing themselves from Cuba, thereby making a way for the restructuring of the political relationship of the island with the Mother Country using the argument of racial harmony.[83]

Acosta was born to Spanish parents on the island in 1825; as a young man, he had studied in Spain, alongside Ruiz Belvis and Betances.[84] Piñeiro de Rivera (1989) notes that in 1851, while there, he co-founded the Sociedad recolectora de documentos históricos, a group whose goal was the gathering of Puerto Rican historical documents.[85] This speaks to what Lisa Sánchez González has named as "paperlessness," a condition that, in her estimation, defines Puerto Rican subjectivity. She writes:

> *Paperlessness* is a serious metaphor, it is a metaphor that frowns, yet it is *the* Boricua dilemma implicitly broached in our authors' early twentieth-century narratives. Paperlessness denotes a chronically alienated subjectivity, a hermeneutical crisis based in an endless cycle of deferral in U.S. national imaginaries, a cycle that perpetuates Boricua alterity despite documents that should guarantee a legitimate referent (citizenship) and an enunciative center (literature).[86]

While she refers to the period following the granting of United States citizenship on the island in 1917, after it had been annexed by the United States in 1898, the existence of the Sociedad recolectora de documentos históricos reveals that this sensibility of being without papers, being invalid as it were, had existed for Puerto Rican creoles in the mid-nineteenth century. Utilizing Sánchez González's metaphor suggests that one aspect of a particularly Puerto Rican subjectivity is alienation from the metropole, irrespective of whether the colonial seat of power is Madrid or Washington, D.C. Having papers, having documentation, grants legitimacy to one's existence; in a culture that values the written word over oral tradition, papers, documents, archives serve as testimony to one's history. Thus, we witness the pursuit of pamphlets, letters, books, treatises, anything that speaks to the existence of a people. While Schomburg's lifelong passion has traditionally been contextualized within an African American setting where he was one of a number of black collectors and bibliophiles who held the same goal of combating white supremacy by creating alternate archives, here we see an additional inspiration for this impulse in an educator with whom he had contact as a child in Puerto Rico.

In the aftermath of the failure to secure immediate abolition in Puerto Rico, Acosta returned to the island and the following year was arrested and jailed on suspicion of being a part of the insurrection known as El Grito de Lares. After securing amnesty, he would go on to be a politician, an educator, and founder of a bookstore and printing shop, the latter of which would employ Sotero Figueroa. In addition to schools, Acosta co-founded the Ateneo Puertorriqueño, which is dedicated to the promotion of Puerto Rican culture, and which, in 1891, saw the official recognition of an Afro-Puerto Rican, Rafael Cordero, as contributor to the nation. The official speaker of the day, Salvador Brau, dedicated his tribute instead to the men whose actions had paved the way for eventual abolition in the country: Segundo Ruiz Belvis, Francisco Mariano Quiñones, and José Julián Acosta.[87]

Salvador Brau
(Cabo Rojo, PR, 1842–San Juan, PR, 1912)

Esa concordia en las voluntades, esa harmonía en los afectos, esa reciprocidad en los servicios, esos respetos mútuos que fincan su abolengo en las necesidades impuestas á los viejos colonos de esta comarca por el aislamiento social a que se vieron reducidos, ha llegado á constituir cualidad característica de nuestro temperamento....Procuremos cultivar esos afectos; esforcémonos en hacerlos reverdecer; ¡qué no mueran, no! ya que gracias á ellos la historia de Puerto Rico, que no enrojece sus páginas con los nombres de un Touissant ó de un Dessalines, se ilumina con los destellos del espíritu bienhechor de un Rafael Cordero.

[That agreement of wills, that harmony of sentiment, that reciprocity of service, that mutual respect that rests its lineage in the necessities imposed on that generation of colonists of this region by the social isolation to which they were reduced, all of this has come to constitute the characteristic attribute of our temperament....We will strive to cultivate those feelings; let us force ourselves to make them come alive again; may they never die! It is due to those sentiments that Puerto Rico's history, the pages of which are not reddened by such names as a Toussaint or a Dessalines, is illuminated by the achievements of the generous spirit of one Rafael Cordero.]

—SALVADOR BRAU, "Rafael Cordero: elógio póstumo con que se iniciara en el Ateneo Puertorriqueño la velada del 31 de octubre de 1891."

Salvador Brau's 1891 homage to Rafael Cordero (1790–1868) is emblematic of the complicated attitudes toward the Afro–Puerto Rican population held by the liberal elite of that island. An autodidact, Cordero was a *tabaquero,* a tobacco worker who opened a primary school for boys, irrespective of race and class, in 1810. (His older sister Celestina opened a school for girls in 1820; hers was the first school for girls on the island.) As Suárez Findlay (1999) reminds her audience, fifteen years earlier there had been an attempt to nominate Cordero for election in the Ateneo Puertorriqueño.[88] A cultural institution founded in 1876, the Ateneo only allows those who have made lasting contributions to the culture; being named to this body is an appointment to a national academy. As 1876 marked the true end of slavery (those freed under the 1873 law were forced to work for three subsequent years), Cordero was deemed unfit to receive such an honor. In 1891, however, Brau cited him as a "generous spirit" for having founded a school thirty-five years before primary schools were established by Spanish authorities on the island; among the boys who attended the school were José Julián Acosta.[89] Brau honored Cordero, therefore, as someone who had created a space whereby racial and class difference were disregarded in favor of education, doing so decades before the Mother Country thought Puerto Rico merited a system of schooling.[90]

In Brau's tribute to Cordero, we see that the educator was the "right kind" of black: he did not represent the horror that were the named leaders of the Haitian Revolution, but instead was a humble and generous man. Haiti, once again, was the measure against which one determined appropriate black behavior; whereas Toussaint and Dessalines stained the pages of history with the blood they shed waging war against a supposedly helpless generation that enslaved solely because of the economic necessities imposed upon them, no such occurrence had come to pass in Puerto Rico. Brau invoked the violence of the Haitian Revolution and the terror that was felt throughout the hemisphere in its aftermath; his tribute epitomizes what Rodríguez-Silva has termed as the "politics of gratitude" that defined Liberal writings in postabolition Puerto Rico: "Representations of docility and gratitude…were not just descriptive, a depiction of social relations, but also prescriptive, a cultural technology for structuring sociopolitical relations."[91] She goes on to demonstrate in her article how such political thought allowed for the expansion of a highly racialized stratified social order whereby dissent was effectively marginalized; the reverberations of such discursive practices utilized more than a century ago are still felt at the present moment, when there remain those who question Schomburg's loyalty to the land of his birth given behavior that was audacious in that it was not keeping within strictly defined boundaries. As Hilda Lloréns observes, "In Puerto Rico [and its diaspora, I argue], blackness is subversive when it refuses to remain muted against attempts to minimize its relevance and existence" (16).[92] Schomburg's life project was a refutation of silence, as he expended his time, energy, and resources to broadcast recognition of the contributions of black men and women throughout the hemisphere.

Schomburg cites Brau as an inspiration for his study of black history. Placing Brau within the context of other Puerto Rican nineteenth-century intellectuals such as José Julián Acosta, historian Arcadio Díaz-Quiñones comments: "Unlike

José Martí, Hostos, and other radical revolutionaries in exile, these journalists, politicians, doctors, and poets resisted identification with armed rebellion. Instead they demanded liberal, progressive reforms and seemed committed to mediate between modernization and imperialism."[93] Díaz-Quiñones makes a striking distinction once again between those intellectuals who stayed on the island and those who lived in exile: the argument has been made that exile, especially that which is enforced due to political difference with the state, is tied to utopia, to a nostalgia that allows for the creation of alternative spaces that incorporate the émigré's visions of that state.[94] Per this thinking, radicals could afford to think of armed rebellion, as the presumption was that they were in no position to contend with the material realities of life on the island.

Schomburg, of course, was an exception to this train of thought, as his interest in the histories of people of African descent began when he was a child.[95] In her study on Boricua literature, Lisa Sánchez González features a letter dated November 5, 1933, from Schomburg to Joaquín Becerril, the editor of *La Voz del Obrero* (*The Worker's Voice*), a newspaper published in Puerto Rico's capital of San Juan, in which he expressed his interest in acquiring more texts written by and about the Afro–Puerto Rican population. In describing his collection at the 135th Street Branch, he names a work by Salvador Brau (the pamphlet honoring Rafael Cordero) among the scarce resources about blacks in Puerto Rico that the library has in its possession.[96] Brau's influence on Schomburg is most clearly seen when examining these facts about him: first, Brau was an autodidact, a self-taught man who went on to be named Puerto Rico's official historian; second, unlike many of his peers, Brau acknowledged the contributions of peoples of African descent to the formation of the nation in his writings, though once again, these portraits are problematic and emblematic of his own intellectual heritage. Granted, his portrayal of blacks is a complex one, as scholars such as Rodríguez-Silva emphasize, "Brau was one of the main architects of the Puerto Rican version of the myth of racial harmony."[97] Nevertheless, on the island, Brau is a canonical figure, one whose work is considered foundational in the field of Puerto Rican historiography.[98]

Within a year or so after the posthumous tribute to Cordero, while Puerto Rico was still a Spanish colony, Brau traveled to Spain, visiting the Archivo de las Indias in Seville for the commemoration of the four hundredth anniversary of Columbus's arrival in the region. Díaz-Quiñones comments, "The Archivo was for Brau a monument to the ancient grandeur of Spain and a compelling emblem of unity. But there was also a colonial reason for his enthusiasm: Puerto Rico lacked archives of its own."[99] Brau would go on to correct this deficiency with his writings, publishing *Puerto Rico y su historia: investigaciones críticas* (1892), *Historia de Puerto Rico* (1904), and *La colonización de Puerto Rico* (1907). His studies, therefore, are an archive unto itself, a collection that seeks to firmly establish Puerto Rico's vibrant nationhood, despite its political realities.

Schomburg would himself go to the Archivo de las Indias in 1926, after the sale of his private collection to the Carnegie Corporation. His subsequent writings recuperate little-known histories of African men and women in Spain and the Americas from the sixteenth century onward. Published in *The Crisis* and *Opportunity* magazines, these articles broadened his audience's awareness of the African diaspora, which included those who had lived in the Spanish-speaking world for centuries. Brau and Schomburg, then, shared deep-seated motivations for their pursuits of history: for Brau, it was a means by which to demonstrate the enduring intellectual legacies of Spain in Puerto Rico, even after the change in colonial power. For Schomburg, history was the means by which to combat virulent white supremacist thought and action that had deliberately sought to relegate black lives to the lowest echelons of their societies in the name of natural order.[100]

These men and women served as some of the foundations of Schomburg's intellectual development: the accommodating, assimilationist face of the island intellectuals, and the more radical, militant face of the revolutionaries exiled in New York City. While the influence of the island intellectuals is easier to discern in the work of Schomburg as a more mature man, in his youth he quickly joined the cause of Antillean independence soon after his arrival in New York at seventeen years of age, and so was more immediately inspired by men such as Martí, Hostos, and Betances.

SCHOMBURG AND NEW YORK'S ANTILLEAN LIBERATION EFFORTS

Schomburg arrived in New York on April 17, 1891; within the year, he was involved with several clubs dedicated to the cause of Antillean independence.[101] He joined both Club Borinquen and the Partido Revolucionario Cubano; weeks later, on April 3, 1892, he assisted in the founding of Las Dos Antillas (the Two Antilles), a reference to Cuba and Puerto Rico.[102] Along with Rosendo Rodríguez, an Afro–Puerto Rican, Schomburg served as secretary of this club, recording minutes for an organization that helped "to collect money, weapons, and medical supplies for an armed struggle against Spain."[103] Club Borinquen, Las Dos Antillas, and Club Mercedes Varona, a women's club, were the only three clubs reflective of the still-small Puerto Rican community in New York within the larger Cuban one.[104] Virginia Sánchez Korrol emphasizes that Club Mercedes Varona, founded by Inocencia Martínez de Figueroa, Sotero's wife, was the "only women's club to fully exercise its right to vote within the PRC administrative structure, it was also the first venue where New York women cast their vote in a political organization."[105] Among the most prominent members of this club, in addition to its founder, was Lola Rodríguez del Tió.

While these clubs incorporated men and women of all races and ethnicities from these islands, it is significant that those of African descent played prominent roles, not only in the establishment in these clubs but in the administration and continued operation of them. [106] Jesse Hoffnung-Garskof characterizes the exile revolutionary movement in this way: "Within the movement, activists of color and artisans worked to construct their own histories, placing the black race and the working class in the center of national progress."[107] Schomburg, then, was only one of a group of men and women, Puerto Rican and Cuban alike, who were reconstituting the histories of the nations of their birth so as to be more inclusive of their lived realities; such efforts, of which this study is an example, continue into the present day.

Schomburg's revolutionary activities continued until 1898, when the war concluded and the United States claimed as its own Spain's remaining colonies. August 2, 1898, marked the final meeting of the Puerto Rican Section of the Cuban Revolutionary Party; there, members approved immediate dissolution.[108] As Bernardo Vega recounts: "Once the thunder of revolutionary struggle against Spain subsided in the Antilles, the Cuban and Puerto Rican emigrant community in New York fell silent."[109] Virginia Sánchez Korrol writes: "Like leaves scattered to the wind, the dissolution of the Puerto Rican section of the PRC on August 2, 1898, also signaled the end of an era but ushered in a new period in the flowering of the city's Puerto Rican *colonias*."[110] Schomburg was present that night, witness to the disbanding of this assembled body.[111] He was twenty-four years old: in the years since his arrival in 1891, he had worked as "an elevator operator, bellhop, porter, and printer; took night classes at Manhattan Central High; and helped organize the club on Third Avenue [Las Dos Antillas] to collect money, weapons, and medical supplies for armed struggle against Spain."[112] He was initiated into the Prince Hall Masons in 1892 through El Sol de Cuba Lodge, Number 38, in Brooklyn; many of the Hispanic Caribbean men who influenced Schomburg were also Masons, including Martí and Betances.[113] Freemasonry would come to be an organizing principle of Schomburg's life, and for that reason it is the focus of the following chapter. He married Elizabeth Hatcher in 1895, and saw the birth of the first two of his eight children, Máximo Gómez (1897) and Arturo Alfonso Jr. (1898).[114]

His biographer records that it was at this time that he began to employ "Arthur" rather than "Arturo";[115] for her, this gesture signals a repudiation of the Hispanic Caribbean. Yet the remainder of this study will demonstrate that Schomburg personified Edward Said's observation about the exiled: "Because the exile sees things both in terms of what has been left behind and what is actual here and now, there is a double perspective that never sees things in isolation. Every scene or situation in the new country necessarily draws on its counterpart in the old country."[116] In his public and private life, in his work, even in the naming of his children, Schomburg revealed that he never forgot or rejected his Caribbean, and in particular Hispanic Caribbean, origins; if anything, the Antillean liberation effort highlighted the dynamics of race, class, and nationalism in the envisioning of a new nation.[117] In his interactions with men and women from different countries and class backgrounds, he came away with a more ample understanding of the importance of history and the control of the narrative for African diasporic peoples.

PUERTO RICO: "FOREIGN IN A DOMESTIC SENSE"

The exchange of Puerto Rico from Spanish control to that of the United States was not a straightforward one; rather, the struggle for equality with the colonizer that Liberals had begun under Spain would continue for decades with the new Mother Country.[118] In her incisive study *The Anarchy of Empire in the Making of U.S. Culture* (2002), Amy Kaplan writes of the Supreme Court deliberations that characterized the lawsuits that would come to be known as the *Insular Cases*: these are the set of suits fought before the High Court from 1901 to 1905 that determined the political status of Puerto Rico and its inhabitants. The outcome of this litigation was the creation of the category "unincorporated territory," a classification that still stands today and which means that a Congressional act is needed for the island to join the Union. As Kaplan highlights: "This new doctrine positioned Puerto Rico in a liminal space both inside and outside the boundaries of the Constitution, both 'belonging to' but 'not a part' of the United States. *The Insular Cases* thereby relegated the peoples of Puerto Rico to a state of limbo in space and time, where they were neither citizen at home nor aliens from another nation."[119] This ambiguity is one that has defined Puerto Rico's relationship to the United States since its annexation in 1898.[120]

Part of the successful arguments for the arrival at this designation was the racialization of the island's populace: as Kaplan points out, the first of these cases, *Downes v. Bidwell*, took place only five years after *Plessy v. Ferguson* dismantled Reconstruction efforts by enacting de jure segregation.[121] She notes: "At the same moment that former slaves and their descendants were stripped of full citizenship at home, the inclusion of nonwhite citizens from abroad was rendered as the enslavement and darkening of white Americans, thereby placing them outside the domain of the proper citizen."[122] The war against Spain ended in 1898 for Cuba and Puerto Rico (the same year that Hawaii was annexed) but it quickly sparked a Philippine resistance that lasted until 1902; during those years, Puerto Rican bodies, like their Cuban, Hawaiian, and Filipino counterparts, were all racialized in the press at the time. Political cartoonists in periodicals across the country utilized caricatures of African Americans as idle, incompetent, happy slaves—the image of the Old Negro, as it were, that intellectuals and image makers of the Harlem Renaissance were later determined to combat—to create the images of these newly acquired lands in order to legitimize the imperial ambitions of United States politicians. They drew sketches of dark petulant male children as a means of infantilizing these populations, thereby showing them to be incapable of self-government due to their presumed immaturity.[123] These territories were deemed "barbarous," populated by "uncivilized" or "less civilized" human beings; Cuba and Puerto Rico were considered the latter.

This was the era of Manifest Destiny in the United States, whereby territorial expansionism was justified in terms of the exceptionalism of the peoples of this country as bestowed by God Himself. The "White Man's Burden," as Rudyard Kipling's 1899 poem urged, was to save the "new-caught sullen peoples,/ Half devil and half child."[124] From the perspective of the Europeans, or at least the British, their former colony had graduated to adulthood with these new possessions; and with adulthood, with manhood more specifically, came the responsibilities of being a man. Civilizing the primitive element of the Americas was considered an obligation that the U.S. government had willingly taken on in an attempt to surpass the vastness of Queen Victoria's dominion.

It must be pointed out that a good part of the Latin American elite also felt that their populations were uncivilized and in need of the light of illumination that would come from more supposedly refined cultures.[125] While they often looked to Europe as the source of such cure, some did look to the United States, ignoring Martí's admonition about the growing danger of the supposed purveyor of modernity and civilization. In Puerto Rico, many landowners, even those within the autonomist movement of the 1880s and 1890s, favored annexation to the

United States; this was especially true for those whose crop was sugar.[126] Luis García Gervasio emphasizes that the discourse of inferiority regarding Puerto Rico held by U.S. politicians only built upon similar sentiments held by the upper classes of the island:

> The discourse of imperial hegemony borrowed the rhetoric that had already been developed by the subalterns, namely the Creole elite of professional men and landholders....The invader did not have to devalue Puerto Ricans in order to dominate because the islanders were already seen as unworthy in the eyes of the leaders and intellectuals of the country.[127]

This perhaps explains the reverence with which Betances, Hostos, Rodríguez de Tió and the like are held even in the contemporary moment: their imagined nations were inclusive of all segments of the population, irrespective of class. The revolutionary clubs composed of exiles and migrants in the United States were predominantly working-class; *tabaqueros*, artisans, and the like financially supported the liberation of these islands during a historical moment when such mobilization was deemed impossible in Puerto Rico itself.[128]

Arturo Schomburg was one such *tabaquero*; he arrived in New York at seventeen years old, a young man of phenotypical African heritage from an island that at the highest levels denied the existence of the segment of the population of which he was a part. He came to a neighboring country that employed violence to keep the populace of the formerly enslaved Africans and their descendants in check. In both the United States and Puerto Rico, politicians and other stakeholders castigated, marginalized, demonized, and terrorized the African diasporic populations within their borders; in the face of both physical and discursive violence, men and women in both places risked their lives in order to draw attention and fight in defense of the humanity of peoples of African descent. For Schomburg, his contributions to this effort began with the establishment of institutions that would gather and preserve the history of this populace.

2

The Diasporic Race Man as Institution Builder

I am here with a sincere desire to awaken the sensibilities, to rekindle the dormant fibers in the soul, and to fire the racial patriotism by the study of Negro books.

—ARTHUR SCHOMBURG, "Racial Integrity: A Plea for the Establishment of a Chair of *Negro History in Our Schools and Colleges, etc.*"

What of it if the darker races are getting consciousness, isn't the world large enough for the people of all bloods to dwell therein?

—ARTHUR SCHOMBURG, "Masonic Truths: A Letter and a Document."

———————

IN JULY 1913, a year that marked the fiftieth anniversary of the Emancipation Proclamation, Arthur Schomburg delivered a rousing call to the Teachers' Summer Class at the Cheyney Institute in Pennsylvania. Today known as Cheyney University of Pennsylvania, it was founded in 1837 first as the African Institute and next as the Institute of Colored Youth; Cheyney is the oldest African American institution of higher learning in the United States. For Schomburg, education was a key in the ongoing quest for freedom for peoples of African descent, not only in this country but indeed, throughout the world. In this speech, which he later published as an occasional paper of the Negro Society for Historical Research, he laid out the need for black historians, and indeed, the establishment of a chair of Negro History, so as to "teach our people our own history."[1] For Schomburg, this would actively negate the lacunae in white supremacist texts that had removed whole episodes of the achievements of Africans and their descendants; instead of being "at the mercy of the 'flotsam and jetsam' of the white writers,"[2] black writers would manifest their agency in the production and publication of their own histories, thereby empowering children and adults alike as they learned of ancestors who had made contributions to all of the countries where they have lived.

Though we have no documentation regarding reactions to his address, one wonders how the audience of graduates and their families received Arthur Schomburg. To date, we have no recording of Schomburg, and so have no idea how he sounded, and yet we can speculate that perhaps his voice carried an accent conveying a youth spent in the Caribbean, one that was accustomed to speaking Spanish fluently. In his critical text *Phonographies: Grooves in Sonic Afro-Modernity* (2005), Alexander G. Weheliye interrogates "how blackness is sounded and heard by a whole range of cultural, philosophical, political, social, and economic discourses."[3] In the case of Schomburg, one considers how his physical presence implicitly required his audience to acknowledge and incorporate peoples of African descent from other spaces of the African diaspora, particularly those of Hispanophone regions, in their conceptions of blackness. Antonio López comments on the sonic resonances of blackness of Afro-Latino populations, pointing out that "Afro-Latinas/os manage their racialization by vocalizing themselves in certain ways across the multilinguistic spaces of the United States."[4] That is to say that for populations of simultaneous African and Hispanic descent, there was then, and there continues to be now, a persistent negotiation of legibility when in contact with other populations of African descent. Schomburg's conception of blackness was one that was not predicated on national identification but instead on an insistence on its expansiveness; when he spoke of "Negro books," he talked not only about those written in English, but instead, of those written in all of the languages of the African diaspora. He insisted, then, that his audience, consisting of those physically present as well as those who read his speech as text, consider the diaspora in its greatest breadth.

A decade later, in a Masonic publication, Schomburg more bluntly posed the rhetorical question used as an epigraph for this chapter; he was fully aware that the education of African diasporic peoples threatened the continuation of white supremacist thought. He went on to respond to his own inquiry: "The force of resistance with the whites is the consciousness of having robbed the weaker races of all that was lootable, their consciousness squeams with the animus furandi and they are afraid the worm will some day turn, for a thousand and one wrongs unjustly inflicted."[5] Schomburg's frank criticism was notable because it occurred, again, in a Masonic publication; in comparison to the tone of his articles published in *Opportunity* and *The Crisis*, here Schomburg directed his comments to an audience of men who were dedicated to "a militant tradition of protest and resistance."[6]

While his writings are the focus of the third chapter of this study, this chapter examines Schomburg's subject position as a Race Man; in particular, it reassesses his participation in three institutions, the Prince Hall Freemasons, the Negro

Society for Historical Research, and the American Negro Academy. Each of these three organizations was known to be an "uplift" organization, that is, each adhered to a doctrine that sought the social, economic, and political advancement of men and women of African descent. Arthur Schomburg held office in each of these organizations: initiated into the Freemasons in 1892, by 1918 Schomburg had ascended the organizational hierarchy to be named Grand Secretary of the Grand Lodge of the State of New York, a title that he held for eight years.[7] A co-founder of the Negro Society for Historical Research, Schomburg served as secretary and treasurer, assuming responsibilities that he had held in the Antillean revolutionary clubs of his youth.[8] Three years later, at the recommendation of two friends and mentors, John Edward Bruce, president of the Negro Society for Historical Research, and John Wesley Cromwell, Schomburg was admitted into the American Negro Academy, the first scholarly research organization for men of African descent in the country. On December 30, 1920, he assumed the presidency of this association, a position he would hold until 1928.[9]

Schomburg is known primarily for the library that was named in his honor years after the purchase of his extraordinary private collection; certainly his passion for peoples of African descent is clear from his collecting habits. This chapter examines the professional activities that stimulated and fortified his dedication to the pursuit, purchase, and assemblage of books, pamphlets, posters, lyric sheets, plastic arts, all creative endeavors that served as evidence of the accomplishments of men and women of African descent around the globe. Remarkably, Schomburg participated in these organizations in addition to holding a position at the Bankers Trust Company, where he was employed for more than two decades, beginning in 1906; also, during these years he married twice more, to Elizabeth Morrow Taylor in 1902 and Elizabeth Green in 1914, and fathered five additional children: Reginald Stanfield (1903), Nathaniel José (1907), Fernando Alfonso (1912), Dolores María (1914), and Carlos Plácido (1916).[10] As evident from the names of several of his children, Schomburg continued to honor the land of his birth, as well as his family members (he named his daughter after his sister Dolores); this remembrance is evident in his participation in these institutions as well, where he continued to bring attention to the Spanish-speaking world. While these organizations were ethnically diverse, given that they included members from throughout the African diaspora including the United States, the British West Indies, and the African continent, nevertheless, Schomburg's involvement meant a commitment to the further diversification of these spaces, thereby ensuring the inclusion of the histories of Afro-Latinos.[11]

THE RACE MAN

In her 1998 study *Race Men*, Hazel V. Carby traces this term to St. Clair Drake and Horace R. Cayton's *Black Metropolis* (1945), a now-classic study of Chicago's South Side. For them, since the passage of the Thirteenth Amendment, which emancipated all the enslaved in the United States, "black people have had to prove, actively and consistently, that they were not the inferior beings that their status as second-class citizens declared them to be: hence an aggressive demonstration of their superiority in some field of achievement, either individually or collectively, was what established race pride: 'the success of one Negro' was interpreted as 'the success of all.'"[12] In order to prove their humanity in a racist environment which labored to prove the contrary, then, black men and women had to succeed at all costs; while the correlation of excellence to humanity has proven to be a tenuous one in the face of white supremacist thought and systemic racism, nevertheless this has been the calculus employed by peoples of African descent for more than a century in the United States (indeed, throughout the Americas). As Mark Anthony Neal observes: "Race men inspire pride; their work, their actions, and their speech represent excellence instead of evoking shame and embarrassment."[13]

"Race man" is, of course, an explicitly gendered terminology, one that focuses on contemporary ideologies of masculinity and manhood. In his study *Manliness and Its Discontents* (2004), Martin Summers highlights how manhood was embedded in discourses surrounding such notions as "independence, citizenship, engagement in the marketplace, mastery over self and the environment, and patriarchy."[14] Brittney Cooper provides an important corrective with her 2009 dissertation, "Race Women: The Politics of Black Female Leadership in Nineteenth and Twentieth Century America." There she examines the works of women such as Maria Stewart, Anna Julia Cooper, Ida B. Wells-Barnett, Mary Church Terrell, and Pauli Murray, in order to demonstrate how they engaged the public sphere so as to enact their own uplift narratives; Cooper's study serves as an acknowledgment of the important contributions made by these women to better the Race.[15] This conception of the Race, is, of course, one that has been debated as it varies depending on geographic location and language; nevertheless, for the purposes of this study, the Race, as Schomburg uses it in his writings, references the multilingual African diaspora, a collective to which he returned throughout his participation in the Prince Hall Masons, the Negro Society for Historical Research, and the American Negro Academy.[16]

THE INSTITUTIONS

In her reflection on Harlem's yesteryears and its contemporary presence, *Harlem Is Nowhere: A Journey to the Mecca of Black America* (2011), Sharifa Rhodes-Pitts provides a sketch of Schomburg:

> Schomburg belonged to a circle of "race men" who were also book fiends, sharing and trading recent acquisitions. Before there was such a thing as the New Negro movement, he had cofounded the Negro Society for Historical Research, was a member of the Negro Book Collectors Exchange, and had served as president of the American Negro Academy.... The desire of these men to uncover the forgotten history of black people was matched by a desire to protect and steward that knowledge.[17]

Rhodes-Pitts's contextualization of Schomburg is important, not only in terms of chronology but also in terms of his interactions with others: she demonstrates that he was one of a group of like-minded individuals, all of whom were pursuing the same goal of recuperating overlooked and marginalized historical narratives, then guiding the dissemination of these episodes so that they would not be forgotten. One strategy that served as an attempt to ensure that this knowledge would continue to circulate was the establishment of organizations that would ground these efforts in reality. Each of these associations, which today are perceived as having been homogeneous, was ethnically diverse in their time, given that their members originated from different countries throughout the African diaspora. Schomburg's involvement in each of these bodies, the Prince Hall Masons, the American Negro Academy, and the Negro Society for Historical Research, as well as in organizations that survive to this day, the National Urban League and the National Association for the Advancement of Colored People, meant a commitment to the further diversification of these spaces, thereby ensuring the inclusion of peoples of African descent from the Spanish-speaking world.

Prince Hall Masons

Schomburg's biographer, Elinor Des Verney Sinnette, notes that Schomburg's initiation into his Masonic order was one that allowed him entrance into "an ancient secret society whose members were among the most-respected community leaders."[18] Black freemasonry in the United States was established by Prince Hall, a free black man, and fourteen other free black men, who were initiated by a group of Irish Freemasons within a British regiment in Boston on March 6, 1775, weeks before the start of the revolution.[19] Shortly thereafter, they organized a lodge of their own, the Provisional African Lodge No. 1; they were formally incorporated into the organization when they secured a charter from the Grand Lodge of England, which was accomplished on September 29, 1784, and so the Provisional African Lodge No. 1 became the African Lodge No. 459, with Prince Hall elected Grand Master. A year after Great Britain had formally lost the thirteen colonies with the revolution, it is, ironically, an English lodge that facilitated the legitimation of this one; Hall had spent the nine years petitioning lodges throughout the colonies, and had been uniformly rejected, as white lodges here prohibited satisfaction of his request.[20] From its founding, then, what would come to be known as Prince Hall masonry was looking outside the national borders of the United States, finding support from their brethren internationally.

From its formation, black Freemasons were involved in the social issues of the day: Hall himself was a fervent abolitionist who also petitioned that enslaved and free black men be allowed to enlist in the U.S. Continental Army. Though this idea was initially rejected due to fears that black soldiers would rebel against their white counterparts (notably, a fear that predates the Haitian Revolution but one that was only heightened in the aftermath of that event), it was later reconsidered, so that free and enslaved men were allowed to fight. Given that the British Army was accepting black soldiers, this was a pragmatic decision based on the needs of the rebel army. Nevertheless, in his study *Constructing the Black Masculine: Identity and Ideality in African American Men's Literature and Culture, 1775-1995* (2002), Maurice O. Wallace highlights how Hall's actions within the realm of Freemasonry and the military "secur[ed] New England's enslaved and free men of color a meaningful place in two of the most crucial spheres of masculine authentication in colonial American culture...Hall's efforts point up the single-minded earnest with which African American men in the colonial period aimed to prove and link their manliness to the building of nationhood."[21] Enlistment in the military was an important strategy for men of African descent, free and enslaved, throughout the hemisphere, including the Spanish-speaking lands: for the enslaved, it was an important tactic for securing their freedom, and for both groups it was a means by which to secure equal rights of citizenship in the eyes of the law.[22]

The founding of the African Lodge No. 459 (renamed the Prince Hall Grand Lodge after his death in 1807) quickly led to the establishment of lodges throughout the country in the following decades. These men became acknowledged leaders in their communities, as they fought to end slavery and the slave trade, as well as labored to secure the full rights of citizenship for African men and women and their descendants. They also established schools for their children, whose formal education was banned by law under slavery.[23] The end of the Civil War meant the proliferation of lodges in the U.S. South; Black Freemasonry continued to expand well into the twentieth century and continues in this day and age to serve as an important fraternal order for black men in the United States.

In this organization men found not only an alternate space whereby they could participate meaningfully in the political matters of their day; indeed, Prince Hall Freemasonry, and their auxiliary organizations for women, such as the Orders of the Eastern Star (founded in 1874), provided emotional and material support for black communities across the country.[24] These organizations, from the time of their founding, offered a means by which to counterbalance the racist carica- tures created and perpetuated in a culture sustained by spurious science that attested to the primitivism of the Negro (craniometry, for example, which linked brain size, race, and intelligence); social Darwinism that declared that the natural order meant the survival and success of the civilized (i.e., those closest to the white Anglo Saxon Protestant) races; Manifest Destiny that conveyed that God had ordained the systematic enslavement and destruction of populations indigenous to the Americas and the African continent in the course of the continental expan- sion of the nation's borders from the Atlantic to Pacific Oceans; and physical vio- lence in the forms of lynchings and indiscriminate murder.

In Prince Hall Freemasonry and the Order of the Eastern Star, for example, men and women of African descent had a metaphorical space (and a physical space, in the form of the lodges themselves) that recognized their full humanity and that labored for their full rights as citizens, which one scholar articulates as "enfranchisement, inclusion, and employment."[25] The systemic racism and dis- crimination they experienced gave rise to a politics of respectability, whereby they would comport themselves at all times with dignity and honor.[26] Writing about Prince Hall Freemasonry in the United States in the first decades of the twentieth century, Martin Summers argues that these men "concretely and symbolically constructed their gender identities within the paradigms of providership, pro- duction, and respectability....Symbolically, Masonry provided black men with an imaginary claim to traditional, nineteenth-century notions of manhood."[27] Still, black Freemasonry provided for its initiates an important platform, one that served as "a school for leadership and a vehicle for collective expression outside the channel of formal politics."[28]

This held true in the United States as well as in the Hispanic Caribbean; in her groundbreaking and singular 2013 study, *Writing Secrecy in Caribbean Freemasonry*, Jossianna Arroyo writes that for Afro-Latinos of this region, initiation into this order allowed for the devising of new approaches for true liberation. She puts forth: "Like their African-American counterparts Afro-Caribbean Freemasons used literacy—and their membership at the lodge—to acquire social power, citizenship, and respectability."[29] Throughout her study, she emphasizes the role of the written word as a technology that linked these men to a "life of active citizenship, intellectual creativity, spiritual, and political knowledge."[30] For men of African descent in the eighteenth and nineteenth centuries, many of them, like Schomburg, with limited formal schooling, Freemasonry trained them in the importance of education, not only with their participation in Masonic ritual but also with their active involvement in the dominant culture. Self-education was promoted as an alternative to that which the given state would not provide. Arroyo notes: "Language, writing, and translation—fitted for different venues, and in different styles and vernaculars—became a source of revelation and political praxis."[31]

In addition to literacy, part of the sense of pride experienced by these men of African descent was due to the prominent role given to the figure of the artisan in Masonic literature. Wallace notes that this figure was the emblematic personage of American Freemasonry: "The artisan had emerged definitively as a national figure for republic citizenship. Deeply esteemed, he personified values of muscular labor, capitalist productivity, economic independence, and masculine self-sufficiency....In becoming a Mason in America, in fact, a man became a figurative craftsman, whatever his actual trade or office."[32] In fact, many black men throughout the Americas in the nineteenth and early twentieth centuries, enslaved or free, were actual artisans, craftsmen who had specialized in fields such as carpentry, blacksmithing, shoemaking, woodwork, tailoring, and printmaking, for example. Arroyo notes: "Indeed, Masonic rituals posited artisan labor as the very foundation of civilization, art, and philosophy."[33] Whereas their dominant societies demonstrated to these men that they were to be marginalized and ignored, Freemasonry taught them instead that their contributions were critical to the societies in which they lived and that it was in fact their civic duty to participate in a meaningful way.

In his attempt to trace the evolution of Schomburg's personal identifications, Jesse Hoffnung-Garskof writes that Schomburg's involvement in black fraternal organizations, particularly the Prince Hall Masons, was instrumental in his development: "Aside from his family life, masonry was the primary institutional framework that organized his social, political, and intellectual migrations into black Harlem and Brooklyn."[34] In the same article, Hoffnung-Garskof emphasizes that these spaces were African diasporic in nature: examining the surnames of the founders of the El Sol de Cuba Lodge, (Schomburg's lodge in Brooklyn), he encounters both Spanish surnames, reflective of the principally Afro-Cuban founders, as well as English ones that belonged to Latin American men whose families had migrated there from the British West Indies.[35]

When he was initiated, then, Schomburg was once again surrounded by the diasporic fullness of the black experience of the Americas. Two decades after he joined, with membership decreasing, Schomburg and his brothers actively recruited Anglophone men who had been born in the United States as well as in the British West Indies; as Summers emphasizes, "When a black Barbadian migrated to Brooklyn and joined Carthaginian [a brother lodge], he probably thought of himself as an individual who was joining an institution that had a history and a presence throughout the diaspora rather than as an African Caribbean who was joining an African American institution."[36] Schomburg, then, played a critical role in an institution that is representative of African diasporic migration to the United States in general, and to New York City in particular, in the first decades of the twentieth century.[37]

In 1914, El Sol de Cuba Lodge was renamed the Prince Hall Lodge No. 38, in honor of its founder. By this year, Schomburg had been named Master of the lodge; in this capacity, as Sinnette comments, "Schomburg's concern for the preservation of its records induced him to gather and organize its documents and papers along with books, pamphlets, correspondence, photographs, and other data pertaining to the black freemasonry movement in the United States."[38] She later notes that he served as the first chairman of his lodge's Committee on Foreign Relations; he utilized his Spanish fluency to contact his brother masons throughout the Americas.[39] This is in addition to his role as translator of all of the founding documents of the lodge, so that those English speakers who did not know Spanish might participate in those rituals requiring the memorization of the facts related to the origins of the group.[40] Hoffnung-Garskof underscores that well into the 1920s, it was as a high-ranking official within the Prince Hall Masons upon which Schomburg's recognition rested; his passion as a collector and historian was not particularly well known outside of certain circles until the 1920s, when his collection was purchased by the Carnegie Corporation as a donation for the New York Public Library.[41]

For men of African descent in the Americas, Freemasonry was an organization that provided them a stronger sense of self as men, as productive contributors to their respective societies. Corey D. B. Walker writes: "As male bodies became ritually pure and upright through initiation and membership in the order, black male bodies assembled in this fraternal order could counter the prevailing sentiment of the black body as a social and political problem. Through Freemasonry, the black body could be seen in a positive light—as a contributing and respectful member of a new social and civic order."[42]

The Negro Society for Historical Research

Through his involvement with the Prince Hall Masons, Schomburg participated in a global network of men of African descent who were focused on making significant contributions to their societies; one of these men, a brother in Schomburg's Masonic lodge, was John Edward Bruce.[43] Born into enslavement in 1856, he labored to educate himself after emancipation. A self-taught man, he founded and ran several newspapers, as well as contributed "newspaper articles, authored pamphlets and books, delivered numerous speeches, collected evidence, undertook research, and advocated the adoption of Black history courses in Negro colleges and secondary schools."[44] For Bruce, as for many advocates of black history being integrated in school curricula, including Schomburg, the study of African diasporic history "legitimized Black humanity, reinforced Black pride, and underpinned Black protest and civil rights struggles."[45] History therefore was, and is, an implement of resistance against white supremacist thought that suffused mainstream culture.

To that end, Bruce and Schomburg co-founded the Negro Society for Historical Research; it was established in April 1911, with John Edward Bruce serving as president and Schomburg as secretary and treasurer.[46] Sinnette writes:

> One of the major goals of the society was "to collect useful historical data relating to the Negro race, books written by or about Negroes, rare pictures of prominent men and women...letters of noted Negroes or of white men friendly to the Negro, Africa curios of native manufacture, etc., etc." The society's purpose, as stated in the preamble to its constitution, was "to show that the Negro race has a history which antedates that of the proud Anglo-Saxon race."[47]

Another goal was "to teach, enlighten, and instruct [black] people [in their own] history and achievement."[48] In his biography of John Edward Bruce, William Seraile writes: "Bruce aimed to make black New York City the cultural and intellectual center for research by forming libraries and art collections to collect data, pamphlets, books, and other pertinent materials chronicling the race's achievements in the African America."[49] While David Fulton (1861–1941), a writer, journalist, and fellow Mason, was named the official librarian of the group, it was

Schomburg who assumed the responsibilities of the office, both acquiring new materials as well as managing a circulating library for members.[50]

In John Edward Bruce, Schomburg found a mentor who himself appreciated African diasporic history; Ralph L. Crowder writes how in 1893, Bruce prepared a reader for children composed of biographical sketches of prominent figures such as Benjamin Banneker, Frederick Douglass, Martin Delany, and Toussaint L'Ouverture. The book would later be published in 1910 as *Short Biographical Sketches of Eminent Negro Men and Women*.[51] Schomburg wrote about this association in his most widely distributed essay, "The Negro Digs up His Past" (1925); he observes that the Negro Society for Historical Research "has succeeded in stimulating the collection from all parts of the world of books and documents dealing with the Negro. It has also brought together for the first time co-operatively in a single society African, West Indian, and Afro-American scholars."[52] In the context of the essay, Schomburg was writing about the development of three historical organizations focused on peoples of African descent, the other two being the American Negro Academy and Carter G. Woodson's Association for the Study of Negro Life and History (notably, the only such intellectual society that survives to this day). Schomburg's emphasis on the diasporic nature of the participants of the Negro Society for Historical Research distinguishes it from the other two; this institution is, therefore, the one that unites men from across national and cultural boundaries, an achievement that highlights the potential of such unification in the political realm.

Indeed, Crowder notes that the association had corresponding and honorary members who lived in Europe, the African continent, and throughout the Americas.[53] It also included university-produced scholars: both W. E. B. Du Bois and Alain Locke were corresponding members, for example.[54] In an unpublished commemoration of Schomburg written after his death, Locke would go on to recall his time spent with members of a society that was, in his word, "cosmopolitan"; he writes: "Africans, American Negroes, Negroes from all the Antilles composed it together with a few booklovers and antiquarians from New York."[55] Noting that the Hispanic Caribbean was "an area relatively new to them," Locke goes on to emphasize how these men were the "real founders of Negro historical scholarship before the heyday of the professional race historians."[56] This was another distinction about Bruce's organization: a good number of the founding members were autodidacts, men who were denied the opportunity to seek formal education on a higher level and so who instead pursued history, and often book collecting, as their passion. Nonetheless, both self-taught and university-educated men were brought together under the auspices of the Negro Society for Historical Research, an association that survived until Bruce's death in 1924.[57]

The American Negro Academy

Founded on March 5, 1897, by Alexander Crummell, John Edward Bruce, W. E. B. Du Bois, poet Paul Laurence Dunbar, and fourteen others, the American Negro Academy sought

a. To promote the publication of scholarly work;
b. To aid youths of genius in the attainment of the higher culture, at home or abroad;
c. To gather into its archives valuable data, and the works of Negro authors;
d. To aid, by publications, the dissemination of the truth and the vindication of the Negro race by vicious assaults;
e. To publish, if possible, an "Annual" designed to raise the standard of intellectual endeavors among American Negroes.[58]

The emphasis of this organization, then, was explicitly the production of academic scholarship by men of African descent; again, there was the emphasis on the need for the establishment of institutions that could combat the virulent racism that had curtailed the promise of emancipation in the aftermath of the U.S. Civil War. Indeed, its constitution unequivocally states that it was to be populated by "authors, scholars, artists, and those distinguished in other walks of life, men of African descent, for the promotion of Letters, Science, and Art."[59]

Certainly the academy's membership was populated by such men: though perhaps remembered primarily for the essay of which he is a focus in Du Bois's *The Souls of Black Folk* (1903), Alexander Crummell (1819–1898) was an Episcopal minister who had been educated at Cambridge University. A missionary in Liberia for twenty years, from 1853 to 1873, he returned to the United States, leading a congregation in Washington, D.C. It was in this city that the American Negro Academy was established, with Crummell elected its first president; as per Schomburg's biographer, this academy was the "most prestigious organization dedicated to encouraging research in black history."[60] Crowder observes: "The establishment of this Black historical association was part of a larger movement in America that encouraged not only the forming of professional and learned organizations but also the founding of ethnic cultural societies."[61]

Schomburg's election into this elite body was based on the recommendation of his mentor John Edward Bruce, who as one of the original eighteen members had been actively involved since its founding in 1897. Schomburg became a part of the American Negro Academy in 1914, three years after he co-founded the Negro Society for Historical Research. In "The Negro Digs up His Past," he honors Crummell's accomplishment by writing that since its founding, the academy "has continued ever since to be one of the bulwarks of our intellectual life, though unfortunately its members have had to spend too much of their energy and effort answering detractors and disproving popular fallacies. Only gradually have the men of this group been able to work toward pure scholarship."[62] At their annual meetings, held in December, members had the opportunity to present their research, which, in keeping with the organization's constitution, were published as occasional papers. Of Schomburg's involvement in the association, Sinnette writes: "Schomburg was the only presenter before the American Negro Academy who consistently reminded the membership of the role of blacks in Spain, Central America, South America, and the West Indies. For his participation in the annual meetings Schomburg prepared at least four papers to present to the academy, each dealing with some aspect of the history and contribution of blacks not native to the United States."[63]

By 1914, when he joined this body, Schomburg had already published several articles in the *Crisis* and other outlets about the Afro-Latinxs in the Caribbean; in 1915, he presented a paper entitled "The Economic Contribution by the Negro to America," which was later published, where he details the system of African enslavement as controlled by the Iberian regents. While Schomburg's writings are the focus of the next chapter, suffice it to say that with this paper, he attempts to rewrite the mythological foundations of the United States that dictate that the first Africans on these shores landed in Virginia in 1619. He highlights the Spanish and Portuguese colonization efforts, rather than the British ones, reminding his audience that Columbus's landing in this hemisphere had catastrophic effects, not only on the indigenous populations he found in the Caribbean but also on those inhabitants of the African continent that were enslaved and transported as forced labor.

Schomburg's insistence on making this history of enslavement public knowledge reflects his passion for a fuller rendering of the history of Africans in this hemisphere. His contribution was unusual in the context of the academy given that it had little interaction with men outside of the United States; Alfred A. Moss Jr. comments, "Its members were physically far removed from their counterparts in Africa, Latin America, the West Indies, and Europe. Most of them had never met or mingled with educated blacks in these places, and even the few who had, as well as those who followed developments in black communities abroad, frequently had only limited understanding of the cultures, governmental systems, or concerns of their inhabitants."[64] Schomburg, then, as a translator within his Masonic lodge, as head of the foreign language section of the mailing division within the Bankers Trust Company, as an Afro-Latino with active ties to multilingual communities both within and outside the borders of the continental United States, defied the profile of most of the membership of the American Negro Academy.

His commitment to including men who would contribute other perspectives to the academy is made evident by his recommendations for membership. In 1916, for example, he nominated Pedro C. Timothee, professor of Latin at the University of Puerto Rico, a translator of French, an attorney and a pharmacist; Moss records that Timothee was not invited to join the association, as he was not elected.[65] Four years after his attempt to bring Timothee into the association, Schomburg was elected president; in his study of the academy, Alfred A. Moss Jr. reveals the stark differences between Schomburg and the previous presidents (among which were Crummell and Du Bois). Moss names outright his birth on the Spanish colony of Puerto Rico, his migration to the United States, his lack of formal education, and his white collar job, which, though respectable, was not in the same grouping as his colleagues, many of whom were scholars, lawyers, and doctors.[66] Within this space, composed entirely of men of African descent, some of whom were his Masonic brothers, Schomburg remained an outsider, a transgressive figure who headed the organization until its final meeting in 1928.[67]

The National Association for the Advancement of Colored People and the National Urban League

> We need in the coming dawn the man, who will give us the background for our future, it matters not whether he comes from the cloisters of the university or from the rank and file of the fields.
>
> —ARTHUR SCHOMBURG, "Racial Integrity: A Plea for the Establishment of a Chair of Negro History in Our Schools and Colleges, etc."

While he did not hold office in these organizations, Schomburg was quite involved in both the NAACP and the Urban League; certainly both of the associations supported his ideas by publishing his articles in *The Crisis* and *Opportunity*, respectively. While this study examines those written pieces in greater length in the next chapter, it is important to note the philosophies of these two influential groups, both dedicated to the social, economic, and political development of peoples of African descent within the United States. The NAACP was founded in 1909, with the establishment of the Urban League occurring the next year. Both organizations depended on the support of white progressives of the upper middle class who were dedicated to racial reform, and both had integrated boards of directors.

Nevertheless, their differences were important: while the NAACP was focused on the attainment of social justice reforms through protest and the legal system, the Urban League concentrated on "vocational education, social work training, and social service."[68] Nancy J. Weiss details how the NAACP focused more on securing the equal rights for peoples of African descent through legal and political channels, fighting housing and education discrimination in the court system, as well as inaugurating an antilynching campaign that revealed the extent of the violence suffered by blacks in the United States.[69] Touré F. Reed directly states that the Urban League was a "social-work organization" which "attempted to prepare Afro-Americans for life in the industrial city" through vocational training; additionally, it served as a lobbying group that "encouraged employers, unions, and landlords to open jobs and housing to blacks."[70]

Interestingly, though both organizations depended on the social sciences for the collection of data from which they could labor to enact change in the United States, both also had publications that featured not only these facts and figures but also creative contributions by both established and emerging writers. In fact, in Moss's opinion, the successful publications launched by these two organizations challenged the success of the American Negro Academy, insofar as both *The Crisis* and *Opportunity* were "lively, well-edited publications which printed a range of materials, including articles by and about black artists, scholars, and scientists."[71] Indeed, whereas Schomburg published a long essay providing an extensive historical overview of the contributions of Africans and their descendants in the Western hemisphere beginning in the fourteenth century for inclusion in the ANA's Occasional Papers series, in the publications of the NAACP and the Urban League he provided shorter pieces, chronicles that included biographical sketches of highly accomplished Afro-Latinxs whose names and histories may not have been known by a wider Anglophone audience, as well as first-person accounts of his travels to Hispanophone lands where he successfully recovered marginalized narratives.

Returning to Schomburg's 1913 speech with which this chapter began, he makes clear the task at hand for the graduating class of educators, who face the vast challenge of equipping future generations with the indispensable knowledge needed to combat white supremacy. For Schomburg, education is not found solely within the walls of a classroom; on the contrary, his involvement with both the

Prince Hall Freemasons and the Negro Society for Historical Research had demonstrated to him the significance of self-taught men such as himself. Liberated from hegemonic discourses that were often reproduced in classrooms, they could instead produce articles, essays, pamphlets, and speeches that were free from such constraint. These men recognized and respected the pedagogical value of texts that affirmed the humanity of peoples of African descent, and their participation in these organizations meant their dedication to this cause.

For Schomburg, black history meant an inherently African diasporic history, that is, one that recognized not only the contributions of peoples of the African continent or even Haiti but also those of Spanish-speaking men and women of African descent. As Kevin Meeham writes:

> Schomburg places the contribution of people of African descent at the center of any inquiry concerning culture, history, and politics in the hemisphere….[T]his is both an epistemological and political claim. It is epistemological in the sense that his essays imply that we cannot come to know Latin American history in any meaningful way without centering the African presence in that history. At the same time…he consider[s] the political fortunes of people of African descent to be fundamentally linked—both across the hemisphere and globally.[72]

Schomburg rightfully noted the tension between the black bourgeoisie and the lower classes, and while he surrounded himself with men who had far more formal education than he had, he nevertheless always kept in mind those without such achievement. As much as he actively participated in organizations that were mainstays of the black middle class, at the same time his writings and the physical spaces that he created, namely his collection first in his Brooklyn home and later at the 135th Street Branch, were open and available to everyone, the materials he had gathered accessible to all. Here we see a true liberal democratic impulse, one that underscores his passion for learning, whether it be attained in a formal educational setting or outside of the classroom. This same egalitarian imperative manifests in his published and unpublished writings: there, Schomburg reveals a dedication to sharing the lives and occurrences of peoples of African descent in the Spanish-speaking world.

3

AFRO-LATINX CHRONICLES
Schomburg's Writings

It is the season for us to devote our time in kindling the torches that will inspire us to racial integrity.

—ARTHUR SCHOMBURG, "Racial Integrity: A Plea for the Establishment
of a Chair of Negro History"

INTEGRITY, *n.* 1. a. The condition of having no part or element taken away
or wanting; undivided or unbroken state; material wholeness, completeness,
entirety.

—THE OXFORD ENGLISH DICTIONARY

IN THE MIDST of his 1913 speech to the teachers' summer class at Cheyney
Institute, Schomburg introduces the notion of "racial integrity," that is, a conception whereby peoples of African descent achieve a sense of unification, as opposed
to fragmentation and division. For him, this sense of wholeness as a community
across national boundaries could be accomplished through learning, and in particular, through the formal implementation of history courses focusing on the
narratives of the African diaspora. He uses as a counterpoint the example of the
Jewish people, "who though not a practical nation, live in theory a nation of most
powerful intellects."[1] As Adalaine Holton points out, here Schomburg distinguishes
between the political entity of the nation-state ("a practical nation") and a diasporic existence (a nation in theory).[2] Their continued practice of "customs and
traditions" has allowed for the Jewish diaspora to "cling together and uphold the
maxim that 'in unity there is strength'";[3] Schomburg recommends that the African
diaspora learn from these counterparts; doing so would mean the acknowledgment of the histories of all the peoples of African descent internationally,

71

including those who, like this man himself, are Spanish-speaking. Difference, then, would be an asset rather than a detriment, as the student is able to gain different perspectives about the combating of white supremacy by thriving black communities in other geographic locations. Through the course of his writings, published and unpublished, Schomburg brought concerted attention to the large Afro-Latinx community living in the Western Hemisphere.

In addition to his literal archives (his personal collection as well as the library that he established at Fisk University), Schomburg's writings are themselves an archive, in that here he records in English those events and personages that have contributed substantially to the history of the Americas. The subjects of his writings had previously been overlooked by dominant historical narratives in both English and Spanish; with his chronicles and essays, therefore, he not only salvaged these men and women from obscurity, he also bolstered their prominence by publishing these narratives, both in popular African American publications as well as in the papers circulated within the scholarly communities in which he participated. His essays broaden the parameters of his audience's conceptions of blackness so as to include the Spanish-speaking populations of African descent. While this chapter does not examine every article or essay that Schomburg ever wrote, it does look at representative pieces that reveal not only his dedication and commitment to the acknowledgment of Afro-Latinx contributions to the hemisphere but that also highlight the complexities of Afro-Latinx subjectivity.

THE CRÓNICA

SCHOMBURG'S historical articles fit into the Latin American genre known as *crónicas,* or chronicles, short historical accounts that blend reporting with editorial content and that were (and are) featured in periodicals written in Spanish and Portuguese throughout the hemisphere. In her ground breaking 1992 study *La invención de la crónica,* Susana Rotker explores the development of this hybrid genre during the era of Modernismo, the literary movement of the late nineteenth century ushered in by Rubén Darío and José Martí, among others.[4] In fact, Martí's *crónicas* serve as the foundation for her analysis, in that she argues that he came to the realization that journalism represented the democratization of writing because it was available to a broader audience than the book-buying public.[5] Unlike strict reportage, which assumed a tone of objectivity, the *crónica,* or chronicle, allowed for the inclusion of a more subjective perspective, whereby the writer could reference his/her own personal narratives and emotions;[6] the chronicle, therefore, stood at the juncture between the literary and the journalistic.[7] Later in the study, Rotker writes how the *crónica* threatened the clarity of generic boundaries by transgressing both.[8] In the chronicle, therefore, Schomburg identified a genre that would allow him the opportunity to provide biographical sketches on personages he deemed worthy of such treatment along with the space for subjective expression. Unlike reporting, which takes on mimetic resonance, in that it purports to simply tell the facts, the chronicle also provided the possibility to editorialize, relating quotidian occurrences with larger social and political themes. For Schomburg, the *crónica* afforded a discursive space for the introduction of Spanish-speaking men of African descent in periodicals written and read by an Anglophone African diasporic audience.

Plácido

> There is a sad and tragic chapter in the history of Cuba under Spanish rule, that seems to circle with pathetic recollections the dreadful wrongs done to innocent men....A calm generally precedes these conditions and I will attempt to carry you through the events as they were ushered into existence by the break of day.
>
> —ARTHUR SCHOMBURG, "Plácido: an Epoch in Cuba's Struggle for Liberty"

One of the first historical figures about whom Schomburg wrote is the Afro-Cuban poet Gabriel de la Concepción Valdés (1809–1844), also known as Plácido; a free man, the poet was put to death in 1844 on charges that he was the leader of an antislavery uprising. That year was one of widespread repression in Cuba; only forty years after the successful revolution in Haiti, Spanish authorities were on alert for any disturbance to their labor system. The planned rebellion was known as la Conspiración de la Escalera, or the Conspiracy of the Ladder, a reference to the implement to which conspirators were tied and whipped. After his death, Plácido took on mythological importance for peoples of African descent throughout the region, and indeed, throughout the hemisphere.

Schomburg's portrait of Plácido is noteworthy for several reasons, not the least of which because he primarily emphasizes his prowess as a poet rather than as a presumed revolutionary. He details Plácido's early life as an artisan who worked first at a printing office and later as someone who created portrait holders of tortoise shell. By his sixteenth birthday he was known by his nickname, and his poetic talent was already recognized.[9] Schomburg's focus on this man's artistic talent is interrupted when discussing the imperial powers present on the island, the Spanish authorities and English abolitionist David Turnbull, who was said to have played a key role in the conspiracy as a supporter of abolition. At one point, Schomburg takes the opportunity to introduce his readers to another nineteenth-century Afro-Cuban poet of renown, Juan Francisco Manzano (1797–1854);[10] his mention of Manzano is meaningful because he conveys to the reader that Plácido was not exceptional, that indeed there were other poets of African descent on that island, both enslaved and liberated. In addition to his fame as a poet, Manzano is the author of the only extant slave narrative from Latin America, *Autobiografía de un esclavo*, published in England in translation in 1840, and in Havana almost a century later, in 1937. While Schomburg does not make mention of this, Manzano was also accused in taking part in the 1844 conspiracy; after his release from jail, he seemingly stopped writing. Though he evaded Plácido's fate, he nonetheless suffered the effects of Spanish repression.[11]

Schomburg's Plácido is a man who suffered the "unfortunate fate" of "having been born in Cuba with intelligence";[12] he includes one of his poems, "My Prayer to God," (*Plegaria a Dios*) wherein the poet expresses his surrender to God's will. Schomburg's depiction reveals this man's humanity, out of which developed an art recognized even in his day; in the era of Paul Lawrence Dunbar and James Weldon Johnson, Schomburg offered a sketch of a renowned Spanish-speaking poet of African descent. Like men and women in the United States at the time of the writing, here also was someone who had been persecuted unjustly, who died at the hands of a state that had no regard for his gifts and talents, but that saw him solely as a threat to the established order. Rather than focus on the loss, Schomburg puts emphasis on his art, honoring his memory and his contributions to the world.[13]

THE CRISIS: A RECORD OF THE DARKER RACES

W. E. B. Du Bois published some of Schomburg's earliest writings in the initial issues of his magazine *The Crisis*. The official publication of the National Association for the Advancement of Colored People (NAACP), the object of this periodical was "to set forth those facts and arguments which show the danger of race prejudice, particularly as manifested to-day toward colored people."[14] Consequently, it would be a newspaper in that it reported the news; a literary review; a space for articles; and an editorial page that would "stand for the rights of men, irrespective of color or race, for the highest ideals of American democracy, and for reasonable but earnest and persistent attempt to gain these rights and realize these ideals."[15] In the pages of this periodical, then, Schomburg found an ideal space to relate the violence being inflicted on a group of Afro-Cuban veterans who had fought in the wars for independence only to understand that participation in these efforts had not garnered them equality in the political arena.

General Evaristo Estenoz

> Many Cuban Negroes curse the dawn of the Republic. Negroes were welcomed in the time of oppression, in the time of hardship, during the days of revolution, but in the days of peace and of white immigration they are deprived of positions, ostracized and made political outcasts. The Negro has done much for Cuba; Cuba has done nothing for the Negro.
>
> —ARTHUR SCHOMBURG, "General Evaristo Estenoz"

On May 20, 1912, members of the Partido Independiente de Color (PIC) led armed protests across the Cuban countryside in an effort to force the National Congress to recognize its legality. Formed only four years earlier, this political party was composed primarily of Afro-Cuban veterans and activists pressing for full recognition of their rights. Postindependence Cuba had failed to achieve José Martí's dream of a united nation; in the years following the establishment of the Cuban republic in 1902, the Cuban government had actively encouraged Spanish immigration in efforts to whiten the country, passing over those men who had fought in the Ten Years War of 1868–1878, the Little War of 1879–1880, and what has come to be known as the Spanish-American War of 1898.[16] With a growing Afro-Cuban middle class and the passage of the vote for all men in the country, the Afro-Cuban population had legitimate political clout in the first decade of the new century. Frustration with being ignored by government officials, who provided lucrative incentives to new Spanish immigrants as well as hiring opportunities to white Cubans, resulted in the formation of the new political party in 1908.

In the subsequent two years, it became clear that the PIC posed no true threat to the standing political order. In congressional elections of 1908, PIC candidates received little more than one hundred votes, whereas candidates from the predominant Conservative and Liberal parties received between twenty thousand and fifty thousand.[17] However, representatives from both parties recognized the potential for mobilization on the part of a populace that had been little served in the first decade of the republic, namely the poor and working classes, many of whom were Afro-Cuban. In addition to greater access to jobs in the public sector, the PIC called for

> an end to racial discrimination, equal access for Afro-Cubans to posi-
> tions in public service and the diplomatic corps, and an end to the ban
> on "nonwhite" immigration. Most of the other demands aimed at
> improving the conditions of the popular classes regardless of race:
> expansion of compulsory free education from eight to fourteen years;
> provision of free technical, secondary, and university education; state
> control of private schools; abolition of the death penalty; reform of the
> judicial and penitentiary systems; establishment of the eight-hour work
> day and of a system that gave Cubans priority in employment; and the
> distribution of national lands to Cubans.[18]

In 1910, the Congress passed an amendment outlawing the organization of political parties on the basis of race or class; it was introduced by Afro-Cuban senator
of the Liberal Party Martín Morúa Delgado. Himself a noted writer and activist,
Morúa Delgado had been elected the nation's first Afro-Cuban senator in 1901.
Nine years later, he introduced what would be called the Morúa Amendment on
the Senate floor; as president of the Senate, he ensured the passage of this legislation. Declared unconstitutional, members of the PIC appealed both to Congress
as well as to the United States Department of State to overturn the amendment,
only to be met with opposition.[19] Instead, participants were met with widespread
repression, as party members were arrested, charged with illegal gathering, and
imprisoned. While thousands left the party, the founders of the PIC, among them
Evaristo Estenoz and Pedro Ivonnet, called for an armed demonstration in order
to demand the repeal of the Morúa Amendment on May 20, 1912.[20] This kind of
action was in fact standard for political parties at the turn of the century; rather
than attempt a modicum of negotiation with the leaders of the party, the Cuban
government instead ordered their extermination.[21]

Using the popular press to warn of black rebellions in the eastern provinces,
Cuban soldiers launched a determined attack against all perceived rebels in the
summer of 1912. In addition to three battleships in the waters of the Oriente
region, the United States deployed more than two thousand troops for its second
military intervention into Cuba (following an occupation of the island from 1906–
09).[22] The military not only attacked PIC members, they also killed thousands
who had no relation to the party: on May 31, 1912, 150 Afro-Cuban peasants were
killed in La Maya, signaling an assault on the black populace as a whole.[23] Men
and women of African descent were arrested and imprisoned throughout the island,

as whites were allowed to arm themselves without permits or licenses and were allowed to form civil guards under the eyes of authorities.[24] Within two months, demonstrations had been crushed and all perceived threats of armed resistance on the part of the Afro-Cuban population ended; thousands had been killed, among them Evaristo Estenoz, who was shot at point-blank range on June 27, 1912. Newspapers across the country featured photographs of his corpse, as they celebrated his death, which effectively ended what has come to be known as the Race War of 1912.

By 1912, Arturo Alfonso Schomburg was already recognized within certain circles as one of the most important collectors of objects documenting the global black experience; he carried this commitment to bringing to light the contributions of men and women of African descent in all of the Americas to his writing. Writing for an English-speaking audience, Schomburg offered a summary of contemporary events in Cuba: "The cable has flashed over the world the news that in Cuba General Evaristo Estenoz has taken up the gage of battle for the rights of his dark fellowmen, and that a crisis in Cuba is the result."[25] By the time of the publication of this issue of the *Crisis*, Estenoz had already been killed; nevertheless, Schomburg reviewed for his audience the founding of the Independent Colored Party, its stated goals on the part of its constituents, the popularity of the party, the passage of the Morúa Amendment, and the subsequent crisis caused by this law. From New York City, Schomburg indicts the deceased Morúa Delgado:

> The new party was a success and it augured no good to President Gómez. When the government found that it could not deal with the situation, it turned to the late Negro senator, M. Morúa Delgado, the president of the senate.…For this perfidy, Delgado was rewarded with the appointment to the portfolio of secretary of war, but he was ever afterward looked upon by the Negroes of Cuba as a Judas to his race. Although he did not, like Judas, go out and hang himself, he died, it is said, of a broken heart.[26]

While this opinion had been expressed on the part of activists and those intimately involved with the fight for full citizenship on behalf of the Afro-Cuban population, it was by no means popularly expressed in publications at the time. Schomburg therefore introduced his audience to the figure of a man of African descent betraying his people. That this man, Morúa Delgado, had ascended to political heights and was ostensibly accepted by his political contemporaries at the time, only to seemingly deceive the constituency that had elected him, served as an implicit warning to African Americans serving in politics at the time, men such as George Washington Ellis, William Henry Hunt, and Mifflin Wistar Gibbs.[27]

His words act as a cautionary tale to an audience mobilizing in part through the very publication in which the article appears.

Schomburg ends his essay debunking the myth of racial unity that had been circulated within Cuba at the conclusion of the nineteenth century: "The Negroes began to realize, when their leaders were thrown into prison on the eve of election, that the white Cubans had determined that they should not have any representation save what was bestowed on them as charity."[28] While popular literature of the time spoke only of "Cuba" using José Martí's vision of unification of the island, Schomburg, who had hosted Martí in New York and who was deeply involved in the independence of Cuba and Puerto Rico in his teenage years, separates the two groups, those of European and African descent. Again, he strikes a chord of caution to his audience regarding the placement of hope solely in political officials; in addition, he emphasizes the distinction between the two communities within Cuba, thereby underscoring the commonalities between the Afro-Cuban and African American populations.

Toward the conclusion of the article, Schomburg unleashes his criticism of U.S. foreign policy: "During the colonial days of Spain, the Negroes were better treated, enjoyed a greater measure of freedom and happiness than they do to-day."[29] This sentence, indeed the article itself, is a stinging indictment of the United States, as it was heavily involved in expansion of its empire into Latin America at the time. Men and women like Schomburg himself, who had been engaged in the fight for liberation of the island of his birth and her sister island of Cuba, had greeted the end of the Spanish-Cuban-American War of 1898 with trepidation. Martí's articles written about the United States had offered warning of the Colossus of the North and its expansionist interests three decades earlier; noting the establishment of racial segregation in the United States, there had been trepidation about the presumed imposition of such laws in these islands. Writing in 1912, Schomburg composed his chronicle as news reports emerged about mass killings of those of African descent in Cuba; he closes his article utilizing the motif of the runaway slave: "The black men in Cuba have taken to the woods because conditions are intolerable, because, as my friend, the late José Martí, the apostle of Cuban freedom said: 'So long as there remains one injustice to repair in Cuba the revolutionary redemption has not finished its work.'"[30] Invoking the figure of the escaped enslaved man (the *cimarrón*), Schomburg again emphasizes that Cubans of African descent are similarly occupied in their own struggle for civil rights. Cuba, then, is not simply a foreign country that has nothing to do with the African American community; instead, it is an additional site for emancipation in the Americas. Despite differences of language, Schomburg calls on his audience not only to be empathetic to the cause, but also to contextualize the Afro-Cuban struggle for equal rights as a hemispheric one.

SCHOLARSHIP

This study has examined Schomburg's participation in the Negro Society for Historical Research and the American Negro Academy; within both institutions, participants circulated speeches that members had made within the association. The American Negro Academy in particular was intent on the distribution of these papers, which "were selected for publication because the academy believed them to be excellent examples of black intellectual ability, correctives to distorted or prejudiced opinions concerning their race, and significant contributions to the general body of knowledge about black Americans."[31] Arthur Schomburg offered to these bodies a wider definition of "black Americans" to include narratives of men and women of African descent in the Spanish-speaking Americas.

Negro Society for Historical Research

> We often feel that so many things around us are warped and alienated. Let us see, if we cannot agree to arrange a formula or create a basic construction, for the establishment of a substantial method of instruction for our young women and men in the material and the useful.
>
> —ARTHUR SCHOMBURG, "Racial Integrity: A Plea for the Establishment of a Chair of Negro History"

One of Schomburg's clearest statements about the importance of education and learning emerges in this speech, which was later circulated within the membership of the Negro Society for Historical Research. Indeed, for him, the study of history and of the accomplishments of peoples of African descent served as a balm in the midst of the madness of white supremacy and systemic racism. His recommendation for the formalization of the study of black history, in all of its facets, was therefore one that sought the creation of safe spaces within institutions of learning. While he was delivering his remarks to a historically Black college, he did not qualify his proposal by stating that these spaces of learning should be located solely in black institutions such as Tuskegee or Fisk; instead, it was a broad proposition, offered at a time when the educational landscape was changing, as more black men and women were graduating from college and more nonprofit organizations such as the Carnegie Corporation and the Rosenwald Fund were investing in higher education, particularly in the former Confederate states. The first decades of the twentieth century, then, were opportune for discussions about the training of educators and the establishment of new schools throughout the country.

Schomburg begins his speech by recalling the existence of the Rosetta Stone: "The cuneiform characters and kindred systems of writing have remained to this day enveloped in a veil of mystery, which the light of reason can only overcome with spasmodic success....[A]round those letters…hinges the riddle of African civilization."[32] Schomburg here implies that Africa and the cultural productions of her children are the keys by which to understand civilization; this stands in direct opposition to works of scientific racism such as Karl Vogt's *Lectures on Man* (1864), which proposed that whites and blacks were separate races, and Ernst Haeckel's *The History of Creation* (1876), which identified Caucasians as the highest evolved race. The refutation is a strong one: whereas Hegel proclaimed that Africa "is no historical part of the World; [and] it has no movement or development to exhibit,"[33] here Schomburg responds to the charge by saying not only that this history exists, but that it has also yet to be deciphered. He therefore tacitly charges his audience with this task. He continues: "The object of this paper is not to revolutionize existing standards, but simply to improve them by amending them, so that they will include the practical history of the Negro Race, from the dawn of civilization to the present time."[34] Once more, Schomburg contests the claim that Africans and their descendants are primitive beings who produced nothing of substance, instead contextualizing the origins of the continent's history to the beginning of time itself.

Throughout the speech, Schomburg emboldens his audience not only to rediscover history but also to produce texts about those narratives that have been lost or ignored or marginalized. He says: "We need a collection or list of books written by our men and women. If they lack style, let the children of tomorrow correct the omission of their sires. Let them build upon the crude work. Let them, because of the opportunities that colleges and universities grant, crystalize the crude work and bring it out flawless."[35] Schomburg here addresses a class division present even today, between those who pursue higher education and those, such as himself, who could not; for him, this is a deceptive division, one that threatens the production of texts from peoples of African descent, men and women alike. Instead of the anticipation of a future moment that might bring censure on a spurious charge about lack of style, he offers as an alternative the present moment as a focal point. For him, then, there is no reason that exonerates an absence of writing by black men and women.

With this, he offers a list of writers of African descent in fields as disparate as poetry and fiction, science, historical treatises, slave narratives, educational and religious texts, and scientific theorems. In the same text where he highlights the contributions to the culture made by Phyllis Wheatley, Frederick Douglass, Frances E. Watkins Harper, and Paul Laurence Dunbar, for example, he also highlights the work of Juan Latino, a sixteenth-century professor of classics at the University of Granada in Spain; Alexander Pushkin, Russian writer and author of *Eugene Onegin*; and Alexandre Dumas, author of *The Three Musketeers*. All of these men and women were of African descent; Schomburg's naming of them here exposes the breadth of the African diaspora.

In 1934, this speech was one of two essays by Schomburg (the other being "African Exploration") that appeared in *Negro: An Anthology*. Edited by British heiress and political activist Nancy Cunard, this 855-page tome is a stunning tribute to African diasporic writing; with seven parts devoted to authors from the United States, the West Indies, South America, Europe, and the African continent, Cunard's collection serves as a "recording of the struggles and achievements, the persecutions and the revolts against them, of the Negro peoples."[36] In addition to Schomburg's writings, one sees his influence in the sheer assortment of writers gathered here, including works by Langston Hughes, Zora Neale Hurston, Sterling Brown, Countee Cullen, and W. E. B. Du Bois, as well as writers from Cuba (Nicolás Guillén and Gustavo Urrutia), Haiti (Jacques Roumain), Brazil (Mario de Andrade), Trinidad (George Padmore), and Uruguay (Elemo Cabral and Ildefonso Pereda Valdés). More than two decades after his speech, then, Schomburg played an integral part in the creation of a text that underscores the depth of African diasporic writing.[37]

The American Negro Academy

We have been instructed to look at the Negro as "idle, worthless, indolent and disloyal," but a careful examination of the West Indies and South America does not show this to be true. Many instances of advancement by hard industry can be noted in any of the many spots of the New World. There is not a single field of industrial activity in which the descendants of the African have not contributed their mite toward an improvement of conditions which the gold seekers and pleasure hunters were wont to overlook.

—ARTHUR SCHOMBURG, "The Economic Contribution by
the Negro to America"

Irrespective of its seemingly innocuous title, Schomburg's paper to the American Negro Academy challenged U.S. parochialism by engaging its audience to acknowledge the history of enslavement outside of these borders. While the America of the heading might lead one to believe that his discussion would focus on the United States, instead Schomburg used the word much as inhabitants in the rest of the hemisphere do, that is, in reference to the entirety of this landmass that is the Americas. Instead of discussions about Jamestown or Plymouth Rock, he directs his attention to Santo Domingo (Hispaniola), a site of Christopher Columbus's landing.[38] Immediately, then, he suggests to his audience that the place of Columbus's arrival was as important, if not more so, than simply the fact that he landed somewhere. He highlights not only some amorphous region known as the Caribbean, but indeed, calls attention to the Hispanic Caribbean as the womb of the "New World."

Within the first paragraph, Schomburg names the person responsible for the trafficking of enslaved men and women from the African continent: Father Bartolomé De las Casas. While in Latin American historiography De las Casas is recognized as a savior of the indigenous (which Schomburg references here with his phrase "the Apostle of the Indians"), for Schomburg, it is important to lay at his feet the sin of having initiated the Middle Passage.[39] Schomburg then moves to a conversation about Columbus's Iberian sponsors, citing the history of an African settlement in southern Spain in the fifteenth century and additionally referencing the seven hundred year Moorish presence there.[40] Again implicitly, Schomburg contests discussions about civilization that identify the European continent as the progenitor of all culture, instead making the subtle argument that not only was there an African presence in Europe but also that they lived within the Iberian peninsula.

In the remainder of the essay, Schomburg goes on to examine the "work that no historian or economist has given them the credit which is their due for blazing the path of wealth into which the nations of Europe have ridden upon the lucrative backs of the Africans."[41] He expands his historical narrative from Santo Domingo to the remainder of the South American continent, referencing revolts that took place as well.[42] He anticipates what would later be known as the Tannenbaum slavery thesis by comparing systems of enslavement in the British- and Spanish-controlled territories.[43] Finally, he offers a review of the areas in which Africans and their descendants have excelled, from food management to military service, in areas of culture such as song and storytelling.[44] From the Hispanic Caribbean to the continent itself, Schomburg revises historiography about slavery written in the United States, amply demonstrating that historians must necessarily take into account the experiences and narratives of their neighbors in the rest of the Americas. As his biographer comments about this essay, "To Schomburg the United States was merely a part, albeit an important one, of the wider American nexus, and he regarded himself as an historian of that greater southern land mass which was also America."[45]

THE NEW NEGRO

A highlight of the literary movement that came to be known as the Harlem Renaissance was the publication of *The New Negro*, an anthology edited by Alain L. Locke. Published in the fall of 1925 after the success of a special issue of *Survey Graphic* in March of the same year, this collection of poems, short stories, illustrations, and essays has come to be representative of a cultural moment in African diasporic literary history in the United States. Schomburg's essay, "The Negro Digs up His Past," which appears both in the journal and in the anthology, has come to be regarded as a directive about the necessity for the study of history in the midst of enthusiasm about African American cultural production. Sinnette notes:

> For Arthur Schomburg, the Harlem Renaissance proved to be an excellent environment for conducting his bibliophilic research and an ideal opportunity to promote interest in black history and culture. Responding to the urgent desire of black writers and artists to use "black themes," Schomburg supplied information both from his encyclopedic knowledge and from his private collection. The Harlem Renaissance also stimulated Schomburg himself to write more for publication, and this proved to be his most prolific period.[46]

"The Negro Digs up His Past"

> The American Negro must remake his past in order to make his future. Though it is unorthodox to think of America as the one country where it is unnecessary to have a past, what is a luxury for the nation as a whole becomes a prime social necessity for the Negro. For him, a group tradition must supply compensation for persecution, and pride of race the antidote for prejudice. History must restore what slavery took away, for it is the social damage of slavery that the present generation must repair and offset.
>
> —ARTHUR SCHOMBURG, "The Negro Digs up His Past" (1925)

With these words, Schomburg opens what is his most widely disseminated text; in calling for the study of history, he makes the argument that this knowledge is a worthy defense against white supremacist thought and its attendant violence. While he seemingly wrote specifically about the person of African descent living in the United States, there remains the broader resonance of his words; in the Spanish-speaking Americas, a shared history of enslavement had, by the publication date of this essay, already been systematically erased from nationalist narratives that, ironically, deified a discourse of *mestizaje*. More than two decades after the conclusion of the War of 1898, he was well aware of the representations of peoples of African descent not only in the Hispanic Caribbean but indeed throughout the continent; ideologies of mixture would continue into the 1920s and 1930s, all emphasizing the contributions of indigenous, African, and European populations to Latin American cultures, and all marginalizing the African element in aspiration for the attainment of whiteness.

In his essay, Schomburg summarizes the results of decades of the study of history: (1) that peoples of African descent have long been agents in their own liberation; (2) that those who reach a certain level of achievement are regarded as "exceptional," are ostracized from the larger group, and the group as a whole is not credited with influencing that person; and (3) that excellence has characterized peoples of African descent since the beginning of time, a fact that needs to be acknowledged in order to more fully understand humanity as a whole.[47] His points are significant, given the historical context in which they were offered: writing a history highlighting the agency of peoples of African descent in their own emancipation counters the perception that they were the passive recipients of white largesse. Effectively, Schomburg writes against the stereotype of the white savior, promulgated throughout the nineteenth century as the United States expanded its territorial boundaries with its imperialistic ambitions.

His second conclusion, about the estrangement experienced by those who reach a particular level of success, may be his most personal. Indeed, he had firsthand experience with having been (and to this day, being) considered extraordinary, the effect of which is an assignment to a limbo whereby the person is cast aside and the impact of the group on the person is no longer considered. In his case, his Hispanic Caribbean heritage, specifically his Puerto Rican heritage, has been overlooked and ignored, the result of which is that members of these communities are almost completely unaware of his existence. In his final point, Schomburg argues for the recognition and restoration of peoples of African descent to the history of humankind. Notably, he does not argue that those of African descent are better than any other group—indeed, he later conveys impatience with the notion of bias or counterbias.[48] Instead, he puts forth that the recovery of these historical facts is not solely as a restorative effort ("not merely that we may not wrongfully be deprived of the spiritual nourishment of our cultural past") but indeed a means by which to appreciate the depth of human accomplishment, irrespective of racial identification ("but also that the full story of human collaboration and interdependence may be told and realized").[49]

OPPORTUNITY: A JOURNAL OF NEGRO LIFE

While the NAACP's publication was the *Crisis*, the National Urban League's accompanying periodical was *Opportunity*; one historian offers that these titles reflected the disparate views held by the two most prominent organizations dedicated to the social, political, and economic improvement of the African American population. Whereas for the NAACP, the situation for this population was indeed catastrophic, the Urban League's outlook was decidedly more optimistic: "Believing that the obstacles to socio-economic progress among [African Americans] lay not in their own innate deficiencies but in the way whites treated them, the League determined to create conditions of economic opportunity that would enable [African Americans] who took advantage of them to achieve their rightful places in urban society."[50] The publication itself reflected this view, featuring articles that addressed economic conditions in the country but also providing a space to showcase the talents of young writers who would go on to be some of the most well known of the Harlem Renaissance, such as Langston Hughes, Countee Cullen, Eric Walrond, and Zora Neale Hurston. The first issue appeared January 1, 1923; edited by Charles S. Johnson, *Opportunity* would be the setting of several of Schomburg's chronicles, particularly after the sale of his collection to the Carnegie Corporation in the summer of 1926.

"West Indian Composers and Musicians"

> The African brought to America among his patrimony musical instruments.... The African fetiches with their religious dancing has had its counterpart in the Voodoo ceremonies in Haiti and the Nanigoz societies of Cuba, known to exist in those islands as late as 1890. It is quite true that the Church, not knowing the true interpretation of music and dancing carried on by the African has dubbed it with the term savagery.
>
> —ARTHUR SCHOMBURG, "West Indian Composers and Musicians"

In his second paragraph of a *crónica* that offers portraits of musicians from Cuba and Puerto Rico, Schomburg provides these sentences, which reveal his awareness of conversations about primitivism in relation to African diasporic religions in the early decades of the twentieth century. As Carla Kaplan writes, "Primitivism, a mostly white and highly idealized view of blacks, was an especially knotty collection of ideas in this context. Primitivists often carried on a tradition of romantic racialism that saw blackness as an antidote to atomistic, joyless modern life, based on ideas of blacks as a more childlike and natural people."[51] These ideas developed in the aftermath of the Great War, which had prompted a crisis of faith in civilization as the supposedly civilized countries of the European continent had destroyed each other in one of the bloodiest conflicts to that point. The primitive, as embodied literally by peoples of African descent, therefore served as sources of inspiration for those devastated by World War I.

African diasporic religions such as Vodou of Haiti and Abakuá of Cuba were sites of intense curiosity for anthropologists of the time, perhaps most famously Franz Boas of Columbia University, and his student Melville Herskovits. Practitioners of these spiritual systems had been criminalized for centuries, as they engaged in ceremonies that were not sanctioned by the Catholic Church. In Haiti, Vodou was connected with the Haitian Revolution, as the first slave uprising was reportedly planned during a religious ceremony; the religion would later go on to be outlawed in 1835. In Cuba, Abakuá was also criminalized, most famously in 1906, with the publication of Fernando Ortiz's first book, *Hampa afro-cubana: Los negros brujos (apuntes para un estudio de etnología criminal)* [*Afro-Cuban Underworld: Black Witches (Notes for a Study of Criminal Ethnology)*]. The practitioners of Abakuá, an all-male Afro-Cuban secret society, are known as *ñáñigos*. As George Reid Andrews writes, "In Cuba as in Africa, Abakuá was an urban-based religion closely tied to seaports and oceangoing commerce... [It] was a membership society organized into local lodges or chapters and based on a body of secret ritual knowledge that members paid high fees to learn and promised never to divulge."[52]

As a Freemason, Schomburg was well aware of the power of secret societies and their ability to affect change in the lives of men through the promotion of economic and political advancement. His acknowledgment of these religions is striking, particularly given their maligned reputations in upper-class Caribbean culture, and particularly within the pages of a publication whose audience was predominantly middle-class African Americans. This brief paragraph is revelatory: he demonstrates once again his continued connection with the region of his birth.

∼

Schomburg's decision to publish his *crónicas* in *Opportunity* and *Crisis* as well as his scholarly papers reveals his understanding about audience; whereas the scholarly papers reached the members of those organizations and possibly a few others with whom those members might have shared their works, the readers of *Opportunity* and *Crisis* were greater in number. His efforts to complicate contemporary notions of blackness had a wider reach with these publications: as Elmer Anderson Carter, the editor of *Opportunity*, notes in the February 1933 issue, "The art and literature of the Negro in the New World is not confined to the United States as Mr. Schomburg, the distinguished bibliophile demonstrates."[53] Questions about dissemination of knowledge remain a vibrant debate for scholars today: to whom are they writing and for what purpose? In his biographical portrait of John Edward Bruce, Ralph L. Crowder points out that historical articles in the newspapers reached a working-class audience that scholarly papers and expensive texts did not.[54] Gerald E. Poyo makes a related argument with regard to José Martí's involvement with *Patria*; while Martí had already been publishing in periodicals for more than a decade before the creation of the Partido Revolucionario Cubano and its newspaper, it was here in *Patria* where he could more forcefully emphasize the need for alliances across race and class.[55] Publishing in two of the most important African American periodicals of the early twentieth century allowed Schomburg to reach not only his fellow scholars but also a larger audience who were all invested in the attainment of social, political, and economic equality for peoples of African descent.[56]

MASONIC WRITINGS

[T]he souls of white men did not revolt when they were raising millions of mixed breeds in the country; when they were bleaching or whitening up the masses of blacks, making possible such a large number of individuals whose racial nomenclature is uninterminable by any rule; they do not belong to the black, and have by all rights a better position with those in whose veins courses the best blood of the southland.

—ARTHUR SCHOMBURG, "Masonic Truths: A Letter and a Document"

In an article defending not only the Prince Hall Masons but presumably the existence of peoples of African descent, Schomburg emphasizes the history of rape, miscegenation, and deliberate whitening of populations of Africans in the Americas. While certainly questions of colorism were discussed within communities of

African descent throughout the hemisphere, here Schomburg's declaration high-lights the hypocrisy of the white supremacist thought that marginalizes men and women of African descent as primitive and barbaric, and at the same time char-acterizes these bodies as lust-filled and animalistic, worthy only of degraded sexual interaction between the races. Schomburg's "Masonic Truths" is a response to an article by a white Mason, Arnold P. Whiting, entitled "Rousing of Inferior Races," that had appeared in a Masonic publication, *National Trestle Board*. This is, as Jossianna Arroyo points out, perhaps his most famous defense of the social body that had acted as a main organizing principle of his life.[57] He composed this article in the 1920s, when he was serving as the Grand Secretary of Prince Hall Masons of the State of the New York, as well as the editor of the *Masonic Quarterly Review*, a fact that the editor of *National Trestle Board* highlights at the conclusion of Schomburg's essay.[58]

Arroyo provides a radical, and much-needed, reassessment of Schomburg's Masonic writings in her 2013 study, *Writing Secrecy in Caribbean Freemasonry*. There, she establishes the importance of writing in general for Masons; she observes, "Language, writing, and translation—fitted for different venues, and in different styles and vernaculars—became a source of revelation and political praxis."[59] She notes that for Afro-Latinos,

> the written word became a technology of advancement and resistance. Like their African-American counterparts Afro Caribbean Freemasons used literacy—and their membership at the lodge—to acquire social power, citizenship, and respectability. These elements seemed to them not merely utilitarian, but redemptive, as though they had saved their individuality and given pride to the social black collective.[60]

In this article, we see the weight of responsibility Schomburg bears as he speaks on behalf of not only himself, as a man of African and European descent, but also on behalf of his brothers and indeed of all who have been characterized as being of African heritage.

One aspect of the strength of Schomburg's defense of peoples of African descent in the Americas is his forthrightness with regard to policies of whitening across the Americas: in this passage, he does not refer to surreptitious relation-ships between white men and women of African descent that have been roman-ticized in some quarters but instead to factual political strategies utilized by countries throughout this hemisphere as a means by which to "treat" the illness that was the presence of peoples of African descent. Here, he explicitly writes about a history of sexual contact between men and women across the Americas, interactions that encompassed every possible kind of relation, including rape and violation, resulting in the emergence of millions of people such as Schomburg himself who, depending on their geographic location, were not easily identifiable as either white or black. Schomburg also touches on the realities not only of colorism but also of the attendant material privileges that came (and come) with a phenotypical appearance that conveys white heritage.

In this passage, Schomburg also alludes to policies put in place by politicians across the hemisphere in efforts to whiten their populations (known as *blanquea-miento* in Spanish and *branqueamento* in Portuguese). As George Reid Andrews writes of the final decades of the nineteenth century and the first decades of twentieth century in Latin America:

> Scientific racism was immediately embraced by turn-of-the-century elites confronting the challenge of how to transform their "backward," underdeveloped nations into modern, "civilized" republics. Such a transformation, they concluded, would have to be more than just political or economic; it would have to be racial as well. In order to be civilized, Latin America would have to become white.[61]

Andrews goes on to describe how European immigration was but one resolution to this issue (policies of which had begun in the mid-nineteenth century); other solutions included the destruction of the housing structures of urban communities of peoples of African descent, the subsequent construction of European-like boulevards and other physical structures, and the suppression of African diasporic religions and the musical forms that evolved from those spiritual systems such as rumba and son in Cuba and samba in Brazil.[62] Whitening, then, was a strategic political approach that had as an aim the complete suppression of all realms of life for those of African descent in the name of civilization, modernization, and progress. Schomburg rejected such policies and the ideologies and discourses that accompanied them, instead making his life's work the recuperation and restoration of censored and repressed histories that would facilitate the acknowledgment of a history of black excellence and the recognition of the full humanity of peoples of African descent. It was this driving impulse that would lead him to create not one but two repositories, one in the capital of black America, the other in the Jim Crow South, both of which were accessible to the larger surrounding communities to educate themselves and revel in the richness of black excellence.

Published first in his newspaper *La Doctrina de Martí* and later in his collection *Ensayos políticos* (1899), Rafael Serra here makes clear the necessity for the complete destruction and the construction of new social structures through revolution; reminiscent of Audre Lorde's admonition that the "master's tools will never dismantle the master's house,"[47] Serra underscores that the amendment of existing structures will inevitably lead to the replication of those structures, irrespective of intent to the contrary. After the 1898 war and the establishment of the Cuban Republic in 1902, Serra witnessed the infiltration of white supremacist thought in the creation of a new Cuba that systematically excluded Afro-Cuban civic participation; in his writings, which included articles and essays, in the newspapers he created, and in the schools he founded, Serra personally took on the task of creating a more educated populace of African descent who would be able to contribute to their nation in new ways, ones that would allow for both its progress and its salvation.

Serra was one of the two men to whom Schomburg presented himself upon his arrival in New York, the other being Flor Baerga.[48] An Afro-Cuban and an autodidact, Serra was a *tabaquero* and activist whose dedication to the independence of both islands was notable, as was his commitment to the education of men and women of African descent. Born free in Havana, Serra founded a free school, *Armonía*, and a newspaper of the same name in 1879 while living in Matanzas, at the age of twenty-one; his goal for this mutual aid society was the "modeling of citizen consciousness."[49] Within a year, he was exiled to New York, where he lived until the turn of the century. There he co-founded a number of organizations that supported the Antillean insurgency, including Los Independientes (a revolutionary club), the Partido Revolucionario Cubano (Martí's political party) and Las Dos Antillas; Schomburg was a member of the latter two and, and in the case of Las Dos Antillas, served as secretary.[50] In 1890, Serra founded La Liga, which was modeled after the Directorio Central de las Sociedades de la Raza de Color, an Afro-Cuban association founded three years earlier in Cuba with the explicit goal of establishing the "moral and material well-being of the raza de color through the promotion of formal education and 'better habits.'"[51]

Writing about Serra's organization, Aline Helg observes, "The society of La Liga brought together working-class Cubans and Puerto Ricans of African descent living in New York and provided them with general education, a propaganda against Spanish colonialism, and family entertainment."[52] Despite challenges, including the racism of white Cuban exiles, with Martí's support Serra was able to open a similar organization in Tampa for Afro-Cubans there in 1892.[53] Martí himself taught at La Liga, and was named head supervisor and honorary president; it was at this time that his nickname of "Maestro" began to circulate.[54] Serra's passion for the education of peoples of African descent was connected to his ideas of the responsibilities of citizens; Alejandra Bronfman observes, "His was a liberal notion of citizenship, premised on equality but also on a sense that citizens had obligations that could be met only if they began their civic lives with adequate education and preparation."[55] A lingering legacy of racism and enslavement had been the woeful state of educational systems for peoples of African descent on the island, free or enslaved. Serra's schools and newspapers therefore provided an alternative to racist declarations that peoples of African descent could not reach the intellectual capacity of those of European descent. Again, we see an emphasis on education as fundamental for the decolonization of the mind, a theme Schomburg would take up in his own work.

After Martí's death, Serra founded the newspaper *La Doctrina de Martí*, which stood as an important and necessary corrective to those who had willfully misinterpreted Martí's efforts to create a Cuban nation that was inclusive of everyone. Naming Serra's paper as "the most influential of the numerous newspapers that advanced Martí's thought," Gerald E. Poyo writes: "During its existence *La Doctrina* reminded Cubans of Martí's broader nationalist ideals that included creating a republic based on social justice, mutual respect among the social classes, and racial harmony."[56] Serra launched this newspaper in New York in 1896, where it was published with regularity until 1898; this was only one of the several periodicals of which he was in charge.[57] He then published *La Doctrina* in Cuba, to which he returned after the conclusion of the war. In the first decade of the twentieth century, he was elected to the legislative body twice, in 1904 and 1909; in 1907, he published a collection of essays, *Para blancos y negros. Ensayos politicos, sociales y económicos.* The title of the compendium is an indication of the stratification of Cuban society in the first decades of the twentieth century, when Cuban nationalist rhetoric had encouraged racial fraternity by attempting to silence and marginalize the population of African descent. Until his death in 1909, Serra continued to write explicitly about civil rights and social justice issues in language that reflected his liberal beliefs: as Bronfman writes, "his model for equal citizenship was based…on the reality of a conscience that was moral, virtuous, and educated."[58] Citizenship, then had nothing to do with race but instead with the inherent equality of one's soul.[59]

"WITNESS FOR THE FUTURE"

Schomburg and his Archives

> Not long ago, the Public Library at Harlem housed a special exhibition of
> books, pamphlet prints and old engravings, that simply said, to skeptic and
> believer alike, to scholar and school-child, to proud black and astonished
> white, "Here is your evidence."
>
> —ARTHUR SCHOMBURG, "The Negro Digs up His Past"

SCHOMBURG HAS BEEN an elusive figure for scholars and students alike, a
man who rarely publicly spoke about himself, who instead occupied his time doing
the work of writing, collecting, assembling, exhibiting, and promoting documentary evidence of black excellence from throughout the African diaspora. He
remained in the background as others gained credit for works they produced
having utilized his famous collection. Here he allows us a glimpse of his work with
these lines that appear in the midst of his most well-known essay; as was his
custom, he highlights the fruits of his labor, the "evidence," as it were, of excellence, material documentation of histories and cultures disparaged by white
supremacist thought that had consigned Africa and its dispersed peoples to the
peripheries of its recorded history. Note that Schomburg does not identify himself
as the person who had curated the 1924 exhibit at the 135th Street Branch library
and who had purchased the majority, if not all, of the objects that had been put
on display. On the contrary, he brings attention to those articles that irrefutably
testify, as if in the court of public opinion, to the existence of these cultural products and, more importantly, to the lived experiences of their creators. He continues: "Assembled from the rapidly growing collections of the leading Negro
book-collectors and research societies, there were in these cases, materials not

91

only for the first true writing of Negro history, but for the rewriting of many important paragraphs of our common American history."[1] Again, Schomburg pivots away from the opportunity to call attention to himself and his roles as a book collector and officer of such institutions as these research societies; instead, he offers a vision of an archive as matrix of source material, one that is accessible to all, "skeptic and believer alike," of all ages and all races and yet from which new historical considerations could take form.

More than five decades later, in a 1978 interview, Jean Blackwell Hutson, the first director of the Schomburg Center for Research in Black Culture after it was declared a research library by the New York Public Library in 1972, spoke about Schomburg and his collection. She commented:

> I guess it was a little naïve, because Mr. Schomburg thought that if everybody could really read about the exploits of the black people and the achievements that racial prejudice would not continue. He really thought that racial prejudice was based on ignorance and that dissemination of truth would change the United States. So he didn't think so much of preservation as of dissemination and widespread use.[2]

Named the third curator of the Division of Negro Literature, History, and Prints in 1948, after Schomburg himself and then Lawrence Reddick, Hutson would remain the curator of the collection until 1972; she held the position of director until her retirement. Hutson had worked alongside Schomburg earlier in her library career, after graduating from Columbia University's famed School of Library Science in 1936. During the course of the interview she compares the Schomburg Center to Yale University's Beinecke Library, where Carl Van Vechten had established the James Weldon Johnson Collection in 1941 and where Langston Hughes's papers rest alongside those of other luminaries. She calls the Beinecke a "mausoleum," a space devoid of life, which preserves and honors that which is considered valuable.

Such a characterization also speaks to questions of access: whereas many archives discourage engagement with the masses, the Schomburg Center throughout its incarnations, first as a collection in a private home, next a collection within a branch library, to finally the research library that it currently is, has always actively engaged the largest number of people possible, starting with the inhabitants of the surrounding community. In commenting on the democratic impulse that guided his collecting habits, Sinnette observes: "Schomburg viewed his collecting as a serious avocation firmly linked to combatting ignorance and prejudice. He was as generous with his collection as he was with the time and energy he devoted to locating the books and materials for it."[3] With the collections that he established both in Harlem at the 135th Street Branch Library in Harlem and the Fisk University Library in Nashville, Arturo Schomburg actively created liberatory spaces, whereby students, scholars, and the general public gain access to emancipatory narratives gone untold in mainstream texts. In his collecting, we see the multiplicity of the black experience in the Americas and indeed, throughout the world.

ARCHIVE THEORY

In her discussion of Schomburg's archive, which she characterizes as "Afrodiasporic," Adalaine Holton writes: "Schomburg's accumulation of documents is an archive that extends and complicates our understanding of what an archive is and the role that it plays in the production of knowledge and in the creation and maintenance of political power."[4] The archive as a thing unto itself first and foremost is a site of preservation, a memorial to the past; as Jacques Derrida reminds us in his 1995 article "Archive Fever: A Freudian Impression," the archive in ancient Greece was the house of the magistrates, those beings who were empowered by the state to physically embody the law and whose domiciles therefore housed state documents.[5] In her study on the power of performance as its own archive, Diana Taylor writes, "[W]e might conclude that the archival, from the beginning, sustains power."[6] Archives therefore have always had an explicit relation to power, though one that has garnered comment only in the last few decades; Michel Foucault interrogates this relationship in his *The Archeology of Knowledge* (1972), whereby he animates the archive so that we come to understand it not simply as a repository but as an agent active in the production of knowledge. This is what Ann Laura Stoler has described as the "archival turn," so that we now understand the archive as "subject" rather than simply as "source."[7] It is not simply a repository for collections of materials, but rather a physical space whose items have been selected for inclusion, as well as those that have been explicitly excluded. In calling attention to the myths that have been constitutive of the archive, Derrida and Foucault both also shed light for a wider audience on the role such spaces play in the construction of history.

Indeed, the relationship between the creation of historical narrative and the collection and preservation of the documents that reveal these accounts as trustworthy was the critical imperative that motivated black collectors and bibliophiles in the United States to engage in these activities since the nineteenth century. Dorothy Porter Wesley provides a brief overview of the history of black collectors in her article "Black Antiquarians and Bibliophiles Revisited, with a Glance at Today's Lovers of Books and Memorabilia"; there she documents the establishment of the Reading Room Society of Philadelphia in 1828, a gathering of free men of color that exchanged books and materials for no longer than a week.[8] She states the impetus behind such gatherings was "to meet the need for intellectual and moral improvement."[9] In his piece on the history of Philadelphia bibliophiles beginning in the nineteenth century in the same collection of essays, Tony Martin enumerates the many reasons for the pursuit of collecting rare books, documents, pamphlets, art, and other materials by and about black men and women; among them, to "counter the pseudo-scientific racism that was so prevalent during that time, when so-called scholars and writers were claiming that black people were by nature inferior"; "to provide a body of information for posterity"; "to restore, perhaps even initiate, an 'African consciousness,' an African perspective on black history."[10] There was, then, not only an acknowledgment about the necessity for the recuperation of these texts, but also a sense of urgency to do so: "The reasons for collecting books, then, were not only academic; they were also highly political. These books were being collected with a view of uplifting a downtrodden race of people."[11] During the centuries when white supremacist thought systematically negated the humanity of peoples of African descent, these men and women gathered written evidence to the contrary as testimonies of not only the existence of these populations around the world but also of their achievements. These documents were testaments of black excellence.

Returning to Schomburg, Holton notes: "Schomburg's writings, as well as those of other black book collectors and archivists, exhibit an awareness of the relationship between power and the archive that Foucault identifies."[12] Here she references his personal correspondence, as Schomburg had significant relationships not only with booksellers and fellow bibliophiles throughout New York City, but also with established networks of collectors throughout the Eastern seaboard and, indeed, internationally.[13] She goes on to reference Thomas Osbourne's conceptualization of the "principle of archival credibility," whereby one gains certain standing by working in and engaging with the archive. Osbourne reveals that the "status of such principles of credibility is at once epistemological and ethical: epistemological credibility because the archive is a site for particular kinds of knowledge…and ethical credibility because knowledge of the archive is a sign of status, of authority, of a certain right to speak, a certain kind of author-function."[14] Schomburg himself was well aware of the high stakes of collecting materials that demonstrated without question the accomplishments of men and women of the African diaspora. In an article about Schomburg that appears in the collection of essays about black collectors, Sinnette references them when she writes: "Those men and women were faced with the historical imperative of black self-definition and regarded their bibliophilia as a mission, a commitment to a social cause."[15] Arturo Schomburg was but one of a number of men and women in the last decades of the nineteenth century and continuing into the first decades of the twentieth century who were passionate about recovering historical texts that could attest to black subjectivity; unlike many of his colleagues, his interests included but also went beyond salvaging materials from Anglophone and Francophone lands. In these circles and networks that he frequented, he was passionate about also retrieving materials about peoples of African descent in the Spanish-speaking territories of Europe and the Americas.

INFLUENCES

Jesse Hoffnung-Garskof traces Schomburg's collection and preservation of materials to his involvement with the Antillean revolutionary cause in the 1890s: "History in general and collecting in particular had, in fact, been something of a mania among the émigré nationalists in New York. It was as if colonialism and displacement produced uneasiness about belonging that could only be assuaged by lists of books, biographical sketches, and other testaments to the achievements of national progenitors."[16] Among those he names as collectors were José Martí, Flor Baerga, and José González Font, who had owned a stationery shop in San Juan at which Schomburg had been employed in his youth. Indeed, it was González Font who had written a letter of introduction about Schomburg, which he presented to Flor Baerga and Rafael Serra upon meeting them.[17] Hoffnung-Garskof continues: "They sought to construct a Puerto Rican patrimony, writing a history to inspire unity and self-consciousness among members of the national community."[18] There was already at this time in the late nineteenth century an awareness of the necessity to document and preserve materials about the small Puerto Rican population in New York City.[19] These pioneers, a good number of whom had been exiled due to their activities in favor of the end of Spanish colonial rule, were therefore cognizant of the imperative to record this community's activities in an effort to argue that they had remained part of the Puerto Rican nation, even in exile.

This recognized need to write one's way into existence can also been seen in the work of Salvador Brau (1842–1912), Puerto Rico's national historian in the first decade of the twentieth century and one of Schomburg's influences. Arcadio Díaz-Quiñones writes that Brau exhibited some ambivalence and self-conscious-ness in writing about Spain's role in Puerto Rican history and culture during the first years of United States government. Brau himself reflected on this sense of contradiction while visiting Spain's archives in 1892, when there already existed a strong independence movement in the Puerto Rican exile community in New York; he understood the archive as foundational in the construction of a nation. Díaz-Quiñones observes: "The founding of an archive was not, therefore, only the result of a pure and erudite will; it was a moral and historical idea."[20] Brau himself was a student of private collections: at a time when the island had neither an offi-cial (i.e., state-sponsored) archive nor a system of higher education, he had ben-efited from private collections of books that had been deemed contraband by the colonial government.[21]

Brau recognized the need for an official repository of documents, in that it would assist in an authoritative recognition of the existence of the Puerto Rican nation: "The remaking of history, the diligent publication and analysis of sources, was a political task imperative to the 'nation imagined' by the *autonomistas*."[22] Puerto Ricans on both sides of the Atlantic Ocean, then, and across class and racial lines were highly aware of the opportunity to influence the historical narrative at the close of the nineteenth century and the first decades of the twentieth; while Brau's writings would come to function as an archive, firmly establishing Puerto Rico as an inheritor of Spanish cultural values, Schomburg's collecting project was not attached to a given political state but instead to the collective histories of peoples of African descent, irrespective of national origin. As Adalaine Holton points out, in Schomburg's archive, "objects from across the diaspora exist side by side, allowing archivists, scholars, and the public to identify differences and similarities between the objects and their contexts."[23]

THE 135TH STREET BRANCH LIBRARY AND THE DIVISION OF NEGRO HISTORY, LITERATURE, AND PRINTS

Returning to her study on the literature of the Puerto Rican diaspora of the United States, Lisa Sánchez González argues that a defining condition of early migrants was one of paperlessness, that is, the denial of a "legitimate existential pedigree in our colonial metropole's socio-symbolic order" whereby both citizenship and the literature produced assured a sense of belonging.[24] She argues that Schomburg's collection was his response to this dilemma:

His goals in this archival project are to identify and celebrate Black contributions to transamerican civilization, and he was particularly (though not exclusively) prone to research concerning men of African descent. In these lifelong pursuits, Schomburg was extremely successful; the papers and artifacts he gathered became the world's first major collection of transamerican and transatlantic Africana, which is today the African diaspora's largest combined archives.[25]

Sánchez González cites Schomburg's personal correspondence, which offers testimony to his letters to booksellers, publishers, antique dealers, and others of the publishing apparatus, asking for books in Spanish. "What this does indicate is that Schomburg felt a compelling interest in maintaining the representational scope of the collection he founded, inclusive of Spanish language texts, as well as his more specific personal and political interest in providing Harlem's Spanish-speaking community with books by or about people of color in Puerto Rico."[26]

The first public incarnation of this collection was as a critical part of the Division of Negro History, Literature and Prints at the 135th Street Branch Library. Writing about this library during the years of the Harlem Renaissance, Victoria Núñez comments: "The library is present as public space in which interracial cooperation and alliances could and did form."[27] Indeed, the 135th Street branch fostered relationships across racial groups; it was led by Ernestine Rose, who had previously found success as a librarian in the Chatham Square and Seward Park branches, serving the growing Jewish immigrant communities of the Lower East Side in the first decades of the century. In her first book about those experiences, she writes: "Yet the library is and must remain an aggressively American institution, or fail in its patriotic and educational function."[28] For Rose, the public library in general was an establishment that was imbued with the national values of the United States, namely those of liberty and justice.[29] The library, then, was a space not only for personal edification but indeed for the rectification of whole communities.

Rose continues: "Accurate knowledge of the people, their backgrounds, social and human, is the first essential. By this I mean an intimate acquaintance on the part of every member of the library with the history, traditions and literature of each nationality that the library expects to serve."[30] It was with this passion that Rose arrived at the 135th Street branch, to which she was appointed as librarian in 1920; in addition to integrating her staff (among those who worked with her were Nella Larsen, who would be a noted novelist of the Harlem Renaissance in her own right, Catherine Allen Latimer, and Pura Belpré, respectively the first accredited black and first accredited Puerto Rican librarians hired by the New York Public Library system), Rose arranged for talks and exhibitions, and played an integral role in the establishment in 1925 of the Division of Negro History, Literature and Prints, the reference collection that was located on the library's third floor.[31] It was this division that would be the foundation for what would become the Schomburg Center: Schomburg himself, who had already been lending materials to the branch, headed the citizens committee that had formed the reference division. As Howard Dodson, former director of the center, notes, "the Committee agreed to establish an organization 'to collect books and documents relating to the Negro race and keep them on exhibit for the public, and allow them to be used as a reference library for scholars.'"[32]

In the formation of the division, Rose, Schomburg, and the other committee members (among whom were John Edward Bruce, writer James Weldon Johnson, and well-known socialist Hubert Harrison) all demonstrated their dedication to not only serving the needs of the African diasporic communities in Harlem but also their passion for an education centered on black excellence. Dodson comments: "A place where the evidence of black thought, ability, and development was collected, stored, preserved and made accessible to scholars, the Schomburg, from its inception, was also a place where such knowledge was offered to the public in presentational and representational education, performance, and visual arts programs."[33] Schomburg's space, the collection and, subsequently, the archive that he created, was, and remains, a space for potentiality, for the actualization of the self. In an article juxtaposing the archive and the public library, Patrick Joyce observes: "The archive is always a place where authority resides. It was the public library that truly constituted the democratic public in this sphere."[34] The Schomburg Center strikes a balance between these two stark positions: it is fertile ground for the possibility of equality. Particularly because Schomburg's archive was not (and is not) closed off, it was a democratizing (i.e., an equal, egalitarian) space.

Later in her article about Pura Belpré, Núñez writes of this branch as a safe space: "the library as an institutional space in which members of Harlem's community could resist the policies and protocols of Jim Crow America."[35] The creation of the Division of Negro History, Literature and Prints by Ernestine Rose and the citizens committee and its subsequent incarnation after Schomburg's death as the Schomburg Collection, and later as the Schomburg Center of Research in Black Culture, was (and is) a secure physical space that served as solace for its patrons: outside its walls, the surrounding community has faced uncertain economic fortune, racial discrimination, and a dominant culture that insisted on mediocrity as an adequate standard for African diasporic lives. Within the space, men and women, boys and girls see material objects that serve as a testament to black excellence; in this way, they may connect to the energy of the decade in which the Negro Division was created, a time of creative resurgence known as the Harlem Renaissance.

THE SPIRIT OF THE HARLEM RENAISSANCE

Scholarly consensus identifies the dinner held in honor of the publication of Jessie Fauset's first novel, *There Is Confusion*, at Manhattan's Civic Club on March 21, 1924, as the birth of the Harlem Renaissance.[36] In addition to being a writer herself, Fauset served as the literary editor of *The Crisis* magazine, and was responsible for publishing a number of young writers, including Langston Hughes, Claude McKay, Countee Cullen, and Jean Toomer.[37] Organized by Charles S. Johnson of the Urban League, the event brought together black writers and artists with luminaries from the white publishing industry. One outcome of the dinner was the selection of Alain Locke as editor of a special issue of *Survey Graphic* dedicated to Harlem; Schomburg's famous "The Negro Digs up His Past" is included in both this issue, which appeared the following March, and the expanded anthology, published later in 1925. Locke begins the issue with an assessment of Harlem itself; he concludes the first paragraph by stating: "Harlem represents the Negro's latest thrust towards Democracy."[38] Locke was writing in the midst of what would come to be known as the Great Migration, when hundreds of thousands of African Americans moved from the rural South to Northern and Western cities such as Chicago, Detroit, and Los Angeles, in addition to New York, fleeing the racial terrorism of the South in search of greater economic and political opportunities in other parts of the country.[39] In addition, returning black veterans of the Great War were met with the political intransigence and violence of the United States, as they faced a country that was unwilling to extend to them the universally acknowledged rights and liberties for which they had been fighting in Europe.[40] While Locke concedes that migration is a factor contributing to the dynamism of the times, for him, "The wash and rush of this human tide on the beach line of the northern city centers is to be explained primarily in terms of a new vision of opportunity, of social and economic freedom, of a spirit to seize, even in the face of an extortionate and heavy toll, a chance for the improvement of conditions."[41] It is this image of the fresh and novel that enlivens the concept of the "New Negro."

Locke provides his conception of this term in the second article of *Survey Graphic*'s special issue (in the anthology itself he combines the two commentaries); there he writes that the "younger generation is vibrant with a new psychology; the new spirit is awake in the masses, and under the very eyes of the professional observers is transforming what has been a perennial problem into the progressive phases of contemporary Negro life."[42] He contrasts this with the image of the "Old Negro," that figure which had been conceived of predominantly as a problem, as "more of a formula than a human being—a something to be argued about, condemned or defended, to be 'kept down,' or 'in his place,' or 'helped up,' to be worried with or worried over, harassed or patronized, a social bogey or a social burden."[43] The New Negro instead is, first of all, a person, a human being who is self-sufficient rather than a societal encumbrance; secondly, Locke focuses on the consciousness of this population, employing words such as "spirit" and "psychology": "By shedding the old chrysalis of the Negro problem we are achieving something like a spiritual emancipation."[44]

The manifestation of this sense of renewal and rejuvenation was the marked increase in the publication and distribution of different kinds of black cultural forms: from art to music, from literature to drama, the Harlem Renaissance marked a moment whereby peoples of African descent entered the public sphere in a new way, making a significant contribution to the dominant culture of the United States.[45] Howard Dodson himself relates the creation of the Negro Division to this period of time when he writes that it was "at one and the same time a product of the Renaissance and a forum for it.... [It] became both the repository for a unique collection of book and non-book materials by and both blacks and the setting in which the study and interpretation of black history and culture were given new meaning for scholars, artists, intellectuals, and the general public alike."[46]

Indeed, artists and writers made great use of Schomburg's collection, both prior to the 1926 sale to the Carnegie Corporation, when it was primarily located in his home in Brooklyn (though he had already lent items to the 135th Street library), and in the subsequent years. Schomburg's biographer writes that the artists who conferred with Schomburg and accessed his collection included "Gwendolyn Bennett, Georgia Douglas Johnson, Arna Bontemps, Langston Hughes, and Jessie Redmon Fauset."[47] Sinnette goes on to point out that: "In addition to providing information, advice, and encouragement, Schomburg gave financial assistance to young black writers and artists."[48] Some of the writers and scholars he assisted include Claude McKay, Carter G. Woodson, James Weldon Johnson, and W. E. B. Du Bois.[49] Among the artists who benefited from exhibitions at the 135th Street Branch was Aaron Douglas, who had a one-man show there, and among the artists whose work was shown were "Laura Wheeler Waring, Louis Latimer, William Ernest Braxton, and Albert Smith."[50] Schomburg's personal correspondence with writers and artists attests to how integral he was in the Harlem Renaissance: he and his collections were at the heart of this literary and cultural movement.

THE NEGRO COLLECTION AT
THE LIBRARY OF FISK UNIVERSITY

In the late 1920s, Schomburg began a relationship with administrators at Fisk University; his friend Charles S. Johnson had moved to Nashville in 1928, having been named head of the Department of Social Science at the institution.[51] In 1926, following the sale of his private collection, Schomburg traveled to Europe; his recovery of documents attesting to the history of the African presence in Spain resulted in the articles "In Quest of Juan Pareja" (about the student of Spanish Baroque painter Diego Velázquez, published in *The Crisis*); "The Negro Brotherhood of Sevilla" (concerning a Catholic ecclesiastical group with roots in fifteenth-century southern Spain, published in *Opportunity*); "Negroes in Sevilla" (providing a general history of this population, published in *Opportunity*); and "Notes on Panama and the Negro" (offering a history of the African presence in central America beginning in the sixteenth century, published in *Opportunity*). Schomburg desired to continue this investigation and in 1929 expressed his interest in doing so in correspondence with Thomas Elsa Jones, the president of Fisk; in the same letter, Schomburg expressed his desire to assist in the expansion of Fisk's library by developing its holdings concerning "Negro life."[52] Over the following months, he prepared bibliographies for the newly named librarian Louis S. Shores so as to assist in the acquisition of texts about the African diaspora, and had begun to contribute to the expansion of the library's collections.[53] Shores acknowledged Schomburg's contributions in his annual report to the university for the 1929–30 academic year, writing that booksellers around the world had been alerted to the university's interest in shoring up their holdings in the Negro Collection.[54] In a communication with the president of the university, Shores emphasized that Fisk's collection, as opposed to being solely focused on slavery, was one that concentrated on the presence of peoples of African descent internationally.[55]

In 1931, Schomburg applied to the Carnegie Corporation for funding that would allow him to assist in the expansion of Fisk's library as well as act as a consultant for other interested institutions.[56] Later that year, Schomburg moved to

Nashville to establish the Negro Collection within Fisk University's library, assuming the title of curator of said collection. In addition to overseeing the purchase of books and other materials, Schomburg led the reorganization of the existing collection, so that texts were removed from the stacks and placed in the Negro Collection Reading Room itself, a space dedicated specifically for that purpose in the newly constructed library building and designed with murals by Aaron Douglas.[57] As his biographer notes: "With his broad international perspective, the collection at Fisk began to reflect a global character. A great many books and manuscripts were ordered from foreign bookdealers, and among the collection's earliest acquisitions were items about black domestic servants in Europe, along with extensive finds relating to blacks in African and the Caribbean."[58] While Schomburg's activities in Harlem receives the bulk of critical attention, it should not be overlooked that he replicated this task in a different setting, in the Jim Crow South, decades after he had firmly established his place in the New York cultural scene. And whereas New York was, and is, a center for a multitude of African diasporic populations, Nashville at the time was populated predominantly by families who had lived there for generations; the students at Fisk may have arrived from different states, but they all in general came from states in the U.S. South.[59] Schomburg's accomplishment, therefore, was his ability to create a second collection of books and other materials that emphasized the global black experience; in so doing, he ably demonstrated that this could be done in a number of settings. Though almost certainly facilitated by the number of publishers and booksellers in the city, the Harlem collection, Schomburg proved, was not an exceptional accomplishment; he established a prototype for it to be replicated in other places throughout the country, and indeed, throughout the world.

Schomburg's contribution to the library itself was significant: "In 1931 Louis Shores [the school's librarian] reported that the Negro Collection totaled 4,630 volumes, of which 4,524 had been added by Arthur Schomburg."[60] There were one hundred and six books in the library when Schomburg arrived; within months, he had instituted a collection that rivaled better-funded schools in the area. In 1932, after Schomburg had already returned to New York to assume responsibilities as curator of the Division of Negro History, Literature and Prints, Shores was in communication with W. D. Wentworth, president of the YMCA Graduate School in Nashville about establishing a cooperative relationship between the libraries of the two schools. Whereas the YMCA school would be known for their materials focusing on the "Negro" in the United States after the conclusion of the U.S. Civil War, Fisk's specialties included those items focused on the "Negro outside of America and prior to 1865."[61] These areas of expertise are a direct reflection of

Schomburg's efforts to establish another reference collection that emphasized the global black experience. After his death in 1938, Charles S. Johnson acknowledged Schomburg's work at Fisk in his tribute to his friend: "As we have profited by his constant and intimate help in the past, we are grateful to be permitted by his generosity and foresight to continue to benefit through the great institution which he has established in the incomparable Schomburg collection."[62]

SCHOMBURG AND THE PRODUCTION OF KNOWLEDGE

A consideration of Arturo Schomburg's collecting habits compels us as scholars and students alike to consider different modes of scholarship when we think of knowledge production. Indeed, we are perhaps so accustomed to explicit modes of scholarly assemblage—e.g., pamphlets, articles, books, presentations, etc.—all of which serve as examples of deliberation and reflection on a given subject, that at times we fail to consider what could be termed an implicit mode of knowledge production, which in Schomburg's case meant the assembly of materials around a defined theme. Whereas Schomburg was fairly clear in his writings that his definition of "Negro" transcended national boundaries and limitations, he published this conception of blackness mostly in popular publications instead of codifying it in a book, where it potentially would have had greater impact in academic circles.[63] Both Schomburg's collecting as well as the exhibits he organized, including two major exhibitions about black culture at the New York Public Library on Forty Second Street and Fifth Avenue in 1925 and 1934, reveal his dedication to the information he gathered reaching the general populace, beyond academic circles.[64] This implicit mode of knowledge production is one that at times escaped notice; as Tony Martin writes,

> Black bibliophiles run through our history like an unseen hand. Their influence is present in many of the major developments of our historical experience, even when a superficial glance does not immediately bring to light their presence. They were the ones who built our first libraries. They were behind our first literary and debating societies. They were the ones who established our first historical societies. They were the unseen influence even in some of our mass political organizations, such as the United Negro Improvement Association. They left us a legacy without which the movement toward black studies in the 1960s and 1970s would have been a much more difficult effort.[65]

In fact, this implicit mode of knowledge production is, in some ways, more elusive and yet more effective, in that the information produced at times becomes communal rather than originating from a more "official" source of authority.

This kind of construction of information could even be considered subversive: in an article about the politics of institutions of memory making, such as archives and museums, Richard Harvey Brown and Beth Davis-Brown take on the question of accessibility and its relationship to power. They point out: "Access includes not only which living persons may enter the library or museum, but which dead ones may be memorialized there. This is because the inclusion or exclusion of exhibits or displays in libraries and archives can seem to signal official approval to the public."[66] Throughout his career, Schomburg consistently highlighted the global scope of the African diaspora in his work, particularly in his writings, in his exhibits, and in his collecting itself. These actions reveal the extent to which Schomburg understood his audience: as Holton observes, "His historical project involved a three-layer approach, simultaneously engaging the past, present, and future."[67] While his writings and his collection of items from the past served both contemporary and future populations, his exhibitions were geared toward men and women of the period in which he lived. Today, the services of the Schomburg Center remain a vibrant part of the surrounding Harlem community.

THE LIVING ARCHIVE

[A]n archive exists because there is a user to give it meaning.
—PATRICK JOYCE, "The Politics of the Liberal Archive."

In *Forging Diaspora*, Frank A. Guridy refers to the Schomburg Center for Black Research as an "Afro-diasporic institution."[68] Indeed, two years after his death, the Negro Division, of which his personal collection was a significant part, was formally renamed the Schomburg Collection; decades later, in 1972, the library was designated a research library by the New York Public Library system, renamed the Schomburg Center for Research in Black Culture, and its status as an archive secured. In the immediate aftermath of his passing, the librarian of the 135th Street branch, Ernestine Rose, with whom Schomburg had collaborated in the purchase of his collection, commented: "Although a popular, branch library, this collection has brought scholars and students from all parts of the nation and the world, and because of this, it has taken on an importance in the community and the library system that could not have been ours under any other circumstances."[69] This has grown truer over the decades, as the Schomburg Center today holds more than ten million objects in its five divisions (Research and Reference; Manuscripts, Archives and Rare Books; Art and Artifacts; Photographs and Prints; and Moving Image and Recorded Sound). In addition to these items available for consultation, the center presents year-round programming consisting of exhibitions and public lectures, as well as fellowship programs for high school students and academics, and teachers' institutes for area educators.

The Schomburg Center is the most visible of Schomburg's legacies; it stands as a testament to his dedication and passion to African diasporic peoples around the world. As Kevin Meehan writes: "Most generally, Schomburg considered archival preservation and research as an integral part of black freedom struggle...For Schomburg, archival work was needed, first and foremost, to help vindicate the racial community from the slanders of so-called scientific racism."[70] This recalls Thomas Osbourne's formulation of the epistemological credibility one earns by engaging the archive, discussed earlier in the chapter; in Schomburg's case, as a creator of a large collection and as curator of both of the collections at Fisk and at the 135th Street Branch Library, he holds the critical position of arbitrator of knowledge. Yet Schomburg remained focused on acquiring items that revealed the depth and breadth of the global black experience, irrespective of language or national origin, and in this way, laid the foundation for renderings of blackness that fully encompassed the complexity of the human experience of African diasporic beings. Meehan views Schomburg's archival work as "a serious avocation possessing not only a basic principle—racial vindication—but also a defining method."[71] He maintained throughout his life the notion that the achievements of black men and women throughout the African diaspora, once made manifest in documentation and disseminated through popular forms, would lead to the successful destabilization of racist discourse; at the heart of this passion is the establishment of an institutional presence such as the research collection that would later grow to become the Schomburg Center for Research in Black Culture.

In considering Schomburg's archive, Holton proposes the notion of a "counter-archive"; she writes:

> By building and popularizing a counter-archive of Afrodiasporic history, Schomburg made a radical intervention in the production of historiographic knowledge. His collection and his essays effectively refuted the dominant ideology of white supremacy and the popular and official forms of historiographic knowledge in which this discourse was embedded.[72]

Like Meeham, Holton highlights the primary motivation of Schomburg's collecting, namely, the disruption and nullification of a discourse about the inferiority of peoples of African descent found in dominant culture in the United States due to the primacy of white supremacist thought. Holton continues: "His efforts to compile a transnational and multilinguistic archive of black history make possible a black international imaginary—a history of people connected to each other not through national belonging, but through the complicated linkages of diaspora."[73] Later in the essay, she observes that "Schomburg's archive is both an imaginary space of diasporic connection and a real location where books, photographs, artwork, and other forms of material culture collected from the African diaspora come together."[74]

In his pioneering study, *Silencing the Past: Power and the Production of History*, Michel-Rolph Trouillot elucidates the role of the archive in the construction of knowledge. He writes: "Archives assemble. Their assembly work is not limited to a more or less passive act of collecting. Rather, it is an active act of production that prepares facts for historical intelligibility. Archives set up both the substantive and formal elements of the narrative. They are the institutionalized sites of mediation between the sociohistorical process and the narrative about that process... [T]hey help select the stories that matter."[75] Earlier in his text, Trouillot reminds his readers that history in and of itself is not self-evident, but rather emerges only after the creation and proliferation of certain narratives: "For what history is changes with time and place, or better said, history reveals itself only through the production of specific narratives."[76] Trouillot makes evident the relationship between the construction of history and the archive itself; it is an association of which Schomburg was himself highly aware, hence his attention to the inclusion of texts and other materials written by and about men and women of African descent in Spanish-speaking lands.

Ada Ferrer responded to Trouillot's characterization of the archive in an interview supporting her 2014 study *Freedom's Mirror: Cuba and Haiti in the Age of Revolution*; there she offers a qualification of Trouillot's formulation, highlighting the disarray of the archive. She says: "Silences exist clearly, but they do not emerge fully formed, or total. In the abundance and outsized character of the archive, we have an incredible resource for tracing the ways in which the very silences that Trouillot writes about are constructed, maintained, challenged day to day, by real people and institutions, in real places under concrete circumstances."[77] For both historians, the archive is a living organism, one that not only contributes to the production of knowledge but that also allows for a self-referentiality about that which has been created. There is no one singular definitive explication about any given subject; rather, the archive allows for multiple readings about the same theme. Schomburg knew this implicitly; he understood with his collection, as he did with his writing, that the value of the work lay in the assembly of the materials. He did this with an eye to future generations, laywomen and men like himself, college- and university-educated students, scholars, journalists, and artists alike—all were welcome in his archives, so that they could witness and testify to the multiplicity of the global African diasporic experience.

5

"FURTIVE AS HE LOOKS"
The Visual Representation of Schomburg

FURTIVE, *adj.* 1. a. Done by stealth or with the hope of escaping observation; clandestine, surreptitious, secret, unperceived. 2. Of a person, etc.: Stealthy, sly. 3. Obtained by theft, stolen; also in milder sense, taken by stealth or secretly. 4. Thievish, pilfering.

—THE OXFORD ENGLISH DICTIONARY

In appearance, he was like an Andalusian gypsy, olive-complexioned and curly-haired, and he might easily have become merged in that considerable class of foreigners who exist on the fringe of the white world.

—CLAUDE MCKAY, *Harlem: Negro Metropolis*

En abril de 1891 Flor Baerga recibió un extraño visitante de Puerto Rico. Se trataba de un joven negro de apenas diecisiete años. Un tabaquero de San Juan lo había recomendado a Baerga: un puertorriqueño más arrojado al exilio.

[In April 1891 Flor Baerga had an unusual visitor from Puerto Rico. He was a young black man, just turned seventeen, who had been recommended to Baerga by a tabaquero back in San Juan—yet another Puerto Rican cast into exile.]

—BERNARDO VEGA, *Memoirs of Bernardo Vega*, trans. *Juan Flores*

WITHIN THE PAGES of the more than one hundred scrapbooks assembled by Arthur Schomburg's contemporary, L. S. Alexander Gumby, that are dedicated to the cultural happenings of peoples of African descent in the United States in the first decades of the twentieth century, one finds Scrapbook 52, dedicated to Schomburg and his collection.[1] In its pages appears a portrait of Schomburg with

FIGURE 5.1 Portrait of Arthur Alfonso Schomburg, as he appears in *Negro: An Anthology* (1934)

the caption that titles this chapter (*Figure 5.1*). He is in full profile, well groomed in a suit and tie, nary a hair out of place. The photograph identifies him ("Arthur A. Schomburg is the world's leading collector of books and pictures dealing with the Negro"), then provides the purpose for which it appears in the publication ("Pictures of famous Negroes and works done by them are, through the generosity of Mr. Schomburg, to be a regular feature of The National News Gravure").[2] Interestingly, there is nothing seemingly "furtive" about Schomburg here, which makes the editorialized heading accompanying the announcement more curious. Is he secretive because he refuses to look at the camera? What about his being invites such judgment? There are, indeed, two strongly worded assessments expressed here, one about the man's countenance and the second about his character itself.

The same photograph accompanies the first of Schomburg's two essays that appear in the 855-page, oversized *Negro: An Anthology*, edited by Nancy Cunard and published in 1934. Without the caption, Schomburg appears to be fleeing the camera altogether, the photograph seemingly taken mid-movement as he is eager to distance himself from the machine itself. The heading, therefore, adds culpability to the photograph; whereas in the absence of those words, he merely appears in great discomfort, if not distress, the words provide an intentionality to that movement, as if he had committed some kind of offense. The photograph's appearance in two separate publications indicates that it was a circulated image of him in his lifetime, which elicits another series of questions: Why would Schomburg choose *this* one as the best representation of him? Why does he not want the viewer to look at his face? What information is conveyed there?

There appears to have been some disagreement about the appearance of Arturo Schomburg, or rather, in how to read him, as made evident from the epigraphs that head this chapter. In the opinion of his friend the prominent black Jamaican writer Claude McKay, Schomburg could have passed for a white man. Granted, it would have been a marginalized whiteness, as Spanish, especially that of the southernmost region of the country (where the gypsies reportedly resided), was not held in the same esteem in the United States as the British or Germanic variety in the first years of the twentieth century.[3] Nevertheless, according to McKay, Schomburg, by virtue of his physical appearance, could have abandoned the African diasporic communities in which he lived without comment. For Bernardo Vega, a white Puerto Rican activist who migrated to New York in 1916 and whose memoirs are considered foundational in Puerto Rican Studies, Schomburg was simply black. Vega offers no commentary on gradation of pigmentation, as McKay does, instead stating that Schomburg was of visible African descent and therefore presumably had no chances of identifying as anything else. The disparate readings of Arturo Schomburg's countenance and, more extensively, of his body itself, highlight once again the bind in which he found himself throughout his life, as neither man, each a representative of the different Caribbean communities prominent in New York at the time, claimed him as one of their own.

In this chapter, I examine the body of portraits that survive Arturo Schomburg, some of which have rarely been seen outside of the center that bears his name. Though in disagreement with the unnamed editor of the captioned photograph that appears in Gumby's scrapbook, I argue that there is something deliberately performative in Schomburg's elusiveness in front of the camera. If performance is a series of repeated gestures, then one has to conclude that Schomburg was, at the very least, uncomfortable in front of the lens. In the majority of the photographs taken of him throughout his life, he willfully looks away from the camera, often sitting or standing in a three-quarter pose. Even when he looks in the direction of the camera, he often looks above the lens. He cannot be captured or pinned down. In this demonstration of defiance, one begins to glimpse beyond the sterling reputation of this famed bibliophile; he allows us to see the man himself, who refused to be apprehended by a medium that had to that point been used to replicate and perpetuate demeaning stereotypes about people of African descent. Unlike many luminaries such as Sojourner Truth, Booker T. Washington, or even his contemporary James Weldon Johnson, Schomburg more often than not rejects the gaze of the camera.[4] He demonstrates agency in exactly how he would be represented in these photographs, seemingly choosing the same pose time and time again. He controls his body, his image. And so he escapes us, flees apprehension by the viewer himself. Unlike subjects of other portraits, he remains closed, shut off from the photographer and, by extension, the audience itself.

PHOTOGRAPHIC PORTRAITURE

The invention of photography, and, more importantly, its accessibility to great numbers of people, quite simply shifted how human beings came to know and understand themselves and the world. Maurice O. Wallace and Shawn Michelle Smith write: "To be sure, photography was a watershed invention. So profound was the influence of photography upon antebellum and postbellum American life and thought that, like today's digital technology, early photography shifted the very ground upon which the production and circulation of knowledges, scientific and philosophical, had set only a half century earlier."[5] With regard to photographic portraiture in the United States, there are two separate traditions that converged when the sitter was a person of African descent in the final decades of the nineteenth century and the beginning in the twentieth: the studio portrait, which was the domain of the middle and upper classes, and the pseudoscientific and criminal. The latter class of photograph had led to the hypervisibility of the black body, in particular the black male body. In her 2011 study *Troubling Vision: Performance, Visuality, and Blackness*, Nicole R. Fleetwood explains: "*Hypervisibility* is an interventionist term to describe processes that produce the overrepresentation of certain images of blacks and the visual currency of these images in public culture. It simultaneously announces the continual invisibility of blacks as ethical and enfleshed subjects in various realms of polity, economies, and discourse, so that blackness remains aligned with negation and decay."[6] Though written in the twenty-first century, Fleetwood's comments recall the history of photography for black subjects in the United States. Writing about the work of James Van Der Zee, one of the renowned photographers of the Harlem Renaissance, Deborah Willis-Brathwaite states: "We need only remember that the bulk of his photographs were created during an era when the overwhelming majority of postcards, greeting cards, comic strips, and other popular cultural artifacts made with images of African Americans consisted of crude, degrading racial caricatures."[7] As a medium, photographs were utilized as a means by which to illuminate that which was touted as the "Truth"; that is, they were bestowed with the presumption of objectivity and imbued with the belief that they could capture reality.

Beginning in the nineteenth century and well into the twentieth, photography was most often used against men and women of African descent as a means of supporting white supremacist thought.[8] In her 2002 dissertation, scholar Camara Dia Holloway notes: "Photography was, in part, conceived and deployed to represent racial difference and to secure and sustain the privileged status and social power of whiteness."[9] Though it has come to be a democratizing medium, initially there were stark differences in the usage of photography, depending on class, race, and gender. For the middle and upper classes, photographic portraiture endowed subjectivity, much like paintings had previously done for centuries; shot in private studios, these images were taken in order to attest to the worth of these subjects, in all of their humanity.[10] One could glean information about their social positioning from their dress, their hair style, their jewelry, and other accessories: anything within the frame of the photograph conveyed critical information about the identity of these men and women. For most men and women of African descent in the Americas as a whole, the majority of whom did not belong to the middle or upper classes, this kind of portraiture was simply outside of their range of opportunity, at least until the early twentieth century, with the advent of the New Negro Movement in the United States.

Writing about how members of the black bourgeoisie in the early twentieth century utilized photography, Holloway comments that for them, the medium was primarily a counterhegemonic tool, one that could most quickly refute the specious notion of innate black inferiority. These men and women were intent on demonstrating how, contrary to allegations of primitivism, they were, in fact, the very embodiment of modernity itself. Stylish, cultured, and intelligent, these portraits provided a stark contrast to the representation of black men and women in popular culture of the day. Photographers such as James Van Der Zee and James Latimer Allen provided this newly emergent group the platform to attest to their rightful place in this country; published often in black periodicals such as the *New York Age*, the *Chicago Defender*, and the *Pittsburgh Courier*, the new images of wealth and affluence were inspirational to readers. Marginalized in a culture that claimed they were of no consequence and cast as powerless in society as a whole, these image producers and their subjects instead revealed themselves to be meaningful contributors to the fabric of the country. From this vantage point, then, they moved forward to demand their full political rights as citizens.

COUNTERVISUALITY AS MODE OF RESISTANCE

Nicole Fleetwood writes: "Visual representations of blacks are meant to substitute for the real experiences of black subjects. The visual manifestations of blackness through technological apparatus or through a material experience of locating blackness in public space equates with an ontological account of black subjects. Visuality, and vision to an extent, in relationship to race becomes a thing-in-itself."[11] Well into this twenty-first century, U.S. society continues to be oversaturated with certain kinds of images of the black male body, most particularly that of the criminal, the athlete, and the entertainer. While the election of President Barack Obama has itself made a serious intervention in the proliferation of these images, nevertheless those three categories are the ones in which the black male body is most "legible," that is, most easily recognizable and therefore the most easily read.[12] To Fleetwood's point, the viewing audience comes to believe that they "know" the person in the image that they are viewing, or at least glean what is knowable about them. Every image is therefore fraught with the weight of burden, as the viewer, in seeing one of these "legible" images, taps into a centuries-old archive. As critic Shawn Michelle Smith observes, "[I]f sight is a social practice, it is also racialized in the United States, shaped and directed by the racial contours and contest of the social sphere."[13] Smith therefore implicates all of us who are in the visual realm—those who take the picture, those who are in the picture, and those who view the picture—we all bring to the world of images a racialized perspective. Objectivity, therefore, does not exist.

In vernacular photos, particularly in the Instagram and the Facebook reality of this second decade of the twenty-first century, the imaged, the photographed, may not have the opportunity to interact with the photographer, that is, the person may simply be on the other end of the lens, his image captured without the possibility of commentary or expression of opinion. (Hence my labeling of that person using a past participle, to denote a more passive positioning in the interaction.) In more formal settings, however, there exists a more heightened awareness of responsibility of the roles of both the photographer and the subject; both wield creative power, that is, the ability to influence the image produced, the end-product.

In Schomburg's portraits, we witness the power of countervisuality, which Nicholas Mirzoeff defines as "the practices of the disempowered when they claim autonomy and assert their 'right to look.'"[14] Whereas the New Negroes, the men and women who are the subjects of portraits by such photographers such as James Van Der Zee and James L. Allen, embraced the medium as a means to offer a corrective to the larger society's misperceptions about race, class, and gender, Schomburg is different. In the majority of his photographs, he chooses to look away from the camera, or look above the line of vision; in those portraits where he does stare at the viewer, he actively challenges the audience to arrive at some kind of cursory judgment about him. His look alternately dares the viewer to offer comment, to enter the dialectical field of visual culture at their own risk. Schomburg will not succumb to easy or lazy categorization; his refusal to comply with the implicit relationship with the viewer underscores his agency. It also makes manifest his rejection of the medium itself.

In his 2008 study *Cutting a Figure: Fashioning Black Portraiture*, Richard J. Powell writes:

> Despite a sobering legacy of scorn and subjugation, peoples of African descent have psychologically "clothed" themselves in fancier attire than others customarily allowed them, enacting personas that inspire awe and provide assurances about their place among life's movers and shakers....Understanding this instrumental use of self requires not only an appropriate way of describing these incisive cultural incursions, but a language for the corporeal and stylistic inventions that fashion catalytic portrayals capable of signifying more than pride, and displaying more than an indexical cluster of physical and sartorial traits.[15]

Schomburg's portraits are not chiefly characterized by his panache or elegance; rather, they are typified by an element of discomfort.[16] In contrast to Powell's description, Schomburg's public persona, at least as it can be gleaned from these photographs, is one in which he prefers to stay out of sight, in the background, away from the glare of the camera and, through that lens, of the viewer.

PORTRAITS OF SCHOMBURG

Arturo Schomburg was well aware of the importance of visual representation with relation to the creation of subjecthood. From the earliest decades of the twentieth century, he had arranged for art exhibitions both in Brooklyn at his YMCA and in Manhattan, at his beloved 135th Street Branch Library, home of the Negro Division of Literature, History and Prints. He was an advisor to the Harmon Foundation, an important patron of black arts, both literary and visual, during the Harlem Renaissance. When the Carnegie Corporation purchased his collection in 1926, he had accumulated thousands of books, manuscripts, prints, and other ephemera celebrating black excellence. It is, therefore, somewhat surprising to discover the small number of portraits of the man himself; nevertheless, this scarcity of images reveals an obvious discomfort with the medium. An examination of these photographs underscores his efforts to elude the "capture" of the viewer, thereby indicating an exertion of agency in the maintenance of privacy and therefore his own personhood.

The photographs under consideration for analysis chronologically span almost the entirety of Schomburg's life, the first taken when he was four years old and the last taken in his final decades. Most of the names of the photographers themselves are unknown, leaving us to focus solely on the subject himself. Two of the photographs were taken in Puerto Rico, and the rest in the United States, presumably in New York City. Rather than examine them in chronological order, I instead first group those photographs in which he chooses not to look at the camera, analyzing them as a whole, then moving to those, though they are fewer in number, in which he does. This comparison allows us to more clearly view Schomburg's different modes of resistance to the medium, which ranges from slightly evading the line of vision of the camera to out-and-out staring down the viewer, daring commentary.

EVASION OF THE GAZE

In one of his earliest portraits (*Figure 5.2*), Schomburg wears full evening dress, his hair neatly coiffed as he is well groomed. Though the context for the photograph has been lost to history, the viewer nevertheless is presented with a young, handsome man of African descent, one who presumably belongs to a then-emerging bourgeoisie. His body is positioned so that he directly faces the camera, confidently, leading the viewer at first glance to think that Schomburg looks directly at him or her.

FIGURE 5.2 Arthur A. Schomburg, ca. 1896, age twenty-two

Yet Schomburg looks slightly above the line of vision, so that he does not look squarely at the lens itself. This is disconcerting to this viewer, who is poised to meet his gaze. His attire and grooming challenge the viewer's conceptions of a black male body in that we are presented with someone who is presumably free, enslaved neither literally nor metaphorically by the legacies of de jure segregation. Nor is it possible to assume him to be a criminal, another overused image of the black male body, both then and now. One imagines a reason for his dress, assuming that he may have been attending a celebration of some kind; there is a dynamism to the image, so that one is left to conjecture that he may have been either arriving from or departing for an important event. Schomburg's apparel appeases any preconceived notion of threat that a viewer might bring to the image; nevertheless, his refusal to fully comply with this gesture of mollification is evident when he evades the scrutiny of the lens.

In contrast to the previous photograph, where it is unclear whether he is standing or seated, in *Figure 5.3,* Schomburg is seated, quite comfortably, it appears. This is more obviously a studio session, as there is a simple neutral backdrop with nothing to distract from the image. He is dressed in a suit, his hair styled in the manner of his day, and he is looking to his left. This is what would

FIGURE 5.3 A. A. Schomburg, writer, "Is Hayti Decadent?" *Unique Advertiser 4* (1904), age thirty

FIGURE 5.4 Arthur A. Schomburg, noted bibliophile

be the standard Schomburg portrait—positioned in three-quarter pose and well dressed. Unlike his tuxedo portrait, here Schomburg appears to be some distance from the camera itself, and is more visibly relaxed within this space. In his grooming and attire, he conveys respectability, dignity, and honor; here is a member of the burgeoning New Negro Movement. Published to accompany his article regarding Haiti in the year of the centennial of the Haitian Revolution, the image serves as an invitation to his viewer, one that expressly conveys a desire for the reconsideration of the standing of this nation. The word *decadent* itself recalls ineptitude and decay; the man who questions whether Haiti suffers without the ability to be healed from this moral ailment seems to answer with a resounding "no." Instead, his own visage provides hope that Haiti will thrive in the future.

Figure 5.4 may be the most widely circulated image of Schomburg; it occupies the cover of Sinnette's biography of him, and when one enters the Schomburg Center for Research in Black Culture, this is the image that greets the visitor. While undated, the affinity for this photograph is understandable: this is Schomburg in all of his command. Still a young man, he nevertheless conveys authority and assuredness. Seated in an elaborately decorated chair against a painted backdrop, Schomburg appears comfortable as he leans into the chair. Legs crossed at the knee, with one hand on his leg and the other on the arm of the chair itself, he remains posed in a three-quarter position. Again, he looks off camera; still, we sense here that he actively allows the photographer to capture this image. This is one instance in which he plainly and unmistakably conveys confidence; this poise and self-possession is not qualified in any way, and his composure is markedly evident.

In his historical examination of the black middle-class male subjectivity in the first three decades of the twentieth centuries, Martin Summers writes about the Freemasons, who, he contends, "[were] also instrumental in contributing to the gender identity formation of large numbers of middle-class black men."[17] He identifies Masons' dress as a critical marker of their manhood: "Through the donning of particular types of clothing and accessories, black Masons literally fashioned an identity that was organized around principles of production and respectability."[18] Through their attire, therefore, these men conveyed to the world that they were, firstly, men who were to be treated with dignity and respect, and secondly, men who were active in being productive for society. Their self-worth was in fact dependent on being both upright in character as well as being a contributor to the larger society and to their fellow Masons through labor. Summers notes about their ceremonial dress: "The standard sartorial ensemble consisted of formal or semiformal dark suits, white leather or lambskin aprons, medallions, white gloves, and, for the most worshipful master, a black top hat. Masons were particularly proud of their dignified attire."[19]

This self-esteem is manifest in the pictures in which Schomburg is in his Masonic regalia (*Figure 5.5*). Head covered, he wears a dark suit with a bowtie and a chain of some kind; he appears to be in a private setting, as this looks to have been a studio session. Despite his formal attire and his Masonic gear, once again he looks distinctly uncomfortable, almost as if he is holding his breath. His semi-closed hands convey a nervousness, as if he does not know how to hold them or where to place them. Though he is standing, again positioned in a three-quarter pose, there is an uncertainty here; the viewer gets the sense that he would rather be elsewhere. Schomburg's dedication to this brotherhood was irrefutable; he was initiated as a young man in 1892, only a year after his arrival in New York, at eighteen years old.[20] Within thirty years, he had risen within the hierarchy of the organization, becoming first Master of the lodge that had initiated him and later, Grand Secretary of the Grand Lodge of the State of New York.[21] In that capacity, he served as the first chairman of the Committee on Foreign Relations, which supplemented his earlier activities as translator of policies and regulations for his fellow brothers.[22] This portrait, taken approximately in 1918, is one

FIGURE 5.5 Arthur A. Schomburg, in Masonic attire, age approximately forty

that conveys his standing within the organization in which he takes such pride, and yet he remains remote, withdrawn into himself, away from the field of vision.

James Latimer Allen was one of the two premier black photographers of the Harlem Renaissance, the other being James Van Der Zee. Unlike Van Der Zee, who sometimes added what Deborah Willis-Brathwaite calls "deliberately fictionalized elements" to his photographs, Allen's pictures were often quite simple in set-up, with a plain backdrop and lighting that drew attention to his subjects' best features.[23] In the catalogue that accompanied the 1999 exhibition at Yale University Art Gallery that brought James L. Allen back to the attention of the public, Holloway writes: "Allen adopted the austere modern portrait format, which presented the subject in a shallow space against a neutral background. This portrait mode eschewed the use of props to convey information about the sitter, relying instead on the belief that the body was legible and could reveal the character of the subject."[24] Once again, we encounter the issue of legibility, of being able to be read. For perhaps the first time, Schomburg appears as though he is enjoying this process. In this portrait, which is featured on the cover of this study, Allen emphasizes Schomburg's physical beauty; Schomburg looks off camera and is shot from his left side. He looks incredibly distinguished, and one can detect a slight smile, as if there is noticeable pleasure in sitting for this particular photographer. As in some of his other portraits of prominent men and women of the Harlem Renaissance, namely those of Alain Locke and Langston Hughes, light falls on Schomburg's forehead, a marker of his intelligence.[25]

Writing about the way Allen positioned his subjects for his portraits, Holloway writes:

> Allen recognized that the appearance and attitude of his sitters as well
> as the setting in which they were placed were crucial to conveying the
> impression of civility, urbanity, and modernity that was the hallmark
> of the New Negro. In virtually all of his photographs, the subjects are
> formally attired. Rejecting the rigid frontality of scientific and criminal
> photography, he photographed them along a diagonal axis to generate
> a dynamism that was associated with the bourgeois, i.e. respectable
> subject. Because posture and gesture were key indices of the racialized
> body, Allen's sitters were invariably posed and self-contained.[26]

While Schomburg is posed in all of these portraits, again, this is the first in which we the viewers bear witness to his pleasure. In this instance, he allows himself a sense of diversion, as we see him relax into the process.

With this portrait, Schomburg's place as a member of the Harlem's privileged class was assured. Holloway: "To commission a portrait from Allen was a deliberate decision to acquire an image most consistent with the Harlem elite's sense of self. Allen's patrons desired images by an artist who shared their world view. Through his lends, they became what they were—serious, creative, and talented human beings, equal *and* black."[27] There was, therefore, a sense of actualization with his photography; the dreams and aspirations of this group of men and women were realized in the act of his taking their photograph.

The Allen portrait of Schomburg is rare in that we know the identity of the photographer and therefore know of the photographer's intention simply by examining his body of work; in the catalogue that accompanied the Allen show at Yale in 1999, there is no mention of this portrait. Holloway, who both curated the show and prepared the catalogue, seemingly did not include Schomburg. It is true that there are more famous artists represented in Allen's body of work, faces that are more recognizable to the public such as those of Langston Hughes and Paul Robeson. Schomburg's portrait is, again, one that conveys physical beauty, as well as self-assurance and clear enjoyment. Though he remains looking away from the viewer, he nevertheless invites the viewer's gaze.

With these portraits, we have glimpsed into the life of Arturo Schomburg and seen a relative discomfort with photography, in spite of the exceptions where he seems to be more actively and positively involved in the process. In these photographs, we see when he does not look at the camera: I argue that this gesture is one that reveals a demonstration of will. The next section examines those few instances when he does look at the camera. Here we catch sight of an impish boy and of a man who is seemingly weary, bearing the burdens of any number of considerations.

DEFIANCE AND RESISTANCE

In the first, a studio portrait taken of him as a child (*Figure 5.6*), Schomburg looks mischievous, curious as to whether or not he is doing the right thing, behaving himself. The fact that he is photographed at all speaks to some means, as a black male child in late-nineteenth-century Puerto Rico, which was still a Spanish territory at the time, did not normally warrant such a luxury. In fact, there were few venues for studio portraiture; in an encyclopedia entry about nineteenth-century photography in Puerto Rico, Abel Alexander and Roberto A. Ferrari write of one French photographer, H. Gautier, who was active in San Juan in the 1870s and

FIGURE 5.6 Arturo Alfonso Schomburg, age four, San Juan, Puerto Rico, 1878

who specialized in the *carte-de-visite* format.[28] (The *carte de visite* "was a photographic visiting card 2½ by 4 inches that arrived once paper prints could be produced from glass negatives.")[29] Against a painted backdrop and leaning against a barrier that simulates an enclosure normally surrounding houses, Schomburg as a child is confident and assured, an innocent as yet unaware of the sometimes conflicting dynamics at play when photographing a body marked by both race and gender.[30]

The second is another studio portrait, this time one in which Schomburg sits with his sister, Lola (*Figure 5.7*). While she appears to be sitting on a chair, Schomburg sits on a stool. Whereas she evades the camera's gaze, looking instead

FIGURE 5.7 Studio portrait of Arturo Alfonso Schomburg and his sister Dolores (Lola) Díaz, circa. 1905, age thirty-one

to her right, he looks directly at the camera, his large eyes almost daring the viewer to comment at the sight of two well-dressed people, a black man sitting alongside a white woman. Again, the fact that a photograph has been taken at all is suggestive of some means, as photography was not available to most of the population on the island. She looks uncomfortable, her face slightly raised as she seemingly looks off into space, and her hands placed in her lap, with her left hand holding onto her right. She seems rather anxious, eager for the session to end, and yet reluctant to provoke a reaction on the part of the viewer. Her brother, limbs akimbo, takes up the space in the photograph, not only with his physical presence but also with his dark suit.

Schomburg's body appears to be all angles, his elbows mirroring the jut of his knees and the direction in which his feet are pointed. His hands are placed uncomfortably between his thighs, and his fingers are curled inward. He is the stable force, the solid one who bears the weight. His posture is indicative of a sense of burden, of heaviness, while his stare is tired and yet daring. It is an unnerving shot, one that may be uncomfortable for the viewer, in the face of Schomburg's silent challenge. 1905, the year in which the portrait was taken, was only seven years after the annexation of the island to the United States; the population of the formerly Spanish territory were accustomed to interactions between *los negros, los trigueños, los mulatos, los blancos*, etc. These interfaces occurred across class lines, as made evident by the sizable number of free men and women of African descent.[31] While racial prejudice existed on the island, it took a form distinct from that which had been established on the mainland, where segregation between the races had been legalized with the *Plessy v. Ferguson* ruling in 1896.[32] Despite claims of a society that did not see difference, this pairing may have raised eyebrows for the viewer unaware of their relationship. Schomburg seems to know this, and in his direct look, invites commentary.

More than twenty years after Schomburg's portrait with his sister, we note the discomfort that notoriously characterizes the passport photo (*Figure 5.8*). It was only in 1914 that then-Secretary of State William Jennings Bryan announced that photographs would have to accompany passport applications in the United States. The State Department continued to issue policies throughout the 1920s that assisted in easing the country's concerns about this new technology that would be used for identification purposes. As Craig Robertson notes in his study *The Passport in America: The History of a Document* (2010): "The purported strength of photographic representation was that it produced a stable and fixed object that provided an accurate point of comparison for state officials."[33] By definition, then, this particular kind of photograph was meant to set a person's identity so that there would be no confusion on the part of the government official viewing it. It was, as Robertson writes, "prepared with the intention of highlighting an individual's unique facial features as part of an attempt by the state to know its population on an individual basis."[34] In 1926, when Schomburg took his picture, the passport photo was still considered a novelty, a genre of

FIGURE 5.8 Portrait of Arthur A. Schomburg from his United States passport, issued in 1926, age fifty-two

portraiture that was engaged predominantly by members of the upper classes who were the most likely to be traveling abroad. For Schomburg, a man who had been accustomed to travel throughout his life, first as a child when he moved between Puerto Rico and the Virgin Islands, and later as an adult, travel was an activity in which he had actively participated. Nevertheless, his discomfort is palpable.

Robertson notes about the genre of the passport photo in the 1920s:

> The promise to deliver accurate identification was based in a faith in the mechanical reproduction of the camera over the lingering sub-jectivity of the written physical description…The "truth" that state officials granted the passport photograph in documenting a person's face and thus their identity coexisted with a public perception of what a newspaper called the "distortion of passport photography." This "distortion" was the product of the clashing of two particular tradi-tions of photographing people: the portrait and the "scientific" image (generally used in criminal identification photographs).[35]

Here, Robertson recalls the class of photography most often used against black bodies in the nineteenth and twentieth centuries, the "scientific" image, of which was purported objectivity. Louis Agassiz's daguerreotypes of enslaved men and women in the nude are but one infamous example of the use of such images: Agassiz, a Swiss naturalist teaching at Harvard, commissioned these portraits as a means by which to further his argument about polygenism, the notion that human beings were divisible by species.[36] Images of the enslaved as well as of criminals, groups that were sometimes conflated in popular imagination in this country, were widely circulated throughout the nineteenth century; in authoriz-ing the mandatory use of a technology that simulated poses already recognizable for members of seemingly undesirable groups, governments in the Western hemi-sphere risked disturbing the comfort of travelers, many of whom were presumed to be engaging in this leisure activity as members of the middle and upper classes and of European heritage. Robertson notes:

> The passport photograph becomes a focal point for these middle-class and upper-class concerns about demands to prove personal identity through official documents and official photographs. The stark frontal image of the passport photograph revealed the unease that many travelers felt towards a required passport. For these travelers this style of photograph indicated the proper target of identification documents should be populations considered suspect and marginal by those who traveled for leisure.[37]

Here, in his passport photo, Schomburg looks perhaps the most ill at ease of all of his photographs. He is as well dressed as ever and is without his moustache, perhaps bowing to social customs of the day. He stares directly at the camera, expressionless, resembling how most of us look in our passport shots. Indeed, this portrait has its own genealogy, understandable given its purpose as a medium that assists in the control of bodies crossing imaginary boundaries. Plainly said, the passport, at its most functional, assists in the regulation and monitoring of bodies; it is no coincidence, therefore, that the passport photograph, that which

FIGURE 5.9 Arturo Alfonso Schomburg, late in life

is used to testify to the claim that the holder of said document is in fact that person, bears a striking resemblance to the mugshot. In this portrait, Schomburg looks entrapped, boxed in, captured in a way that he had resisted all of his life.

In another photograph found in Gumby's scrapbook dedicated to him (*Figure 5.9*), Schomburg does look straight at the camera, in a shot that appears to be a candid one. He looks disturbed, bothered by the actions of a photographer who seemingly interrupts his reading. There is censure in his stare, as if warning his audience to keep away. There is nothing inviting to the viewer here, other than a picture of a well-dressed, well-groomed man, a man engaged in a beloved activity. Though he appears to be in a public place, we as the viewers have transgressed, as we have obviously entered his sanctuary. We are reminded of bell hooks, who writes of what she names the "oppositional gaze":

> Spaces of agency exist for black people, wherein we can both interro-
> gate the gaze of the Other but also look back, and at one another, naming
> what we see. The "gaze" has been and is a site of resistance for colonized
> black people globally. Subordinates in relations of power learn experi-
> entially that there is a critical gaze, one that "looks" to document, one
> that is oppositional. In resistance struggle, the power of the dominated
> to assert agency by claiming and cultivating "awareness" politicizes
> "looking" relations—*one learns to look a certain way in order to resist.*
> (116; my emphasis)[38]

Here is the man Jean Blackwell Hutson called "complex" in a 1978 interview for Columbia University's Oral History Project.[39] He is obviously uncomfortable and has no qualms about relaying that sentiment. Here, Schomburg censures anyone who peeks in on him; though he is performing a public activity, and in spite of the fact that the shot could have very well have been staged, he nevertheless com-municates one singular message with his stare: "Stay back."

QUESTIONS OF LEGIBILITY

In *Troubling Vision*, Nicole Fleetwood comments on "the notion that audiences come to understand black lived experience and black subjects as knowable through visual and performative codes."[40] The emphasis on the visual and the ability to understand, to read and analyze a body, more specifically a racialized body, and to rely on the knowledge ascertained as a kind of "truth" recalls Mark Anthony

Neal's discussion of legibility and illegibility in his 2013 study *Looking for Leroy: Illegible Black Masculinities*. There, Neal offers a persuasive argument for the potential of rendering "illegible" those black male bodies that have been deemed "legible" in U.S. popular culture in the twenty-first century. He writes: "That the most 'legible' black male body is often thought to be a criminal body and/or a body in need of policing and containment—incarceration—is just a reminder that the black male body that so seduces America is just as often the bogeyman that keeps America awake at night."[41] The statement about the criminalization of the black male body and the imagery produced to terrorize the U.S. public as a whole is as true today as it was in the first decades of the twentieth century. An impetus behind the creation of uplifting portraits of black men and women during the Harlem Renaissance was in fact to counter the relentless barrage of images in which this population was portrayed as criminals or bumbling stereotypes, devoid of humanity. Neal's study undertakes two tasks concurrently in that it "suggest[s] the radical potential of rendering 'legible' black male bodies—those bodies that are all too real to us—as illegible, while simultaneously rendering so-called illegible black male bodies—those black male bodies we can't believe are real—legible."[42]

The aim of this chapter is to highlight Schomburg's "illegibility" as a deliberative act; indeed, while he is "read" as a black man in his portraits, I argue that he disturbs the viewer's assurance in the knowledge they have attained in reaching that conclusion. Schomburg does not want to be "read" so easily; he is not an uncomplicated text. On the contrary, in many of his portraits, he evades the audience by being in either full or three-quarter profile; when he looks in the direction of the camera, he often looks beyond the lens, either above or below the camera's line of vision. In those rare portraits where he does look directly at the camera, his gaze is one of daring. He stops the viewer, disturbing his/her ease with his own challenge; ironically, this draws the viewer in to look further, contemplating the nature of the person before them. In Fleetwood's words, he is a "troubling figuration to visual discourse."[43] Powell reminds us: "With portraiture, however, one should not lose sight of the institutional forces that sometimes place the desires, fantasies, and representational will of the subject—especially a socially prominent, renowned, or commissioning subject—above those of the artist."[44] Schomburg defies the spectator to attempt to categorize him, to place him in the same grouping to which they are accustomed. In the end, the nameless writer of the Associated Negro Press might have been correct: the man before us *is* elusive, and has remained so for more than a century. The aim of this project is to honor that elusiveness as well as to understand Arturo Schomburg as a man, a human being, a black Puerto Rican, an Afro-Latino, at this, the beginning of a new century.

CONCLUSION

————◆•◆————

THE DYNAMICS OF AFRO-LATINX SUBJECTIVITY

yo peleo por ti, puerto rico,   ¿sabes?
yo me defiendo por tu nombre, ¿sabes?

—TATO LAVIERA, "nuyorican"

assimilated? qué assimilated,
brother, yo soy asimilao

—TATO LAVIERA, "asimilao"

AMONG THE POEMS FOUND in Tato Laviera's third poetry collection, *AmeRícan* (1985), are these two, "nuyorican" and "asimilao."[1] Born in Santurce, Puerto Rico, almost eight decades after Schomburg's birth in the same area of the island as Schomburg, Laviera came to New York City at ten years of age. One of the most important voices of the Nuyorican poetry scene of the 1970s and 1980s, Laviera would continue to be productive as an artist—a poet and playwright— until his death in 2013. One of the prominent features of his body of work is his full and complete acknowledgment of his African heritage: in many of his poems the poetic voice expresses not only a pride in this heritage but also a challenge to a homogenous Puerto Rican insular identity that dismisses their diasporic coun- terparts living in the mainland United States. With "nuyorican," a poem composed entirely in Spanish (thereby refuting notions that those who live in New York have abandoned the Spanish language), Laviera directly addresses this sense of rejec- tion by asserting an identification with this national identity that encompasses the experience of migration. Also notable in Laviera's poetry is his embrace of a Hispanic Caribbean vernacular that features the elimination of the intervocalic *d* so that the word "asimilado" becomes "asimilao"; in the poem of that name, the poetic voice resists a categorization of assimilation, questioning the label in English and instead answering in Spanglish in a Puerto Rican dialect. With these two poems, then, Laviera, a black Nuyorican, an Afro-Latino, revels in his multilingual multiracial migratory identity, one that defies facile classification.[2]

DIASPORIC BLACKNESS

The title of this study may be, for some, at the very least repetitive: indeed, blackness may be considered inherently diasporic, due to the massive migrations that have occurred not only across the Atlantic Ocean during the Middle Passage but also across all the bodies of water surrounding the African continent as well as within that landmass itself. Still, the heading of this study is deliberate in that it calls attention to this history of migration and to what others have characterized as displacement and uprootedness. As a black man from the Hispanic Caribbean, Schomburg was doubly Othered; at the time of his birth, Latin America as a region was considered a feminized space from the perspective of Progressive-era United States.[3] Blackness in and of itself was considered feminine by leading white sociologists of the time.[4] Black men of the late nineteenth and early twentieth centuries responded in numerous ways, often in highly gendered terms; expressions of manhood were therefore deemed compulsory and exhibitions of that masculinity were thought to be obligatory in order to combat a white supremacist culture that was predicated on the supposed weakness of black men. The establishment of scholarly institutions was one such response. A "foreign Negro," as one critic calls him (employing the parlance of the day), Schomburg, with his German surname and his birth and rearing predominantly in the Hispanic Caribbean, challenged his contemporaries to broaden their notions of blackness so that it could conceivably include him; this challenge continues to this day, as there is growing awareness in the United States of the histories of peoples of African descent in the Spanish-speaking Americas, including the United States itself.

In her examination of Hispanic Caribbean Freemasonry, Jossianna Arroyo observes about Schomburg and his contemporary Rafael Serra:

> In this sense, they confronted subjective and political dilemmas similar to the ones faced by contemporary Afro-Latin@ subjects in the United States, particularly in the ways that black immigrants from the Hispanic Caribbean, do not want to erase their culture, language, or common struggles against racism, even when they identify themselves with

African American civil rights agendas. Their encounter with US racial paradigms creates a new form of consciousness or "transcultural/transnational racial difference" that is not separated from, but that interacts and intermingles with, their notions of race and nation-building brought from the nineteenth-century Hispanic Caribbean.[5]

Recalling Antonio López's theorization of *afrolatinidad*, for Afro-Latinxs there is a sense of overlap, as one experiences not only racialized discourses of being as established by the history of interactions between whites and African Americans within the United States but also, simultaneously, those ideologies of race from the home countries as well within settings marked Hispanic. This is similarly experienced by all peoples of African descent, including those from the West Indies and from the African continent itself, who, upon their arrival in this country, have historically had to develop strategies to navigate the United States in relation to the treatment of the African American community. One of the first communities to face such a challenge was the Puerto Rican community in New York City, of which Schomburg was an early pioneer.

> We do not think that it is too much to ask of the papers that when they write about a Puerto Rican who happened to have done something good to please mention the fact that he is Puerto Rican. Mentioning the many good things done by Puerto Ricans and the Puerto Rican people as a whole will help to destroy their enemies.[6]

In his collection of *crónicas* published as *A Puerto Rican in New York and Other Sketches* (1961), Jesús Colón mentions Schomburg only once; in an article about a bulletin published in 1956 by the New York Public Library highlighting a list of books about Puerto Rico and Puerto Ricans, Colón points out the works, articles, exhibitions, and activities throughout the library system that have been left out. In concluding the article he writes:

> We also missed in the branch library news for February dedicated to Puerto Rico any mention of the Schomburg Collection, at 135th Street and Lenox Avenue. Though the collection itself is dedicated to the Negro people and their history, there is a great deal of material on prominent Negro Puerto Ricans in its files. Besides, Arturo Schomburg, a great figure in the life of the 19th century Puerto Rican in New York was himself a Puerto Rican, born in San Juan, the capital of Puerto

Rico. Its seems to be that one of the main divisions in the New York Public Library system—bearing the name of a great Negro Puerto Rican should at least have been mentioned in a library publication purporting to compile the most important books dealing with the cultural developments and contributions of Puerto Rico and Puerto Ricans in New York.[7]

Schomburg had died in 1938, only eighteen years previous to the article; also, Colón's designation of him as a "19th century Puerto Rican," given that Schomburg lived almost four decades into the twentieth century, implies that those were his "Puerto Rican" years, when he could most easily be identified as such. Finally, the categorization of the collection of having solely to do with "Negro" history, that is, the history of African Americans, again highlights the fight that Schomburg had waged throughout his life, as his emphasis as a bibliophile, as a collector, as a writer, had always been on the global black experience, not just that of those men and women of African descent born and raised in the United States.

In her article on Pura Belpré, the Afro-Latina Puerto Rican librarian who worked alongside Schomburg in the 135th Street Branch Library during the first years of her career, Victoria Núñez writes: "One overlooked theme [of current historiography of Puerto Rican migration] is that of interracial cooperation and alliances that significantly assisted the advancement and settlement of migrant Puerto Rican communities."[8] Earlier in the article she hypothesizes that "Black Puerto Ricans may have moved to Harlem precisely because they perceived it to be a safer haven (not completely safe) from the discrimination they faced in other city neighborhoods" (71). They were there, living outside of the well-established enclaves of Spanish Harlem and the Lower East Side, and they were there in Central and West Harlem earlier than has been accounted for.[9] This led to collaboration and aid from friends and neighbors, fellow migrants from the U.S. South as well as from other islands in the region. The Caribbean itself is not an area defined strictly by language; this notion of immobility and fixedness exists predominantly in universities in the United States that study the region according to the language of the colonizers who settled there. Prospero lives in the halls of academe in the United States. The region itself is one of constant flux, migratory patterns, as people pursue opportunities for better lives; their diasporic settlings in New York are no different.

Lisa Sánchez González writes in *Boricua Literature*: "[Schomburg's] definition of diasporan subjectivity was clearly irreverent toward nationally normed identities (his ideal 'republic' being, after all, bibliographically constituted), and he elaborated this racial constituency along a broad spectrum beyond whiteness and Blackness as they have been legislated, lived, and, consequently, assumed in the United States."[10] Schomburg's collections, particularly the one he established in Fisk University, may seem self-evident—a library emphasizing the contributions of peoples of African descent in a historically black university. Yet this focus was not implemented, even by this group of educational institutions, until the late 1960s, due to the influence of the Black Power movement. The importance of the establishment of the Negro Collection at Fisk lies not only in that people of African descent could see themselves in history, art, literature, etc.; it also established unequivocally that peoples of African descent are worthy of study. This is a fight that continues to go on today, as university systems either downgrade or phase out Black Studies programs started in the fervor of the 1960s. Schomburg was incredibly prescient, then, in creating this space within a university setting dedicated to the subject at hand. It was not something that was replicated in other schools, again, for decades after his death. Even now, the most progressive universities may not have whole sections of their libraries dedicated solely to the black experience.

The City University of New York, for example, has both the Center for Puerto Rican Studies and the Dominican Studies Institute, each of which includes an accompanying library and archives; both of these institutions were created decades after Schomburg's death. Schomburg's insight was that in creating these collections, there could be no doubt that peoples of African descent were worthy of intellectual analysis. In addition, because his collections were international in scope, there was inherently an emphasis on the complexity of the black experience; one is therefore not able to flatten out the cultural productions or intellectual contributions produced by men and women living in different countries, speaking different languages, with different histories. Instead, effort has to be made in order to grasp experiences that challenge established paradigms. The African diaspora as a formulation flies in the face of nationalist identification, and for some, while there is certainly an acknowledgment of the critical importance of Africa, there is no desire for return. Instead, there is an appeal to understand the histories of peoples in the lands they inhabit, to investigate and comprehend their local customs and traditions, to examine what they may have in common and what they do differently; the collections of Arturo Schomburg have facilitated these inquiries, leaving this as his lasting contribution to the Race.

In the summer of 1938, weeks after Schomburg's passing, Arthur Huff Fauset stayed in Harlem; in an editorial published that September in the *Philadelphia Tribune* he praises Schomburg's achievements. Fauset reacts to what was then still known as the Negro Division: "If our children could somehow learn the hundredth part of that which has been accomplished by Negro men and women living in all ages and in all parts of the world, we would not be long in developing an American Negro group which would take its rightful place in this commonwealth. Negro people, we are members of a great and wonderful race!"[11] Here, then, we see the realization of what Adalaine Holton has labeled as Schomburg's decolonial project: it is in learning of past achievements that one learns that one is able to aspire to greatness.[12] In addition, they would know with no uncertain terms that they are a part not only of this country, but of any country to which they are born.

By using "American" as an adjective here, Fauset underscores the geographical breadth of the African diaspora; with his exclamation, he urges an acknowledgment of a relationship that exists beyond national boundaries. Earlier in the piece he writes: "There is scarcely anything that on the Negro that has been written anywhere which is not to be found in this wonderful storehouse. This includes work in French, German and Spanish, in addition to thousands and thousands of English and American volumes."[13] Fauset calls attention to the global scope of the work not only done *about* those of African descent but also *by* men and women of African descent; almost eighty years after his passing, the legacy of Arturo Alfonso Schomburg, an Afro-Latino man of Puerto Rican heritage, of honoring the multilingual, multiethnic, transnational beauty of Africa and its diaspora remains vibrant and continues to flourish.

NOTES

INTRODUCTION

1. There has been great recent discussion about the exclusivity of languages marked by gender, such as Spanish, where nouns with the masculine ending "o" have traditionally been understood to convey members of both genders, male and female, and have therefore been considered universal. By naming Schomburg's subjectivity as "Afro-Latino," rather than "Afro-Latinx," I convey that his was a gendered experience that was the result of being read as a cis heterosexual man during his life. Throughout this project, when referring to general experiences of both men and women of African and Latinx descent, I use the term "Afro-Latinx."

2. Schomburg 201.

3. Sinnette 1989.

4. See Moss.

5. See Hoffnung-Garskof (2010).

6. Sánchez González makes this point in her study *Boricua Literature*.

7. Sinnette 13.

8. In a 1931 letter to the Carnegie Corporation soliciting funding for a fellowship, Schomburg himself writes that he spent two years in St. Thomas College, a secondary institution, from 1886–88, then returned to Puerto Rico to attend the Instituto de Enseñanza Popular from 1889–91. Arthur A. Schomburg, Letter to the Carnegie Corporation. 1/14/1931. Fisk University, John Hope and Aurelia E. Franklin Library, Special Collections, Thomas Elsa Jones Collection, box 39, folder 18.

9. See James (1996) 102–103.

10. A selection of writings on Afro-Hispanic literature includes: Richard L. Jackson, *The Black Image in Latin American Literature* (1976); Miriam

DeCosta-Willis, ed., *Blacks in Hispanic Literature: Critical Essays* (1977/2011); Richard L. Jackson, *Black Writers in Latin America* (1979); Marvin A. Lewis, *Afro-Hispanic Poetry 1940–80: From Slavery to Negritude in South American Verse* (1983); Ian Smart, *Central American Writers of West Indian Origin: A New Hispanic Literature* (1984); William Luis, ed., *Voices from Under: Black Narrative in Latin American and the Caribbean* (1984); Richard L. Jackson, *Black Literature and Humanism in Latin America* (1988/2008); Marvin A. Lewis, *Treading the Ebony Path: Ideology and Violence in Contemporary Afro-Colombian Prose Fiction* (1988); William Luis, *Literary Bondage: Slavery in Cuban Narrative* (1990); Marvin A. Lewis, *Ethnicity and Identity in Contemporary Afro-Venezuelan Literature: A Culturalist Approach* (1992); Vera M. Kutzinski, *Sugar's Secrets: Race and Erotics of Cuban Nationalism* (1993); Lorna V. Williams, *The Representation of Slavery in Cuban Fiction* (1994); Marvin A. Lewis, *Afro-Argentine Discourse: Another Dimension of the Black Diaspora* (1995); Richard L. Jackson, *Black Writers and the Hispanic Canon* (1997); Edward J. Mullen, *Afro-Cuban Literature: Critical Junctures* (1998); Maria Ramos Rosado, *La mujer negra en la literatura puertorriqueña* (1999); Laurence E. Prescott, *Without Hatred or Fear: Jorge Artel and the Struggle for Black Literary Expression in Colombia* (2000); Claudette M. Williams, *Charcoal and Cinnamon: The Politics of Color in Spanish Caribbean Literature* (2000); Miriam DeCosta-Willis, ed., *Singular Like a Bird: The Art of Nancy Morejón* (2002); Marvin A. Lewis, *Afro-Uruguayan Literature: Postcolonial Perspectives* (2003); Miriam DeCosta Willis, ed., *Daughters of the Diaspora: Afra-Hispanic Writers* (2003); Dorothy E. Mosby, *Place, Language, and Identity in Afro–Costa Rican Literature* (2003); Dawn F. Stinchcomb, *The Development of Literary Blackness in the Dominican Republic* (2004); Marco Polo Hernández, *African Mexicans and the Discourse on the Modern Nation* (2004); Antonio D. Tillis, *Manuel Zapata Olivella and the "Darkening" of Latin American Literature* (2005); Jerome Branch, *Colonialism and Race in Luso-Hispanic Literature* (2006); Marvin A. Lewis, *An Introduction to the Literature of Equatorial Guinea: Between Colonialism and Dictatorship* (2007); Marvin A. Lewis, *Adalberto Ortiz: From Margin to Center* (2014). For a selection of Afro-Brazilian literary criticism, Niyi Afolabi, Márcio Barbosa, and Esmeralda Ribeiro, eds., *A Mente Afro-Brasileira: Crítica Literária e Cultural Afro-Brasileira Contemporânea / The Afro-Brazilian Mind: Contemporary Afro-Brazilian Literary and Cultural Criticism* (2007); Niyi Afolabi, *Afro-Brazilians: Cultural Production in a Racial Democracy* (2009). See also the *Afro-Hispanic Review, PALARA (Publication of the Afro-Latin American Research Association),* and *Callaloo.* These titles do not include the studies published in fields other than literary criticism, such as history and Latinx Studies, where there has also been growing interest in the study of Afro-Latinxs.

11. It is fascinating to conjecture Schomburg's reaction to the changing political statuses of the islands of his childhood: the bulk of the personal correspondence that remains preserved at the Schomburg Center is subsequent to the following events. 1917 was a significant year for all of these islands: on March 2, 1917, the Jones-Shafroth Act was signed, conferring U.S. citizenship to inhabitants of Puerto Rico; on April 1, 1917, the Danish West Indies formally became the Virgin Islands of the United States, as the United States had purchased the islands of St. Croix, St. Thomas, and St. John for twenty-five million dollars. The United States awarded citizenship to the inhabitants of these islands a decade later, in 1927. All of these islands are legally unincorporated territories of the United States, meaning their inhabitants are U.S. citizens but are unable to vote for president and do not have a voting representative in Congress, so long as they live on these islands. They assume these rights if they move to the mainland.

12. Torres-Saillant (2010) 455.

13. Sinnette 155.

14. López 11.

15. Urrutia's designation of Schomburg as an "Afro-Puerto Rican" makes sense from his Cuban perspective and within a Cuban context; as Aline Helg points out, "Cubans have perpetuated the mid-nineteenth-century notion of a *raza de color* (race of color) or *clase de color* (class of color) without differentiating mulattoes from blacks and have often referred to both *pardos* (mulattoes) and *morenos* (blacks) as *negros* (blacks)" (3). There was no such comparable discourse on the island of Puerto Rico until the 1970s, and to this day, it remains a rare occurrence to hear such an assertion.

16. In his last known letter dated May 18, 1895, Cuban freedom fighter, essayist, and poet José Martí wrote about his time in the United States: "I have lived inside the monster and know its entrails—and my weapon is only the slingshot of David." See epigraph of collection of Martí's writings on imperialism.

17. See Thomas 26.

18. Victoria Núñez reminds us that there also existed a Puerto Rican enclave in Central Harlem as early as the 1920s, one that might have been Afro–Puerto Rican, but that has been overlooked in Puerto Rican historiography. See Núñez (2009).

19. Hoffnung-Garskof (2010) 76–77.

20. Piñeiro de Rivera, ed. *Arturo Schomburg* 28.

21. Piñeiro de Rivera, ed. *Arthur A. Schomburg* 30. All quotes from Schomburg's writings will come from this English edition.

22. Piñeiro de Rivera, Spanish edition 28.

23. Piñeiro de Rivera, English edition 30.

24. Piñeiro de Rivera, Spanish edition 30.

25. Piñeiro de Rivera, English edition 31–32.

26. For more on the Puerto Rican educational system after the annexation of the island by the United States in 1898, see Moral.

27. Piñeiro de Rivera, Spanish edition 30.

28. Piñeiro de Rivera, English edition 32.

29. In recent years, there has been a reconsideration of Vega's memoirs; in her work on this text, Bridget Kevane has highlighted how its editor, Cesar Andre Iglesias, played a much more active role than his title implies. See Kevane.

30. The details of this brief biographical sketch come from Lisa Sánchez González's first chapter of *Boricua Literature*, titled "For the Sake of Love: Luisa Capetillo, Anarcy, and Boricua Literary History," and from Felix V. Matos-Rodríguez's introduction to his edition of Capetillo's *Mi opinion*. See *Boricua Literature* 16–41 and Matos Rodríguez vii–li.

31. For more on the role of the reader in Cuban and Puerto Rican tobacco factories, see Tinajero.

32. Matos Rodríguez xix.

33. Ibid. xxxvii.

34. There has been growing interest in the life of Belpré, in great part due to the efforts of Sánchez González; in addition to her chapter on Belpré in Boricua Literature, see her 2013 study, *The Stories I Read to Children*.

35. See Hernández-Delgado 427.

36. Núñez (2009), 69.

37. See "About the Pura Belpré Award" N.p. http://www.ala.org/alsc/awards-grants/bookmedia/belpremedal/belpreabout.

38. Sinnette 28.

39. Ibid. 30.

40. Ibid. 50–51.

41. Moss 226.

42. Sinnette 29.

43. Sánchez González, "A Transamerican Intellectual" 140.

44. Ibid.

45. See Boyce Davies.

46. Whereas "afro" is wholly unsatisfying, the existence and successful usage of the prefix at least identifies that there was assimilation of these peoples—the indigenous remain without a linguistic marker in relation to *latinidad,* an indication that in the face of centuries-long campaigns in favor of *mestizaje,* we have not yet developed the language to adequately describe an assimilation that honors indigeneity and that does not result in whitening. Assimilation for the indigenous continues to be constructed of as "loss." All of these terms to some extent are unproductive because they all imply purity and authenticity, which is counterintuitive and counterproductive to how people actually live.

47. Flores and Jiménez Román 1.

48. Ibid 2.

49. Despite this assertion that "Afro-Latin@" is applicable on a hemispheric level, it is notable that the writings collected in this anthology focus solely on the United States, as López does in his study.

50. Flores and Román 2. These scholars use "@" as an attempt at inclusivity, however critics have argued that such a move reinscribes gender binaries, hence the decision of this author to use "x."

51. Ibid 3.

52. Hall 225.

53. López 4–5.

54. For an overview of the creation of this identity as well as a consideration of the impact of this new identity on Puerto Ricans in New York, see Flores (2000) 141–166. In his study of José Martí, Oscar Montero underscores that Martí used the term *latino* in the nineteenth century to mean "people from Latin America, wherever they might be: Mexico, New York, Tampa, or Key West" (2).

55. López 12.

56. Fleetwood 18.

57. Locke (1941).

58. McKay 142.

59. Johnson (2005) 449.

60. Neal 8.

61. Folder 4, Arthur Alfonso Schomburg Collection, Manuscripts, Archives and Rare Books Division, Schomburg Center of Research in Black Culture, The New York Public Library.

62. DeFrantz and Gonzalez 11.

63. Ibid.

64. Iton 195.

65. Ibid 200.

66. For two of the most popular theorizations about Caribbean identity, see Antonio Benítez-Rojo, *The Repeating Island: The Caribbean and the Postmodern Perspective* (1992) and Édouard Glissant, *Poetics of Relation* (1997).

67. Edwards (2007) 691.

68. Ibid. 690.

69. Hall 225.

70. Edwards (2003) 13.

71. Nwankwo 10.

72. Sánchez-Korrol (2014) n.p.

73. Sánchez González, "Transamerican Intellectual" 140–141.

74. Edwards (2003) 7.

75. Sinnette 35.

76. See Kutzinski 2.

77. Edwards (2003) 11–15; Kutzinski 3.

78. Lewis (1995) 783.

79. Ibid. 787.

CHAPTER 1. "PATRIA Y LIBERTAD"

All translations in this chapter are provided by the author of this project.

Sotero Figueroa closes a note, dated March 17, 1893, to Schomburg with the words *patria y libertad,* which mean "Homeland and Freedom"; Figueroa served as president of the Club Político Antillano "Borinquen." Sotero Figueroa, "Note." Reel 3 Frame 00953 Arthur A. Schomburg Papers, Jean Blackwell Hutson Research and Reference Division, Schomburg Center for Research in Black Culture, The New York Public Library. Figueroa (1851–1923) was a fellow Afro-Latino, a Puerto Rican of African descent who worked alongside Schomburg in this revolutionary club; see Edna Acosta Belén's profile of him.

1. In addition to Sinnette, Hoffnung-Garskof and Sanchez González have paid the greatest attention to this period in his life.

2. I use "creole" in accord with its Spanish definition, to mean children of Spanish immigrants born in the Americas. Schomburg himself comments on this when he writes in 1927: "The children of Spaniards who were born and reared in their possessions of Cuba, Santo Domingo, Jamaica, Mexico and Porto Rico are called to this day "criollo" to their respective countries and islands" (137).

3. For a study tracing the development of pro-independence consciousness among the Cuban exile communities from the mid-nineteenth century until the conclusion of the Spanish-American War, see Poyo.

4. See Morales; in his study, Andrews notes that Spain banned immigration from Haiti to Puerto Rico and Cuba in 1806 (68).

5. For an overview of sugar production in Cuba, Puerto Rico, Jamaica, and Brazil, see Yun 11–14; for the classic account of the role of sugar in the Cuban economy in the nineteenth century, see Moreno Fraginals; for an account of sugar expansion in Puerto Rico, see Ramos Mattei (1981). For a discussion about the economic ties between New York and Cuba in the nineteenth century, particularly in terms of the import and refinement of sugar and the import of tobacco, see Pérez (2010).

6. For a classic study of slavery in Puerto Rico, see Díaz Soler; for a study that revised insular historiography to that point, including that of Díaz Soler, see Baralt. The publication of this book in 1982 caused a stir on the island, as common wisdom held that the enslaved of Puerto Rico, as in many other countries, had been docile and had been liberated only through the efforts of white abolitionists; Baralt explored municipal archives and contemporary newspaper accounts in order to demonstrate otherwise. For primary source materials regarding Africans who escaped slavery, see Nistal-Moret (1984).

7. Díaz Soler 218–224.

8. Another law that would affect the lives of working peoples white and black alike, was the passage of the Reglamento de Jornaleros, which decreed that workers of all races had to carry notebooks (libretas) that revealed where they were working, their salary, notes about his/her behavior, and other information deemed pertinent; this was another means by which bodies were highly regulated by the Spanish regime. The law stayed in effect until 1873; resistance to it was a factor in the abolition of slavery. See Bergad. For more information on both laws, see Scarano 414–419 and 450–455. José Curet notes the deleterious effects of the law: "Of a total of 26,223 tenant farmers who had existed on the island in 1849, only 4,437 remained a year later" (120).

9. Andrews 92.

10. See Lidin 113 and Suárez Findlay 53–76. Both strains of thought are visible in Puerto Rico's contemporary political status.

11. See Scarano 543; Wallace (2010) 48–51; Foner; and Pérez (1998).

12. Lidin 62.

13. Suárez Findlay 55.

14. Rodríguez-Silva (2012) 64.

15. Slavery was abolished in Cuba in 1886; for more information, see Scott (2000).

16. Nistal-Moret (1985) 153. Andrews emphasizes that in Cuba, the Moret Law freed children born between 1868 and 1870, but they were obliged to work for their masters until they reached the age of twenty-two, when they would be declared emancipated (78).

17. Nistal-Moret (1985) 151–152.

18. Ramos Mattei (1985) 167–168. This gradual emancipation of the enslaved occurred throughout Latin America; see Andrews 53–84.

19. Suárez Findlay 55.

20. Schools are named after both men; in New York City, the most famous example is Hostos Community College, one of the leading colleges within the City University of New York system.

21. Hoffnung-Garskof (2001) 11; see also Wallace (2010) 43.

22. See Maldonado-Denis 23.

23. In 1840, Betances's father Felipe publicly whitened his heritage by testifying in court about his family background, therefore proving his pure blood (*limpieza de sangre*); this action secured a higher social standing for the family and facilitated his daughter's marriage into a local family. These cases were one course of action men and women of African descent undertook in order to ascend the social hierarchy; see Kinsbruner 36–41. Arroyo points out that this whitening was a successful venture for the older Betances, "that is, until his son Ramón began to reclaim those origins as part of a radical political tradition associated with blackness" (72). In a letter to his sister, who was inquiring about their African heritage, Betances responds unequivocally, "Somos prietuzcos y a orgullo lo tenemos" ("We are black and we have pride"). "Prieto" has pejorative connotations when used, and so here we see Betances reclaim blackness so that it conveys honor; see Arpini 124.

24. Scarano 425.

25. In her most recently published novel *Conquistadora*, famed U.S. Puerto Rican writer Esmeralda Santiago dramatizes this moment in Puerto Rican history, with the protagonist's son being arrested for his involvement in abolitionist activities. See Santiago.

26. Álvarez-López 68.

27. Betances (1983) 58.

28. For more information on this event, see Bergad and Jiménez de Wagenheim.

29. Lewis (2004) 277.

30. Sinnette uses as a basis for his claim that he spent time in St. Thomas, as per Schomburg's own tellings of his life; for Lisa Sánchez González, the evidence that is cited is tenuous ("A Transamerican Intellectual" 142).

31. Sinnette 16.

32. Arroyo 75.

33. For more on Betances, see the works of Ojeda Reyes.

34. Gruesz 187.

35. Ibid.

36. Ibid.

37. See Trouillot and Chancy.

38. This anxiety would lead to the eventual capitulation of white Cuban troops to their Spanish counterparts in 1878; for more, see Helg and Ferrer (1999).

39. Hostos 229, 231.

40. See Maldonado-Denis.

41. Arroyo is the sole scholar to examine this subject in *Writing Secrecy*.

42. Jusino and Torre 150.

43. Scarano points out that between 1892 and 1898, approximately eighty women's clubs were founded in support of the Antillean liberation movement, with roughly one thousand to fifteen hundred members (531).

44. The details of this biographical sketch can be found in Acosta-Belén (2005).

45. Ojeda Reyes 1992.

46. Arroyo 69–102.

47. See Lorde.

48. Sinnette 20.

49. Serra as quoted in Arroyo 147.

50. Sinnette 20–21.

51. Helg 36.

52. Helg 42.

53. Ibid.

54. Cabrera Peña 26.

55. Bronfman 70.

56. Poyo 128.

57. Bronfman 71.

58. Ibid.

59. For more on Serra see Deschamps Chapeaux; this is the only full-length biography of him. See also Fusté, Bronfman, and Arroyo.

60. This chronicle originally appeared in *Crisis* 38 (1931): 155–156.

61. Pérez (2010), 106.

62. "I saw Martí one spring morning at 60th Street and Broadway during the year 1895 soon after the Key-West frustrated attempt to land arms. He voiced the hope that everything would eventually turn out right. He was calm, cheerful and convincing. It was the last time I saw this great man. Previous to this occasion we met at a called meeting of the Club Borinquen at Sotero Figuero home on Second Avenue and 62nd Street, New York....Rosendo Rodríguez and I were selected to escort José Martí out of danger to the West Side of the city where he resided, and see that no harm came to his person" (Schomburg 178–179).

63. Vega (1984) 61.

64. See Redondo de Feldman and Tudisco; Oscar Montero and Anne Fountain focus on the effect that living in the United States had on Martí; see Montero (2004) and Fountain.

65. Montero (2004) 60.

66. Montero highlights how Martí wrote also about indigenous populations in the United States and Latin America as well as Chinese laborers. See Montero (2004) 59–84.

67. Vega (1984) 68–69.

68. Ibid.

69. Montero (2004) 102.

70. Ferrer (1998) 232.

71. Ibid.

72. Ibid. 233.

73. Ibid.

74. Ibid. 234.

75. For a study on the competing nationalisms that shaped the Cuban Republic, see Guerra.

76. Martí (1968) 202.

77. Montero (2004) 66.

78. Martí scholarship is extensive; as Guerra notes, there have been one hundred forty titles published each year since his death (3). For studies that examine Martí's work through the prism of race, see Helg; Ferrer (1999); and de la Fuente.

79. Hoffnung-Garskof (2001) 17.

80. Born free, Barbosa (1857–1922) was a doctor who studied at the University of Michigan in 1880 and went on to have an eminent career as a politician; a member of the Partido Autonomista, he later co-founded the island's Republican Party and its attendant newspaper, *El Tiempo*. He served on the advisory Executive Council from 1900 to 1917 and as a senator from 1917 until his death in 1921.

Along with Rafael Cordero, Barbosa is one of the few blacks outside of the realm of sports and entertainment who are recognized for their contributions to the Puerto Rican nation. For more on Barbosa, see Jiménez Román.

81. See Schmidt-Nowara 44.

82. Scarano 433-435; Bernardo Vega recalls that this document was often read in tobacco factories; see Vega (1984) 48.

83. Upon his return from Madrid in 1867, Ruiz Belvis would go on to collaborate with Betances in the planning of an armed insurrection in Puerto Rico, and together they founded the Comité Revolucionario de Puerto Rico in Santo Domingo, to which they had fled after being exiled by the Spanish government. In November 1867, Ruiz Belvis traveled to Chile to gauge support for the cause of Antillean independence there, and died in Valparaiso (Scarano 436–437).

84. These men were part of a group of Puerto Rican and Cuban students studying in Spain; among the others who were there at the time were Román Baldorioty de Castro (1822–1889), who would go on to be a prominent Liberal politician, abolitionist, and one of the founders of the Autonomist Party in 1887; and Alejandro Tapia y Rivera (1826–1882), writer, abolitionist, and author of the *Biblioteca Histórica de Puerto-Rico,* a collection of documents about the island found in the Spanish archives; see Schmidt-Nowara 44–45.

85. Piñeiro de Rivera 24.

86. Sánchez González, *Boricua Literature,* 69.

87. For more on Acosta, see Schmidt-Nowara.

88. Suárez Findlay 80.

89. Brau (1891) n.p.; Scarano 490.

90. For more on Cordero, see Delano and Delano.

91. Rodríguez-Silva (2013) 622–623.

92. Lloréns (2005) 16.

93. Díaz-Quiñones (1999), 104.

94. In a recently published book, Mihai Spariosu writes that the consciousness of the exile constitutes utopic endeavors in an attempt to ground a sense of lack, which is perceived negatively; for him, modernity itself has been generated by this exile-utopia imaginary.

95. Sinnette 13.

96. Sánchez González, *Boricua Literature* 64–66.

97. Rodríguez–Silva (2012) 76.

98. For a collection of his essays, see Brau (1956); for more on Brau himself, see Córdova Landrón. For more on the creole elite and their role in the

formation of Puerto Rican national identity, see the works of José Luis González and Magali Roy-Féquière.

99. Díaz-Quiñones (1999) 112.

100. An interesting counterpoint to Schomburg arises with the figure of Dominican intellectual Pedro Henríquez Ureña (1884–1946). Born into a family of privilege—his mother, Salomé Ureña de Henríquez (1850–1897) was a poet and the founder of the first school for girls in the country, and his father, Francisco Henríquez y Carvajal (1859–1935) would serve as minister of foreign affairs and later as president of the Dominican Republic—Henríquez Ureña is a critical Latin American intellectual who is often overlooked because he is from the Dominican Republic, a country that has gained greater scholarly attention in the fields of Latin American history and literature only in the last few decades. Both men were from the Spanish Caribbean and were influenced by the formulations of regional identity as proposed by Martí, Betances, and Hostos. Both men also spent the majority of their lives outside of their islands of birth, with Henríquez Ureña living in New York from 1901 to 1904 and again in 1915. While both men were of African descent, Schomburg identified as such, whereas Henríquez Ureña more readily claimed a regional and national identifications that absented African heritage. For more on Henríquez Ureña, see Díaz-Quiñones (2006); Méndez; Victoria Núñez (2011); Torres-Saillant (2001); and Valdez.

101. Sinnette 17.

102. Sinnette 21.

103. Wallace (2010), 44.

104. Hoffnung-Garskof (2001) 11. Sánchez Korrol estimates that by 1910 there were more than one thousand Puerto Ricans in the United States as a whole; we can infer from this, as well as from accounts about the membership of Club Borinquen standing at two hundred, that the Puerto Rican community in New York was approximately a few hundred by the end of the nineteenth century (3). In comparison, the 1870 census recorded almost three thousand Cuban-born residents in New York City alone, according to Lisandro Pérez (104).

105. Sánchez Korrol 112.

106. In addition to Schomburg and Sotero Figueroa, the Antillean revolutionary community in New York included the following Afro-Latinos: Pachín Marín, Rosendo Rodríguez, and Juan Gualberto Gómez, among others. Poyo details how in Florida Afro-Cuban men and women established their own revolutionary clubs and socioeconomic organizations, such as the Colegio Unificación and the Sociedad El Progreso (82). In his dissertation, José I. Fusté provides an intellectual biography of Afro-Cuban and Afro–Puerto Rican intellectuals Rafael

Serra, Tomás Carrión-Maduro and Luis Felipe Dessus in order to highlight how they negotiated affirmations of race and nationalism within a context whereby nationalism was defined by *mestizaje* and racial fraternity. See Fusté.

107. Hoffnung-Garskof (2001) 7.

108. Vega (1984) 79.

109. Ibid 83.

110. Sánchez Korrol 113.

111. Sinnette 22–23.

112. Wallace (2010) 45.

113. For more on Freemasonry in the Spanish Caribbean, see Arroyo.

114. Sinnette 23.

115. Ibid.

116. Said 60.

117. Máximo Gómez was the name of a white Dominican general who was one of the leaders of the Cuban insurgency during the Ten Years War (1868–1878) and the 1895 war effort in Cuba, alongside Antonio Maceo; for more information, see Ferrer (1999). Schomburg therefore named his firstborn after a man who had served as the commander in chief of Cuban military forces for three decades.

118. The phrase "foreign in a domestic sense" comes from Judge Edward Douglas White's assenting opinion regarding the political status of Puerto Rico: "[W]hilst in an international sense Porto Rico was not a foreign country, since it was subject to the sovereignty of and was owned by the United States, it was foreign to the United States in a domestic sense, because the island had not been incorporated into the United States, but was merely appurtenant thereto as a possession." *Downes vs. Bidwell*, 182 U.S. 244 (1901) at 341–342, quoted in Kaplan (2002), 2. After taking control of the island, the United States renamed it to "Porto Rico"; this spelling remained until 1930. For more on this change, see García Gervasio 50.

119. Kaplan (2002) 3.

120. Puerto Rico is not the only land to hold this designation; the other unincorporated territories of the United States are the U.S. Virgin Islands, American Samoa, Wake Island, and the Mariana Islands, the largest of which is Guam.

121. Kaplan (2002) 9.

122. Ibid.

123. See Miller.

124. Kipling, "The White Man's Burden." The Kipling Society n.p. www.kipling-society.co.uk. This poem was originally published in February 1899 with the

heading ""An Address to the United States"; it was completed in the fall of 1898, after the war in the Spanish Caribbean. An unnamed critic draws our attention to the title: "We might bear in mind the fact that in the US the phrase 'white man' was current as a term of commendation, meaning straight or decent."

125. See Trigo.

126. Writing about Luis Muñoz Rivera, a leader of the Autonomist Party and father of the future governor Luis Muñoz Marín, Lidin notes: "Moreover, while Muñoz Rivera was always identified with the autonomist bourgeoisie, his loyalties were with the expanding coffee planters—men who depended on European markets—rather than with the U.S.-dependent sugar producers" (119).

127. García Gervasio 53, 54.

128. In his book on the history of the independence movement in Puerto Rico, Harold Lidin writes of Gerardo Forrest, a member of the Puerto Rican section of the PRC, who traveled to Puerto Rico in 1896 on a reconnaissance mission to investigate the likelihood of an insurrection on the island. He met with José Barbosa and Luis Muñoz Rivera, both of whom cautioned him that he would be unable to find Puerto Ricans to fight on the island. Convinced of the futility of the cause in Puerto Rico, Forrest left to fight in Cuba (129).

CHAPTER 2. THE DIASPORIC RACE MAN AS INSTITUTION BUILDER

1. Schomburg 18.
2. Ibid.
3. Weheliye 6.
4. López 11.
5. Schomburg 105.
6. Hinks and Kantrowitz 17.
7. Sinnette 26.
8. Ibid. 41.
9. Ibid 53–72.
10. Information about his personal life found in the finding aid to the Arthur Alfonso Schomburg Papers; the birth years of his children found in "A Study of the Negro Family" survey by E. Franklin Frazier found in folder 4 of the Arthur Alfonso Schomburg Collection in the Manuscripts, Archives and Rare Books Division, Schomburg Center for Research in Black Culture, The New York Public Library.

11. I use the male term *Afro-Latinos* deliberately, as Schomburg often wrote explicitly about men in the course of his writings.

12. Carby 4.

13. Neal 169.

14. Summers (2004) 7.

15. See Cooper (2009).

16. Adalaine Holton makes the important argument that while the term *African diaspora* was not widely employed in scholarship in English until the 1950s, there is no doubt that this is Schomburg's formulation when he utilizes the term *Negro*, unless he specifies a specific group (220–221).

17. Rhodes-Pitts 59.

18. Sinnette 26.

19. While Prince Hall has been widely identified as a free man born and raised in Barbados, a biographical portrait widely disseminated in William Grimshaw's *Official History of Freemasonry among the Colored People of North America* (1903), subsequent biographies disproved this claim; see Wallace (2002) 56–63.

20. See the second chapter of Wallace (2002) 53–81.

21. Ibid. 56.

22. See Andrews 60–92.

23. Ibid. 4; additionally, see Muraskin 33.

24. For the history of women's organizations, see Brown (1989); Ortiz (2005); Jones (2007); Cooper (2013).

25. See Sesay 38.

26. While this phrase was first articulated in Evelyn Brooks Higginbotham's *Righteous Discontent: The Women's Movement in the Black Baptist Church, 1880–1920* (1993), it was a mode of comportment that predated the middle of the nineteenth century; see Wallace (2002).

27. Summers (2004) 26–27.

28. Hinks and Kantrowitz 17.

29. Arroyo 14. In the course of her study, she highlights the influence of Freemasonry on such revolutionaries as Betances, Martí, Hostos, Serra, and Schomburg himself.

30. Ibid. 7.

31. Ibid. 12.

32. Wallace (2002) 64.

33. Arroyo 20.

34. Hoffnung-Garskof 29.

35. Ibid. 31.

36. Summers (2004) 33.

37. In addition to his involvement with the Freemasons, Schomburg, as per his own telling, also was a member of the Odd Fellows, the Elks, and was a 33° member of the Scottish Rite, meaning he served on its governing body, its Supreme Council; see his "A Study of the Negro Family" survey by E. Franklin Frazier found in folder 4 of the Arthur Alfonso Schomburg Collection, Manuscripts, Archives and Rare Books Division, Schomburg Center for Research in Black Culture, The New York Public Library. All of these bodies were, and are, important fraternal associations and yet they have historically been understudied. See Skocpol, Liazos, and Ganz.

38. Sinnette 26.

39. Ibid. 26–27.

40. Hoffnung-Garskof 32.

41. Ibid. 35.

42. Walker 142.

43. Crowder 117.

44. Ibid. 92.

45. Ibid.

46. Sinnette sets the date as April 9, 1911 (41), while Crowder states the founding of this organization occurred on April 18, 1911 (117).

47. Sinnette 43.

48. Ibid. 44.

49. Seraile 115.

50. For biographical information on Fulton, see Crowder 113–114; for information on Schomburg as the society's librarian, see Crowder 119 and Sinnette 43–44. Sinnette notes, "Since he was not only the custodian of the collection but also its chief contributor, Schomburg retained the books and documents when the society disbanded and incorporated them into his personal collection" (44).

51. Crowder 100–102.

52. Schomburg 236.

53. Crowder 118.

54. Ibid. 107–108, 118.

55. See Locke (1941).

56. Ibid. 3.

57. Sinnette (42), Crowder (122), and Seraile (116) all note that many of the members of the Negro Society for Historical Research, including Bruce himself, would actively participate in Marcus Garvey's Universal Negro Improvement

Association (UNIA). Schomburg did not join the UNIA but did enjoy a personal relationship with Garvey and supported the association's goals (Sinnette 126). Scholarly interest in Marcus Garvey has grown significantly in the past four decades, due, in great part, to Robert A. Hill's multivolume collection of *Marcus Garvey and Universal Negro Improvement Association Papers*. While Garvey scholarship is extensive, the following texts are noteworthy: the 2003 special issue of *Caribbean Studies*, "Garveyism and the Universal Negro Association in the Hispanic Caribbean" (31.1); Stephens (2005); Ewing.

58. Moss 1.

59. Ibid.

60. Sinnette 38; for more on Crummell, see Moss and DuBois; for a critique of Du Bois's essay on Crummell, see Carby.

61. Crowder 108.

62. Schomburg 235–236.

63. Sinnette 55.

64. Moss 132.

65. Ibid. 130.

66. Ibid. 221.

67. For more on Schomburg and the American Negro Academy, see Sinnette and Moss.

68. Weiss 55.

69. Ibid. 66.

70. Reed 5–6.

71. Moss 123.

72. Meeham 58–59.

CHAPTER 3. AFRO-LATINX CHRONICLES

1. Schomburg 6.

2. Holton 222.

3. Schomburg 6–7.

4. For more on Modernismo, see Jrade.

5. See Rotker 113; this argument recalls that which Benedict Anderson put forth in his 1983 opus on nationalism, *Imagined Communities*, where he explores the role of "print capitalism" in the creation of the modern nation. For more, see Anderson.

6. Rotker 128.

7. Ibid. 133–134.

8. Ibid. 226.

9. Schomburg 60.

10. Ibid. 62.

11. For more on Manzano, see his autobiography, as well as the biographies by Mullen and Luis.

12. Schomburg 62, 64.

13. In *Modernity Disavowed*, Sibylle Fischer reads Plácido and his poetry as revelatory of the uneven frictions present in Cuban culture during the revolutionary age; see Fischer 77–106. In *Black Cosmopolitanism*, Ifeoma Kiddoe Nwankwo argues that at the hands of Spanish authorities, English abolitionists and U.S. black abolitionists, Plácido becomes a "race man," which reveals "the extent to which multiple agents shaped the constitution of 'Black' identity in the Americas" (25); she then goes on to examine his poetry so as to glean the poet's own conceptions of race and national identity. See Nwankwo 25–113.

14. "Editorial" *The Crisis* 1:1 (1910–11): 10. The first twenty-five issues of this periodical (spanning the years 1910 to 1922) have been digitized and are easily accessible at the website of the Modernist Journals Project: www.modjourn.org.

15. Ibid.

16. See the fourth chapter of Andrews's study, 117–151.

17. Ibid. 129.

18. Helg 147.

19. Andrews 129. The United States played a critical role in the establishment of the Cuban republic: in 1901, the passage of the Platt Amendment ensured that it could intervene in Cuban affairs, as well as secured the land rights for the establishment of the naval base in Guantanamo Bay. It was incorporated into the Cuban Constitution of 1902. Repealed in 1934, the Platt Amendment allowed for military occupation by U.S. troops on several occasions throughout the first three decades of the twentieth century. In addition to their domestic platform, the PIC was also vehemently against the Platt Amendment, and renewed calls for national sovereignty.

20. Helg estimates that supporters of the party numbered between ten thousand and twenty thousand people by 1910 (156).

21. Andrews 130.

22. Helg 205.

23. Ibid. 211.

24. Ibid. 213.

25. Schomburg 73; this article originally appeared in *The Crisis* 4:3 (July 1912) 143–144.

26. Ibid.

27. Roberts 4–5.

28. Schomburg 74.

29. Ibid. 75.

30. Ibid.

31. Moss 93.

32. Schomburg 3. The Rosetta Stone is a tablet upon which was written one text in three languages: hieroglyphs, Demotic (an Egyptian language), and ancient Greek; found in Egypt, it was used to translate previously undecipherable Egyptian languages. See Ray.

33. See Hegel 99.

34. Schomburg 5.

35. Ibid. 7.

36. Cunard (1934) iii.

37. After his death, Cunard wrote of hours spent with Schomburg, gathering texts in preparation for her anthology; she notes in her tribute published in the *Atlanta Daily World*: "for his was an international mind, imbued with the spice of curiosity and with the spirit of fair-play which made him listen objectively to theories and beliefs that he was not always in accord with," Cunard (1938) 6. For more on her anthology, see Winkiel; for more on Cunard herself, see Kaplan (2013).

38. Schomburg 49.

39. Ibid.

40. Ibid. 49–50.

41. Ibid. 51.

42. Ibid.

43. Ibid. 53–54. The Tannenbaum thesis, proposed by Frank Tannenbaum in his 1947 study *Slave and Citizen*, stated that slavery was harsher in the United States than it was in Latin America; it was subsequently challenged by David Brion Davis in *The Problem of Slavery in Western Culture* (1966), and Carl Degler's *Neither Black nor White: Slavery and Race Relations in Brazil and the United States* (1971). For a summary of these debates, see Frederickson.

44. Schomburg 54–62.

45. Sinnette 55.

46. Ibid. 108.

47. Schomburg 232.

48. Ibid. 236.

49. Ibid. 237.

50. Weiss 55.

51. Kaplan (2013) 17.

52. Andrews 72.

53. Quoted from Piñeiro de Rivera 181; the editorial note opens Schomburg's chronicle, "My Trip to Cuba in Quest of Negro Books," which appeared in *Opportunity* XI (February 1933) 48–50.

54. Crowder 95.

55. Poyo 104–106.

56. Weiss estimates that while *Opportunity* had a monthly circulation of approximately six thousand in its first year to its peak of eleven thousand in 1928, *Crisis* had appealed to approximately that number when it had first appeared in 1910, so that by 1919, it was reaching more than one hundred thousand readers (221). These figures reflect a decidedly larger audience than that of the scholarly organizations of which Schomburg was a part.

57. Arroyo 164.

58. Schomburg 107.

59. Arroyo 11.

60. Ibid. 14.

61. Andrews 118.

62. Ibid. 118–135.

CHAPTER 4. "WITNESS FOR THE FUTURE"

In an article on collecting, historian Emma Jones Lapsansky writes: "On the one hand [collecting] helps to reach back into experience, and thereby reconstruct and connect events, faces, books and gestures. On the other…it allows people to dispatch their 'duty—as *witnesses for the future* to collect them again for the sake of our children,' to solidify familiarity, to create connectedness and continuity" (69; my emphasis).

1. Schomburg 232.

2. Hutson 16.

3. Sinnette 44.

4. Holton 224.

5. Derrida and Prenowitz 9–10.

6. Taylor 19.

7. Stoler 85, 86.

8. Wesley 5.

9. Ibid.

10. Martin 29–32.

11. Ibid. 32.

12. Holton 226.

13. Sinnette 87–96.

14. Osborne 53–54.

15. Sinnette (1990) 35.

16. Hoffnung-Garskof (2001) 26.

17. Ibid. 26; Sinnette (1989) 17, 20. Sinnette details how at the time of his meeting Schomburg in 1891, Flor Baerga "had begun to develop a substantial collection of clippings and photographs relating to the Puerto Rican experience in New York" (20).

18. Hoffnung-Garskof (2001) 26.

19. In her biographical essay about Schomburg, Ortiz writes: "In fact, although as early as 1857 there was a community of Latin American cigar rollers in New York, most of them Cuban and Puerto Rican, by 1910 only 1,500 Puerto Ricans lived in the continental United States. The first major migration from the island was in 1920, and the census registered 11,811 in the country" (25).

20. Díaz-Quiñones (1999) 112.

21. Ibid. 108. The Archivo General de Puerto Rico was only established in 1955, more than four decades after Brau's death.

22. Ibid. 111.

23. Holton 234.

24. Sánchez González, *Boricua Literature* 69.

25. Ibid. 45.

26. Ibid. 66.

27. Núñez (2009) 54.

28. Rose 19–20.

29. New York's branch library system was created in 1901 after the merger with the New York Free Circulating Library (which had been established more than twenty years earlier) in February 1901, but was endowed due to a donation of $5.2 million by Andrew Carnegie in 1901. See "History of The New York Public Library."

30. Rose 14.

31. Sinnette 132–134; for more Rose, see Jenkins.

32. Dodson 9. Dodson served as the director of the Schomburg Center for Research in Black Culture from 1984 until 2011; under his tenure, the center's holdings doubled to ten million items and he raised more than $40 million. He currently serves as the director of the Moorland-Springarn Research Center and the director of the Howard University Library System; see Rowell.

33. Dodson 9–10.

34. Joyce 38.

35. Núñez 72; in a note, she attributes the idea that the "library be placed in the context of institutions of resistance" to Professor Luis Marentes (73).

36. The term "Harlem Renaissance" is contested in scholarship, as studies such as the recent *Escape from New York: The New Negro Renaissance beyond Harlem* (2013) reveal the multiple national and international sites of political protest and vibrant cultural expression of peoples of African descent, including Paris, London, New Orleans, and Havana, for example. For the purpose of this study, which centers on New York City, the term will continue to be employed.

37. Smith (2009) 196.

38. Locke, "Harlem" 629.

39. For the definitive historical account of the Great Migration, see Wilkerson.

40. Sinnette highlights how the summer of 1919 saw twenty-six race riots in the United States (104).

41. Locke 629.

42. Locke, "Enter the New Negro" 631.

43. Ibid.

44. Ibid.

45. While Nathan Huggins is credited with writing some of the first considerations of the Harlem Renaissance in the midst of the Black Arts Movement, scholarly attention to this period began in earnest in the 1980s. Since then, there has been no shortage of critical attention paid to the writers, artists, and scholars themselves; this work has spanned disciplinary boundaries from literary and historical studies to sexuality and performance studies.

46. Dodson 8.

47. Sinnette 115.

48. Ibid.

49. Ibid. 116–122, 126–127.

50. Ibid. 135.

51. Ibid. 149.

52. Arthur A. Schomburg, Letter to Thomas E. Jones, 9/9/1929. Fisk University, John Hope and Aurelia E. Franklin Library, Special Collections, Thomas Elsa Jones Collection, box 39, folder 18.

53. Louis S. Shores, Letter to Thomas E. Jones, 10/1/1929. Fisk University, John Hope and Aurelia E. Franklin Library, Special Collections, Thomas Elsa Jones Collection, box 40, folder 3.

54. Louis S. Shores, Report of the Librarian to Fisk University, 1929–1930. Fisk University, John Hope and Aurelia E. Franklin Library, Special Collections, Thomas Elsa Jones Collection, box 23, folder 9.

55. Louis S. Shores, Letter to Thomas Elsa Jones, 3/19/1930. Fisk University, John Hope and Aurelia E. Franklin Library, Special Collections, Thomas Elsa Jones Collection, box 40, folder 4.

56. Arthur A. Schomburg, Letter to the Carnegie Corporation, 1/14/1931. Fisk University, John Hope and Aurelia E. Franklin Library, Special Collections, Thomas Elsa Jones Collection, box 39, folder 18. This correspondence sheds light on the role of funding sources for institutions of higher education in the early decades of the twentieth century, as the Carnegie Corporation, the Rosenwald Fund, and the Rockefeller General Education Fund all played a key role in the growth of Fisk University.

57. Louis S. Shores, Preliminary Report of the Librarian to the President, July 1, 1930, to April 1, 1931. Fisk University, John Hope and Aurelia E. Franklin Library, Special Collections, Thomas Elsa Jones Collection, box 23, folder 10; Sinnette 157.

58. Ibid. 155.

59. In his study, *Forging Diaspora*, Frank A. Guridy offers the history of Afro-Cuban students at the Tuskegee Institute in the first years of the twentieth century.

60. Sinnette 157–158.

61. Document: Working principles for cooperation between the Fisk University Library and the Library of the Y.M.C.A. Graduate School with special reference to material of the negro. Attached to W. D. Wentworth. Letter to Louis S. Shores, 1/28/1932. Fisk University, John Hope and Aurelia E. Franklin Library, Special Collections, Thomas Elsa Jones Collection, box 40, folder 6.

62. "Schomburg Is Buried while Crowds Mourn; Famous Curator Dead at 64; Collected Rare Books, Prints." *The New York Amsterdam News*, June 18, 1938; *ProQuest Historical Newspapers: New York Amsterdam News* 6.

63. In a letter to Schomburg dated October 12, 1936, his friend Charles S. Johnson, renowned sociologist, one-time editor of *Opportunity* journal, one-time

director of research of the New York office of the National Urban League and later the president of Fisk University in Nashville, Tennessee, encouraged him to expand the biographical portraits he was publishing in periodicals, specifically in the *Amsterdam News*, into book form, given his knowledge about all things related to the African diaspora (Charles S. Johnson, Letter to Arthur A. Schomburg, 10/12/1936. Arthur A. Schomburg Papers, Reel Four Frame 0032, Jean Blackwell Hutson Research and Reference Division, Schomburg Center for Research in Black Culture, the New York Public Library).

64. Sinnette 101, 135–136; Dodson 11.

65. Martin 24.

66. Brown and Davis-Brown 28.

67. Holton 218.

68. Guridy 117.

69. Ibid.

70. Meehan 62.

71. Ibid. 63.

72. Holton 220.

73. Ibid.

74. Ibid. 222.

75. Trouillot 52.

76. Ibid. 25.

77. Public Archive, "Dark Specters and Black Kingdoms: An Interview with Historian Ada Ferrer." February 6, 2015. N.p.

CHAPTER 5. "FURTIVE AS HE LOOKS"

1. For more on Gumby, see Rhodes-Pitt 118–135.

2. The *National News Gravure* was a "photogravure supplement that the ANP designed for distribution by black newspapers throughout the country (although few newspapers actually carried it)" (Evans x). The Associated Negro Press (ANP) was founded by Claude A. Barnett in 1919; in her introduction to the Claude A. Barnett Papers, Linda J. Evans writes: "The ANP was the largest and longest-lived news service to supply black newspapers in the United States with news of interest to black citizens, opinion columns, reviews of books, movies, and records, and occasionally poetry, cartoons, and photographs....It thereby helped create a national black culture and increased black awareness of national news" (v).

3. For more on the historical shifts in definitions of whiteness, see Jacobson; for a recent publication on passing, see Hobbs.

4. In the introduction to their collection of essays about the uses of photography in the construction of U.S. black identity, Maurice O. Wallace and Shawn Michelle Smith contend that men and women such as Washington and Truth "put photographs to striking use in their varied quests for social and political justice, plumbing and expanding the political power of the photograph"; they contend that while they "may not have been photographers, it is fair to say that they *practiced* photography." See Wallace and Smith 4.

5. Ibid. 1–2.

6. Fleetwood 16.

7. Willis-Brathwaite 13.

8. For an argument that photography was often utilized as a means to maintain social order, see Sekula.

9. See Holloway (2002) 4. She goes on to observe that "[photography] was able to assert and represent light as a powerful metaphor for the special essence or property attributed to whites that was proffered as the justification for their hegemonic position. The racial imperatives that drove the development of photographic portraiture optimized the technology for the representation of whiteness to the extent that standard photographic practices do not allow for the successful depiction of people of other races" (4).

10. The space in which photographs were taken was itself a critical element in how the subjects being photographed were viewed; interior spaces in studios conveyed privacy, a luxury enjoyed by the middle and upper classes, as well as order. This could be contrasted with images of urban areas shot at the time, for example, or photographs of the newly acquired territories of Puerto Rico or the Philippines, which often depicted inhabitants outside, in agrarian spaces. For more about what came to be known as social documentary photography, see Yochelson and Czitrom. For more about photography of the Philippines and Puerto Rico, see Rice. To learn more about photographs of Puerto Rico at the turn of the twentieth century, see Duany (2001).

11. Fleetwood 13.

12. For further analysis of "legible" and "illegible" black male bodies, see Neal.

13. Smith (2014) 1.

14. Mirzoeff 1.

15. Powell xvi.

16. There are two exceptions where Schomburg conveys incredible elegance in attire and bearing: the first, where he wears a tuxedo in a photograph taken

in the 1890s, and the second, the James L. Allen portrait of him, taken later in his life. My analyses of those photographs appear later in the chapter.

17. Summers (2004) 26.

18. Ibid. 54.

19. Ibid. With this description we may have found the reason behind Schomburg's formal evening dress in the earlier photograph as a younger man.

20. Sinnette 26.

21. Ibid.

22. Ibid.

23. Willis-Brathwaite 18.

24. Holloway (1999) 7.

25. Holloway makes this observation about Allen's portrait of Alain Locke in the exhibit catalogue (19).

26. Holloway 15.

27. Ibid. 12.

28. Alexander and Ferrari 285.

29. Robertson 82.

30. As far as his dress is concerned, while this appears to be a kind of costume, it could admittedly be indicative of his station.

31. See Kinsbruner.

32. See Rodríguez-Silva (2012).

33. Robertson 90.

34. Ibid. 88. Robertson also identifies Alphone Bertillon as someone who "made one of the first attempts to standardize identification photographs." Among his techniques was the introduction of "direct frontal and profile angles that have come to characterize mug shots" (88).

35. Ibid. 82.

36. These images were discovered in 1976 in Harvard's Peabody Museum; for a fictionalized account that imagines the thoughts of these subjects as well as an overview of the scientific discourses about race at the time, see Rogers.

37. Robertson 87.

38. hooks (1992) 116.

39. Hutson 4.

40. Fleetwood 6.

41. Neal 4.

42. Ibid. 8.

43. Fleetwood 18.

44. Powell 16.

CONCLUSION

1. Laviera 53, 54.
2. For a critical assessment of Tato Laviera's work, see Alvarez and Luis.
3. See King.
4. Robert Park, who later served as mentor to E. Franklin Frazier at the University of Chicago while the latter was completing his doctoral studies, wrote in a 1919 article that the "Negro" was "primarily an artist, loving life for its own sake. His métier is expression rather than action. The Negro is, so to speak, the lady among the races" (130).
5. Arroyo 145.
6. Colón 196.
7. Ibid. 138–140.
8. Núñez (2009) 73.
9. Jesús Colón mentions in his *crónicas* that he and his family lived near 143rd Street and Lenox Avenue during World War I (46).
10. Sánchez González, *Boricua Literature* 56.
11. Fauset 4.
12. See Holton.
13. Fauset 4.

BIBLIOGRAPHY

PRIMARY SOURCES

Alexander Gumby Negroiana Collection, Columbia University Rare Book and Manuscript Library.

Arthur A. Schomburg Collection, Manuscripts, Archives, and Rare Book Division, Schomburg Center for Research in Black Culture. The New York Public Library.

Arthur A. Schomburg Collection, Photographs and Prints Division, Schomburg Center for Research in Black Culture, The New York Public Library.

Arthur A. Schomburg Papers, Research and Reference Division, Schomburg Center for Research in Black Culture, The New York Public Library.

Schomburg Committee of the Trustees of the New York Public Library Papers, Manuscripts, Archives and Rare Book Division, Schomburg Center for Research in Black Culture, The New York Public Library.

Thomas Elsa Jones Collection, Special Collections, John Hope and Aurelia E. Franklin Library, Fisk University.

SECONDARY SOURCES

Acosta-Belén, Edna. "Lola Rodríguez de Tió and the Puerto Rican Struggle for Freedom." *Latina Legacies: Identity, Biography and Community*. New York: Oxford UP, 2005. 84–96.

———. "Puerto Rican Diaspora: Figueroa, Sotero." *Puerto Rico Encyclopedia*, N.p., www.enciclopediapr.org.

Alexander, Abel, and Roberto A. Ferrari, "Central America and the Caribbean (Excluding Mexico and Cuba)," *Encyclopedia of Nineteenth Century Photography*. Ed. John Hannavy. New York: Routledge, 2007.

Álvarez-López, Luis. *The Dominican Republic and the Beginnings of a Revolutionary Cycle in the Spanish Caribbean, 1861–1898*. Lanham, MD: UP of America, 2009.

Alvarez, Stephanie and William Luis, eds. *The AmeRícan Poet: Essays on the Work of Tato Laviera*. New York: Centro Press, 2014.

Anderson, Benedict. *Imagined Communities: Reflections on the Origins and Spread of Nationalism*. New York: Verso, 2006.

Andrews, George Reid. *Afro-Latin America, 1800–2000*. New York: Oxford UP, 2004.

Arpini, Adriana María. "Abolición, independencia y confederación. Los escritos de Ramón Emeterio Betances, 'El Antillano.'" *Cuyo* 25 (2008): 119–144.

Arroyo, Jossianna. *Writing Secrecy in Caribbean Freemasonry*. New York: Palgrave Macmillan, 2013.

Baralt, Guillermo. *Esclavos rebeldes: conspiraciones y sublevaciones de esclavos en Puerto Rico (1795–1873)*. San Juan: Ediciones Huracán, 1982.

———. *Slave Revolts in Puerto Rico: Conspiracies and Uprisings, 1795–1873*. Trans. Christine Ayorinde. Princeton: Markus Weiner, 2014.

Bergad, Laird. "Toward Puerto Rico's *Grito de Lares*," *Hispanic American Historical Review* 60 (1980): 617–642.

Betances, Ramón Emeterio. *Las Antillas para los antillanos*. Ed. Carlos M. Rama. San Juan: Instituto de Cultura Puertorriqueña, 1975.

———. *Ramón Emeterio Betances*. Ed. Haroldo Dilla Alfonso and Emilio Godínez Sosa. Havana: Casa de las Americas, 1983.

Boyce Davies, Carol. *Black Women, Writing, and Identity: Migrations of the Subject*. New York: Routledge, 1994.

Brau, Salvador. *Disquiciones sociológicas, y otros ensayos*. Río Piedras: Editorial de la Universidad de Puerto Rico, 1956.

———. "Rafael Cordero: elógio póstumo con que se iniciara en el Ateneo Puertorriqueño la velada del 31 de octubre de 1891." San Juan: Tipografía de Arturo Cordova, 1891. N.p.

Bronfman, Alejandra. *Measures of Equality: Social Science, Citizenship, and Race in Cuba, 1902–1940*. Chapel Hill and London: U of North Carolina P, 2004.

Brown, Elsa Barkley. "Womanist Consciousness: Maggie Lena Walker and the Independent Order of Saint Luke." *Signs* 14 (Spring 1989): 610–633.

Brown, Richard Harvey, and Beth Davis-Brown. "The Making of Memory: The Politics of Archives, Libraries, and Museums in the Construction of National Consciousness." *History of the Human Sciences* 11: 4 (1998): 17–32.

Cabrera Peña, Miguel. "Alma Fundadora: Rafael Serra y Montalvo." *Islas: Órgano Oficial del Afro-Cuban Alliance, Inc.* 3: 9 (2008): 21–33.

Carby, Hazel V. *Race Men*. Cambridge: Harvard UP, 1998.

Chancy, Myriam J. A. *From Sugar to Revolution: Women's Visions of Haiti, Cuba, and the Dominican Republic*. Waterloo, ON: Wilfred Laurier UP, 2012.

Colón, Jesús. *A Puerto Rican in New York and Other Sketches*. New York: Arno, 1975.

Cooper, Brittney C. "Race Women: The Politics of Black Female Leadership in Nineteenth and Twentieth Century America." Phd diss, Emory University, 2009.

———. "'They are Nevertheless Our Brethren': The Order of the Eastern Star and the Battle for Women's Leadership, 1874–1926." *All Men Free and Brethren: Essays on the History of African American Freemasonry*. Ed. Peter P. Hinks and Stephen Kantrowitz. Ithaca: Cornell UP, 2013. 114–130.

Córdova Landrón, Arturo. *Salvador Brau, su vida y su época*. San Juan: Editorial Coquí, 1968.

Crowder, Ralph L. *John Edward Bruce: The Legacy of a Politician, Journalist, and Self-Trained Historian of the African Diaspora*. New York: New York UP, 2004.

Cunard, Nancy, ed. *Negro: An Anthology*. London: Wishart, 1934.

———. "A Tribute to Arthur Schomburg, Champion of Colored Race." *Atlanta Daily World*. August 2, 1938. 6.

Curet, José. "About Slavery and the Order of Things: Puerto Rico, 1845–1873." *Between Slavery and Free Labor: The Spanish-Speaking Caribbean in the Nineteenth Century*. Ed. Manuel Moreno Fraginals, Frank Moya Pons, and Stanley L. Engerman. Baltimore: Johns Hopkins UP, 1985. 117–140.

Davies, Carol Boyce. *Black Women, Writing and Identity: Migrations of the Subject*. New York: Routledge, 1994.

Davis, James. *Eric Walrond: A Life in the Harlem Renaissance and the Transatlantic Caribbean*. New York: Columbia UP, 2015.

DeCosta-Willis, Miriam. *Blacks in Hispanic Literature: Critical Essays*. 1977. Baltimore: Imprint, 2011.

DeFrantz, Thomas F., and Anita Gonzalez. "Introduction." *Black Performance Theory*. Ed. Thomas F. DeFrantz and Anita González. Durham and London: Duke UP, 2014. 1–15.

De La Fuente, Alejandro. *A Nation for All: Race, Inequality, and Politics in Twentieth-Century Cuba*. Chapel Hill and London: U of North Carolina P, 2001.

Delano, Jack, and Irene Delano, *En busca del Maestro Rafael Cordero / In Search of Maestro Rafael Cordero*. Río Piedras: Editorial de la Universidad de Puerto Rico, 1994.

Derrida, Jacques, and Eric Prenowitz, "Archive Fever: A Freudian Impression." *Diacritics* 25: 2 (1995): 9–63.

Deschamps Chapeaux, Pedro. *Rafael Serra y Montalvo: obrero incansable de nuestra Independencia*. La Habana: Unión de Escritores y Artistas de Cuba, 1975.

Díaz-Quiñones, Arcadio. "Pedro Henríquez Ureña (1884–1946): la tradición y el exilio," *Sobre los principios: los intelectuales caribeños y la tradición*. Bernal, Argentina: Universidad Nacional de Quilmes, 2006. 167–253.

———. "Salvador Brau: The Paradox of the *Autonomista* Tradition." *The Places of History: Regionalism Revisited in Latin America*. Ed. Doris Sommer. Durham and London: Duke UP, 1999. 104–118.

Díaz Soler, Luis M. *Historia de la esclavitud negra en Puerto Rico*. 1953. Río Piedras: Editorial Universitaria, 1981.

Dodson, Howard. "Introduction." *The Legacy of Arthur Alfonso Schomburg: A Celebration of the Past, A Vision for the Future*. New York: New York Public Library, Astor, Lenox, and Tilden Foundations, 1986. 7–15.

Duany, Jorge. "Portraying the Other: Puerto Rican Images in Two American Photographic Collections." *Discourse* 23: 1 (2001): 119–153.

———. *The Puerto Rican Nation on the Move: Identities on the Island and in the United States*. Chapel Hill and London: U of North Carolina P, 2002.

Du Bois, W. E. B. "Of Alexander Crummell." *Norton Anthology of African American Literature*. New York: Norton, 1997. 715–721.

Edwards, Brent Hayes. "Langston Hughes and the Futures of Diaspora." *American Literary History* 19. 3 (2007): 689–711.

———. *The Practice of Diaspora: Literature, Translation, and the Rise of Black Internationalism*. Cambridge and London: Harvard UP, 2003.

Evans, Linda J. "Introduction." The Claude A. Barnett Papers: The Associated Negro Press, 1918–1967. Part Two Associated Negro Press Organizational Files, 1920–1966. Edited by August Meier and Elliott Rudwick. Microfilmed from the holdings of the Chicago Historical Society. v–xi.

Ewing, Adam. *The Age of Garvey: How a Jamaican Activist Created a Mass Movement and Changed Global Black Politics*. Princeton and Oxford: Princeton UP, 2014.

Fauset, Arthur Huff, "I Write as I See: A Summer Experience," *Philadelphia Tribune*; Sept. 1, 1938, 4.

Ferrer, Ada. *Insurgent Cuba: Race, Nation, and Revolution, 1868–1898*. Chapel Hill and London: U of North Carolina P, 1999.

———. "The Silence of Patriots: Race and Nationalism in Martí's Cuba." *José Martí's "Our America": From National to Hemispheric Cultural Studies*. Ed. Jeffrey Belnap and Raúl Fernández. Durham: Duke UP, 1998. 228–249.

Fischer, Sibylle. *Modernity Disavowed: Haiti and the Cultures of Slavery in the Age of Revolution*. Durham: Duke UP, 2004.

Fleetwood, Nicole R. *Troubling Vision: Performance, Visuality, and Blackness*. Chicago and London: U of Chicago P, 2011.

Flores, Juan. "Pan-Latino/Trans-Latino: Puerto Ricans in the "New Nueva York." *From Bomba to Hip-Hop: Puerto Rican Culture and Latino Identity*. New York: Columbia UP, 2000.

———. *Divided Borders: Essays on Puerto Rican Identity*. Houston: Arte Público, 1993.

Flores, Juan, and Miriam Jiménez Román. "Introduction." *The Afro-Latin@ Reader: History and Culture in the United States*. Ed. Juan Flores and Miriam Jiménez Román. Durham and London: Duke UP, 2010. 1–15.

Foner, Philip. *The Spanish-Cuban-American War and the Birth of American Imperialism, Vol 1, 1895–1898*. New York: Monthly Review Press, 1972.

Fountain, Anne. *José Martí, the United States, and Race*. Gainesville: UP of Florida, 2014.

———. *José Martí and U.S. Writers*. Gainesville: UP of Florida, 2003.

Fox, Patricia. *Being and Blackness in Latin America: Uprootedness and Improvisation*. Gainesville: UP of Florida, 2006.

Frederickson, George M. *The Comparative Imagination: On the History of Racism, Nationalism, and Social Movements*. Berkeley: U of California P, 2000.

Fusté, José I. "Possible Republics: Tracing the 'Entanglements' of Race and Nation in Afro-Latina/o Caribbean Thought and Activism, 1870–1930." Phd diss., University of California-San Diego, 2012.

García Gervasio, Luis. "I Am the Other: Puerto Rico in the Eyes of North Americans, 1898." *Journal of American History* 87: 1 (2000): 39–64.

Gatewood, Willard B. Jr. *Black Americans and the White Man's Burden, 1898–1903*. Urbana: U of Illinois P, 1975.

Gilroy, Paul. *The Black Atlantic: Modernity and Double Consciousness*. Cambridge: Harvard UP, 1993.

Giusti Cordero, Juan A. "AfroPuerto Rican Cultural Studies: Beyond *cultura negroide* and *Antillanismo*." *Centro Journal* "Race and Identity" 8: 1–2 (1996): 57–77.

Glasser, Ruth. *My Music is My Flag: Puerto Rican Musicians and Their New York Communities, 1917–1940*. Berkeley: U of California P, 1995.

González, José Luis. *El país de cuatro pisos y otros ensayos*. 1980. Río Piedras, PR: Ediciones Huracán, 1998.

———. *Literatura y sociedad en Puerto Rico: de los cronistas de Indias a la generación del 98*. México: Fondo de Cultura Económica, 1976.

Gruesz, Kirsten Silva. *Ambassadors of Culture: The Transamerican Origins of Latino Writing*. Princeton: Princeton UP, 2002.

Guerra, Lillian. *The Myth of José Martí: Conflicting Nationalisms in Early Twentieth-Century Cuba*. Chapel Hill and London: U of North Carolina P, 2005.

Guridy, Frank. *Forging Diaspora: Afro-Cubans and African Americans in a World of Empire and Jim Crow*. Chapel Hill: U of North Carolina P, 2010.

Hall, Stuart. "Cultural Identity and Diaspora." *Identity: Community, Culture, Difference*. Ed. Jonathan Rutherford. London: Lawrence and Wishart, 1990. 222–237.

Hegel, Georg Wilhelm Friedrich, *The Philosophy of History*. New York: Dover, 1956.

Helg, Aline. *Our Rightful Share: The Afro-Cuban Struggle for Equality, 1886–1912*. Chapel Hill and London: U of North Carolina P, 1995.

Hernández-Delgado, Julio L. "Pura Teresa Belpré, Storyteller and Pioneering Puerto Rican Librarian." *The Library Quarterly: Information, Community, Policy* 62: 4 (1992): 425–440.

Hinks, Peter P., and Stephen Kantrowitz, eds. *All Men Free and Brethren: Essays on the History of African American Freemasonry*. Ithaca and London: Cornell UP, 2013.

"History of The New York Public Library." http://www.nypl.org/help/about-nypl/history, n.p.

Hobbs, Allyson. *A Chosen Exile: A History of Racial Passing in American Life*. Cambridge: Harvard UP, 2014.

Hoffnung-Garskof, Jesse. "The Migrations of Arturo Schomburg: On Being *Antillano*, Negro, and Puerto Rican in New York 1891–1938." *Journal of American Ethnic History* 21: 1 (2001): 3–49.

———. "The World of Arturo Alfonso Schomburg." *The Afro-Latin@ Reader: History and Culture in the United States*. Ed. Juan Flores and Miriam Jiménez Román. Durham and London: Duke UP, 2010. 70–91.

Holloway, Camara Dia. *Portraiture and the Harlem Renaissance: The Photographs of James L. Allen.* New Haven: Yale University Art Gallery, 1999.

————.Race-ing American Moderns: Race and Modernism in Photography between the Two World Wars." PhD diss., Yale University, 2002.

Holton, Adalaine, "Decolonizing History: Arthur Schomburg's Afrodiasporic Archive." *The Journal of African American History* 92: 2 (2007): 218–238.

hooks, bell. *Art on My Mind: Visual Politics.* New York: New Press, 1995.

————. *Black Looks: Race and Representation.* Boston: South End, 1992.

Hostos, Eugenio María de. "El problema de Cuba." 1874. *Pensamiento latinoamericano del siglo XIX: Antología.* Ed. Alberto Saladino García. México: Universidad Autónoma del Estado de México, 2009. 219–234.

Hutchinson, George. *The Harlem Renaissance in Black and White.* Cambridge: Belknap Press of Harvard UP, 1987.

Hutson, Jean Blackwell, Oral History Interview Transcript. Interviewed by Barbara Kline. March 16 and May 5, 1978. Rare Book and Manuscript Library, Columbia University.

Iton, Richard. *In Search of the Black Fantastic: Politics and Popular Culture in the Post-Civil Rights Era.* New York: Oxford UP, 2008.

Jacobson, Matthew Frye. *Whiteness of a Different Color: European Immigrants and the Alchemy of Race.* Cambridge: Harvard UP, 1998.

James, Winston. *Holding aloft the Banner of Ethiopia: Caribbean Radicalism in Early Twentieth-Century America.* New York: Verso, 1998.

————. "Afro–Puerto Rican Radicalism in the United States: Reflections on the Political Trajectories of Arturo Schomburg and Jesús Colón." *Centro Journal* 8: 1/2 (1996): 92–127.

Jenkins, Betty L. "A White Librarian in Black Harlem," *The Library Quarterly: Information, Community, Policy* 60: 3 (1990): 216–231.

Jiménez de Wagenheim, Olga. *Puerto Rico's Revolt for Independence: el Grito de Lares.* 1985. Princeton: Markus Weiner, 1993.

Jiménez Román, Miriam. "*Un hombre (negro) del pueblo*: José Celso Barbosa and the Puerto Rican 'Race' toward Whiteness." *Centro Journal* 8: 1/2 (1996): 8–28.

Johnson, E. Patrick. "Black Performance Studies: Genealogies, Politics, Futures." *Performance Studies Handbook.* Ed. D. Soyini Madison and Judith Hamera. Thousand Oaks, CA: Sage, 2005. 446–463.

Jones, Martha S. *All Bound up Together: The Woman Question in African American Public Culture, 1820–1900.* Chapel Hill: U of North Carolina P, 2007.

Joyce, Patrick. "The Politics of the Liberal Archive." *History of the Human Sciences* 12: 2 (1999): 35–49.

Jrade, Cathy L. *Modernismo, Modernity, and the Development of Spanish American Literature.* Austin: U of Texas P, 1998.

Jusino, Angel Villarini and Carlos Antonio Torre, "Eugenio María de Hostos, 1839–1903." *Fifty Major Thinkers on Education: From Confucius to Dewey.* Ed. Joy Palmer, Liora Brestler, and David Cooper. New York: Routledge, 2002. 146–154.

Kaplan, Amy. *The Anarchy of Empire in the Making of U.S. Culture.* Cambridge: Harvard UP, 2002.

Kaplan, Carla. *Miss Anne in Harlem: The White Women of the Black Renaissance.* New York: Harper Collins, 2013.

Kevane, Bridget. "Confessions of an Editor: Cesar Andreu Iglesias and the 'Memorias de Bernardo Vega.'" *Latin American Literary Review* 27: 53 (1999): 67–80.

———. "The Bernardo Vega Memoir Mystery: The Challenge of Determining Authorship and Meaning." *National Institute for Latino Policy* (April 11, 2013). N.p. http://www.nilpnetwork.org/NiLP_Guest_Commentary_-_Benardo_Vega_Memoirs.pdf.

King, Joshua E. "Reactive Machismo: How Early Twentieth Century Effeminate Stereotypes and Race (Re)constructed Puerto Rican Migrant Men's Identities." MA thesis, University of Wyoming, 2009.

Kinsbruner, Jay. *Not of Pure Blood: The Free People of Color and Racial Prejudice in Nineteenth-Century Puerto Rico.* Durham and London: Duke UP, 1996.

Kipling, Rudyard. "The White Man's Burden." The Kipling Society. N.p. www.kiplingsociety.co.uk.

Kutzinski, Vera. *The Worlds of Langston Hughes: Modernism and Translation in the Americas.* Ithaca and London: Cornell UP, 2012.

Lapsansky, Emma Jones. "Patriotism, Values, and Continuity: Museum Collecting and 'Connectedness,'" *Pennsylvania Magazine of History and Biography* 114 (1990): 67–82.

Laviera, Tato. *AmeRícan.* 2nd ed. Houston: Arte Público, 2003.

Lewis, Earl. "To Turn as on a Pivot: Writing African Americans into a History of Overlapping Diasporas." *The American Historical Review* 100: 3 (1995): 765–787.

Lewis, Gordon K. *Main Currents in Caribbean Thought: The Historical Evolution of Caribbean Society in Its Ideological Aspects, 1492–1900.* Lincoln and London: U of Nebraska P, 2004.

Lidin, Harold J. *History of the Puerto Rican Independence Movement: 19th Century.* Hato Rey, PR: n.p., 1981.

Lloréns, Hilda. "Fugitive Blackness: Representations of Race, Art, and Memory in Arroyo, Puerto Rico." Phd diss., University of Connecticut, 2005.

———. *Imaging the Great Puerto Rican Family: Framing Nation, Race, and Gender during the American Century.* Lanham, MD: Lexington, 2014.

Locke, Alain L. "Enter the New Negro." *Harlem: Mecca of the New Negro.* Spec. issue of *Survey Graphic* 6: 6 (1925): 631–634.

———. "Foreword—In Memoriam: Arthur Alfonso Schomburg 1874–1938." 1941. Folder 3, Arthur Alfonso Schomburg Collection, Manuscripts, Archives and Rare Books Division, Schomburg Center for Research in Black Culture, The New York Public Library.

———. "Harlem." *Harlem: Mecca of the New Negro.* Spec. issue of *Survey Graphic* 6. 6 (1925): 629–630.

———, ed. *The New Negro Anthology.* 1925. New York: Atheneum, 1992.

López, Antonio. *Unbecoming Blackness: The Diaspora Cultures of Afro-Cuban America.* New York and London: New York UP, 2012.

Lorde, Audre. "The Master's Tools Will Never Dismantle the Master's House." *Sister Outsider: Essays and Speeches.* Berkeley: Crossings Press, 2007. 110–114.

Luis, William. *Juan Francisco Manzano, Autobiografía del esclavo poeta y otros escritos.* Madrid: Iberoamericana, 2007.

McKay, Claude. *Harlem: Negro Metropolis.* New York: E. P. Dutton, 1940.

Maldonado-Denis, Manuel. "Introduction to the Social Thought of Eugenio María de Hostos." Eugenio María de Hostos. *America: The Struggle for Freedom, Anthology.* Ed. Manuel Maldonado-Denis. Trans. Vivian Otero and Shannon Lachiotte. Santo Domingo: Editora Corripio, C. x A., 1992. 15–52.

Manzano, Juan Francisco. *Autobiography of a Slave / Autobiografía de un esclavo: A Bilingual Edition.* Trans. Evelyn Picon Garfield. Detroit: Wayne State UP, 1996.

Martí, José. *Inside the Monster: Writings on the United States and American Imperialism.* Trans. Elinor Randall. New York: Monthly Review, 1975.

———. "Mi raza." *José Martí, Antología crítica.* Ed. Susana Redondo de Feldman and Anthony Tudisco. New York: Las Americas Publishing, 1968. 201–203.

Martin, Tony. "Bibliophiles, Activists, and Race Men." *Black Bibliophiles and Collectors: Preservers of Black History.* Ed. Elinor Des Verney Sinnette, W. Paul Coates, and Thomas C. Battle. Washington DC: Howard UP, 1990. 23–34.

Matos Rodríguez, Félix V. "'Mi patria es libertad': Context and Introduction to Puerto Rico's First Feminist Treatise." *A Nation of Women: An Early Feminist Speaks Out. Mi opinión sobre las libertades, derechos y deberes de la* mujer. Ed. Félix V. Matos Rodríguez. By Luisa Capetillo. 1911. Houston: Arte Público Press, 2004. Vii–li.

Meehan, Kevin. *People Get Ready: African American and Caribbean Cultural Exchange.* Jackson: UP of Mississippi, 2009.

Méndez, Danny. "Culture and the City: Pedro Henríquez Ureña's New York City." *Camino Real. Estudios de las Hispanidades Norteamericanas* 3: 4 (2011): 143–168.

Miller, Bonnie M. *From Liberation to Conquest: The Visual and Popular Cultures of the Spanish-American War of 1898.* Amherst and Boston: U of Massachusetts P, 2011.

Mirzoeff, Nicholas. *The Right to Look: A Counterhistory of Visuality.* Durham: Duke UP, 2011. 1–34.

Montero, Oscar. *José Martí: An Introduction.* New York: Palgrave, 2004.

———. "La raza y el racismo en la república imposible de Rafael Serra." *America sin nombre* 19 (2014): 43–52.

Moral, Solsiree del. *Negotiating Empire: The Cultural Politics of Schools in Puerto Rico, 1898–1952.* Madison: U of Wisconsin P, 2013.

Morales, José. "The Hispaniola Diaspora, 1791–1850: Puerto Rico, Cuba, Louisiana, and Other Host Societies." Phd diss., University of Connecticut, 1986.

Moreno Fraginals, Manuel. *El ingenio: complejo económico social cubano del azúcar.* 1964. La Habana: Ciencias Sociales, 1984.

———. *The Sugarmill: The Socioeconomic Complex of Sugar in Cuba.* New York: Monthly Review Press, 1976.

Moses, Wilson Jeremiah. *Creative Conflict in African American Thought: Frederick Douglass, Alexander Crummell, Booker T. Washington, W. E. B. Du Bois, and Marcus Garvey.* New York: Cambridge UP, 2004.

Moss, Alfred A. Jr. *The American Negro Academy: Voice of the Talented Tenth.* Baton Rouge and London: Louisiana State UP, 1981.

Moya Pons, Frank. *Manual de historia dominicana.* 14th ed. Santo Domingo: Caribbean Publishers, 2008.

Mullen, Edward J. *The Life and Poems of a Cuban Slave: Juan Francisco Manzano, 1797–1854.* Hamden, CT: Archon Books, 1981.

Muraskin, William A. *Middle-Class Blacks in a White Society: Prince Hall Freemasonry in America.* Berkeley: U of California P, 1975.

Neal, Mark Anthony. *Looking for Leroy: Illegible Black Masculinities*. New York: New York UP, 2013.

Nistal-Moret, Benjamín. *Esclavos prófugos y cimarrones: Puerto Rico 1770–1870*. Río Piedras: Editorial Universitaria, 1984.

———. "Problems of the Social Structure of Slavery in Puerto Rico during the Process of Abolition, 1872." *Between Slavery and Free Labor: The Spanish-Speaking Caribbean in the Nineteenth Century*. Ed. Manuel Moreno Fraginals, Frank Moya Pons, and Stanley L. Engerman. Baltimore: Johns Hopkins UP, 1985. 141–157.

Núñez, Victoria. "Writing the Migration: Pedro Henríquez Ureña and Early Dominican Migrants to New York." *MELUS Journal* 36: 3 (2011): 111–135.

———. "Remembering Pura Belpré's Early Career at the 135th Street Library: Interracial Cooperation and Puerto Rican Settlement during the Harlem Renaissance." *Centro Journal* 21: 1 (2009): 52–77.

Nwankwo, Ifeoma Kiddoe. *Black Cosmopolitanism: Racial Consciousness and Transnational Identity in the Nineteenth-Century Americas*. Philadelphia: U of Pennsylvania P, 2005.

Ojeda Reyes, Félix. *El desterrado de París: biografía del doctor Ramón Emeterio Betances, 1827–1898*. San Juan: Ediciones Puerto, 2001.

———. *Peregrinos de la libertad*. San Juan: Editorial de la Universidad de Puerto Rico, 1992.

———. *Ramón Emeterio Betances: el anciano maravilloso*. Río Piedras, PR: Universidad de Puerto Rico, 1995.

Ortiz, Paul. *Emancipation Betrayed: The Hidden History of Black Organizing and White Violence in Florida from Reconstruction to the Bloody Election of 1920*. Berkeley: U of California P, 2005.

Ortiz, Victoria. "The Legacy of Arthur Alfonso Schomburg: A Celebration of the Past, A Vision for the Future." *The Legacy of Arthur Alfonso Schomburg: A Celebration of the Past, A Vision for the Future*. New York: New York Public Library, Astor, Lenox, and Tilden Foundations, 1986. 19–111.

Osbourne, Thomas. "The Ordinariness of the Archive." *History of the Human Sciences* 12 (May 1999): 51–64.

Parascandola, Louis J., and Carl A. Wade, eds. *Eric Walrond: The Critical Heritage*. Kingston: U of West Indies P, 2012.

Park, Robert E. "The Conflict and Fusion of Cultures with Special Reference to the Negro." *The Journal of Negro History* 4: 2 (1919): 111–133.

Pérez, Lisandro. "Cubans in Nineteenth-Century New York: A Story of Sugar, War, and Revolution." *Nueva York 1613–1945.* Ed. Edward J. Sullivan. New York: The New York Historical Society and Scala, 2010. 97–107.

Pérez, Louis A. *The War of 1898: The United States and Cuba in History and Historiography.* Chapel Hill: U of North Carolina P, 1998.

Pérez-Rosario, Vanessa. *Becoming Julia de Burgos: The Making of a Puerto Rican Icon.* Urbana: U of Illinois P, 2014.

Phelan, Peggy. *Unmarked: The Politics of Performance.* New York: Routledge, 1993.

Piñeiro de Rivera, Flor, ed. *Arthur A. Schomburg: A Puerto Rican's Quest for His Black Heritage.* San Juan: Centro de Estudios Avanzados de Puerto Rico y el Caribe, 1989.

———. *Arturo Schomburg: un puertorriqueño descubre el legado histórico del negro.* San Juan: Centro de Estudios Avanzados de Puerto Rico y el Caribe, 1989.

Pochmara, Anna. *The Making of the New Negro: Black Authorship, Masculinity, and Sexuality in the Harlem Renaissance.* Amsterdam: Amsterdam UP, 2011.

Powell, Richard J. *Cutting a Figure: Fashioning Black Portraiture.* Chicago: U of Chicago P, 2008.

Poyo, Gerald E. *"With All, and for the Good of All: The Emergence of Popular Nationalism in the Cuban Communities of the United States, 1848–1898.* Durham: Duke UP, 1989.

Public Archive, "Dark Specters and Black Kingdoms: An interview with historian Ada Ferrer." February 6, 2015. N.p.

Ramos, Julio. Introducción, *Amor y anarquía: los escritos de Luisa Capetillo.* Ed. Julio Ramos. Río Piedras, PR: Edición Huracán, 1992. 11–58.

Ramos Mattei, Andrés. *La hacienda azucarera: Su crecimiento y crisis en Puerto Rico.* San Juan: CEREP, 1981.

———. "Technical Innovations and Social Change in the Sugar Industry of Puerto Rico, 1870–1880." *Between Slavery and Free Labor: The Spanish-Speaking Caribbean in the Nineteenth Century.* Ed. Manuel Moreno Fraginals, Frank Moya Pons, and Stanley L. Engerman. Baltimore: Johns Hopkins UP, 1985. 158–178.

Ray, John. *The Rosetta Stone: and the Rebirth of Ancient Egypt.* London: Profile Books, 2008.

Redondo de Feldman, Susana, and Anthony Tudisco, "Semblanza biográfica." *José Martí, Antología crítica.* Eds Susana Redondo de Feldman and Anthony Tudisco. New York: Las Americas Publishing, 1968. 13–34.

Reed, Touré F. *Not Alms but Opportunity: The Urban League and the Politics of Racial Uplift, 1910–1950*. Chapel Hill: U of North Carolina P, 2008.

Rice, Mark. "Colonial Photography across Empires and Islands." *Journal of Transnational American Studies* 3: 2 (2011), n.p.

Roberts, Brian Russell. *Artistic Ambassadors: Literary and International Representation of the New Negro Era*. Charlottesville and London: U of Virginia P, 2013.

Robertson, Craig. *The Passport in America: The History of a Document*. New York: Oxford UP, 2010.

Rodríguez-Silva, Ileana M. "Abolition, Race, and the Politics of Gratitude in Late Nineteenth-Century Puerto Rico." *Hispanic American Historical Review* 93: 4 (2013): 621–657.

———. *Silencing Race: Disentangling Blackness, Colonialism, and National Identities in Puerto Rico*. New York: Palgrave, 2012.

Rodríguez de Tió, Lola. "A Cuba." *Ciudad seva: hogar electrónico del escritor Luis López Nieves*. www.ciudadseva.com. N.p.

Rogers, Molly. *Delia's Tears: Race, Science, and Photography in Nineteenth-Century America*. New Haven: Yale UP, 2010.

Rose, Ernestine. *Bridging the Gulf: Work with Russian Jews and Other Newcomers*. New York: Immigrant Publication Society, 1917.

Rosenfield, Patricia. "Frederick P. Keppel: A Grantmaking Vision Unfolds." Carnegie Corporation of New York. N.p. carnegie.org.

Rotker, Susana. *La invención de la crónica*. Buenos Aires: Ediciones Letra Buena, 1992.

Rowell, Charles Henry. Interview with Howard Dodson Jr. *Callaloo* 38: 1 (2015): 119–138.

Roy-Féquière, Magali. *Women, Creole Identity, and Intellectual Life in Early Twentieth-Century Puerto Rico*. Philadelphia: Temple UP, 2004.

Ruiz Belvis, Segundo, José Julián Acosta, Francisco Mariano Quiñones, *Proyecto para la abolición de la esclavitud en Puerto Rico*. San Juan: Instituto de Cultura Puertorriqueña, 1969.

Said, Edward W. *Representations of the Intellectual: The 1993 Reith Lectures*. 1994. New York: Vintage, 1996.

Sánchez González, Lisa. "Arturo Alfonso Schomburg: A Transamerican Intellectual." *African Roots/American Cultures: Africa in the Creation of the Americas*. Ed. Sheila S. Walker. Lanham, MD: Rowman and Littlefield, 2001. 139–152.

———. *Boricua Literature: A Literary History of the Puerto Rican Diaspora*. New York: New York UP, 2001.

——. *The Stories I Read to Children: The Life and Writing of Pura Belpré, the Legendary Storyteller, Children's Author, and New York Public Librarian.* New York: Centro, 2013.

Sánchez Korrol, Virginia E. "For the Freedom of Enslaved Infants in Puerto Rico." *Huffington Post*, February 5, 2014: N.p.

——. *From Colonia to Community: The History of Puerto Ricans in New York City.* 1983. Berkeley: U of California P, 1994.

Santiago, Esmeralda. *Conquistadora.* New York: Knopf, 2011.

Scarano, Francisco A. *Puerto Rico: Cinco siglos de historia.* San Juan: McGraw-Hill, 1993.

Schmidt-Nowara, Christopher. *Empire and Anti-Slavery: Spain, Cuba, and Puerto Rico, 1833–1874.* Pittsburgh: U of Pittsburgh P, 1999.

Schomburg, Arthur A. "Creole-criollo." Ed. Piñeiro de Rivera 137–138.

——. "The Economic Contribution by the Negro to America." *Papers of the American Negro Academy Read at the Nineteenth Annual Meeting December 28–29, 1915.* Washington, DC: American Negro Academy, 1916. 49–62.

——. "General Antonio Maceo." Ed. Piñeiro de Rivera 175–180.

——. "General Evaristo Estenoz." Ed. Piñeiro de Rivera 73–75.

——. "In Quest of Juan Pareja." Ed. Piñeiro de Rivera 139–143.

——. "José Campeche 1752–1809." Ed. Piñeiro de Rivera 201–208.

——. "Masonic Truths: A Letter and a Document." Ed. Piñeiro de Rivera 101–107.

——. "My Trip to Cuba in Quest of Negro Books." Ed. Piñeiro de Rivera 181–187.

——. "The Negro Brotherhood of Sevilla." Ed. Piñeiro de Rivera 145–151.

——. "The Negro Digs up His Past." *The New Negro.* Ed. Alain Locke. 1925. New York: Atheneum, 1992. 231–237.

——. "Negroes in Sevilla." Ed. Piñeiro de Rivera 153–159.

——. "Notes on Panama and the Negro." Ed. Piñeiro de Rivera 160–168.

——. "Plácido: An Epoch in Cuba's Struggle for Liberty." Ed. Flor Piñeiro de Rivera 59–67.

——. "Racial Integrity: A Plea for the Establishment of a Chair of Negro History in Our Schools and Colleges, etc." *Negro Society for Historical Research, Occasional Papers No. 3.* Yonkers: August Valentine Bernier, 1913. 2–19.

——. "West Indian Composers and Musicians." Ed. Piñeiro de Rivera 127–135.

Skocpol, Theda, Ariane Liazos, and Marshall Ganz, *What a Mighty Power We Can Be: African American Fraternal Groups and the Struggle for Racial Equality.* Princeton: Princeton UP, 2008.

Scott, David. *Refashioning Futures: Criticism after Postcoloniality.* Princeton: Princeton UP, 1999.

Scott, Rebecca J. *Slave Emancipation in Cuba: the Transition to Free Labor, 1860–1899*. 1985. Pittsburgh: U of Pittsburgh P, 2000.

Sekula, Allan. "The Body and the Archive." *October* 39 (1986): 3–64.

Seraile, William. *Bruce Grit: The Black Nationalist Writings of John Edwards Bruce*. Knoxville: U of Tennessee P, 2003.

Sesay, Chernoh M. Jr. "Emancipation and the Social Order of Black Freemasonry, 1775–1800." *All Men Free and Brethren: Essays on the History of African American Freemasonry*. Ed. Peter P. Hinks and Stephen Kantrowitz. Ithaca: Cornell UP, 2013. 21–39.

"A Short History of Carnegie Corporation's Library Program." *Carnegie Reporter* 2: 3 (2003): n.p. carnegie.org.

Sinnette, Elinor Des Verney. "Arthur Alfonso Schomburg (1874–1938), Black Bibliophile and Collector." *Black Bibliophiles and Collectors: Preservers of Black History*. Ed. Elinor Des Verney Sinnette, W. Paul Coates, and Thomas C. Battle. Washington, DC: Howard UP, 1990. 35–45.

———. *Arthur Alfonso Schomburg: Black Bibliophile and Collector*. Detroit: New York Public Library and Wayne State UP, 1989.

Sinnette, Elinor Des Verney, W. Paul Coates, and Thomas C. Battle, eds. *Black Bibliophiles and Collectors: Preservers of Black History*. Washington, DC: Howard UP, 1990.

Smith, Erin A. "Jessie Redmon Fauset." *Harlem Renaissance Lives*. Ed. Henry Louis Gates Jr. and Evelyn Brooks Higginbotham. New York: Oxford University Press, 2009. 196–198.

Smith, Shawn Michelle. "Guest Editor's Introduction: Visual Culture and Race." *MELUS Journal* 39: 2 (2014): 1–11.

Spariosu, Mihai. *Modernism and Exile: Liminality and the Utopia Imagination*. New York: Palgrave Macmillan, 2014.

Stephens, Michelle Ann. "'All Look Alike in Habana': Archaeologies of Blackness across Eric Walrond's Archipelago." *Eric Walrond: The Critical Heritage*. Ed. Louis J. Parascandola and Carl A. Wade. Kingston: U of West Indies P, 2012. 57–71.

———. *Black Empire: The Masculine Global Imaginary of Caribbean Intellectuals in the United States, 1914–1962*. Durham and London: Duke UP, 2005.

Stoler, Ann Laura. "Colonial Archives and the Arts of Governance: On the Content in the Form." *Refiguring the Archive*. Ed. Carolyn Hamilton. Norwell, MA: Kluwer Academic Publishers, 2002.

Suárez Findlay, Eileen J. *Imposing Decency: The Politics of Sexuality and Race in Puerto Rico, 1870–1920*. Durham and London: Duke UP, 1999.

Summers, Martin. "'Arguing for Our Race': The Politics of Nonrecognition and the Public Nature of the Black Masonic Archive." *All Men Free and Brethren: Essays on the History of African American Freemasonry*. Ed. Peter P. Hinks and Stephen Kantrowitz. Ithaca and London: Cornell UP, 2013. 155–174.

———. *Manliness and Its Discontents: The Black Middle Class and the Transformation of Masculinity, 1900–1930*. Chapel Hill and London: U of North Carolina P, 2004.

Taylor, Diana. *The Archive and the Repertoire: Performing Cultural Memory in the Americas*. Durham and London: Duke UP, 2003.

Thomas, Lorrin. *Puerto Rican Citizen: History and Political Identity in Twentieth-Century New York City*. Chicago and London: U of Chicago P, 2010.

Tinajero, Araceli. *El Lector: A History of the Cigar Factory Reader*. Trans. Judith E. Gransberg. Austin: U of Texas P, 2010.

Torres-Saillant, Silvio. "Divisible Blackness: Reflections on Heterogeneity and Racial Identity." *The Afro-Latin@ Reader: History and Culture in the United States*. Ed. Juan Flores and Miriam Jiménez Román. Durham: Duke UP, 2010. 453–466.

———. "The Tribulations of Blackness: Stages in Dominican Racial Identity." *Dominican Republic Literature and Culture*. Spec. issue of *Callaloo* 23: 3 (2000)" 1086–1111.

Trigo, Benigno. *Subjects of Crisis: Race and Gender as Disease in Latin America*. Hanover and London: Wesleyan UP, 2000.

Trouillot, Michel Rolph. *Silencing the Past: Power and the Production of History*. 1995. Boston: Beacon, 2015.

Valdez, Juan R. *Tracing Dominican Identity: The Writings of Pedro Henríquez Ureña*. New York: Palgrave Macmillan, 2011.

Vega, Bernardo. *Memoirs of Bernardo Vega*. Trans. Juan Flores. New York: Monthly Review, 1984.

———. *Memorias de Bernardo Vega*. Ed. César Andreu Iglesias. 5th ed. San Juan: Ediciones Huracán, 1994.

Walker, Corey D. B. *A Noble Fight: African American Freemasonry and the Struggle for Democracy in America*. Chicago: U of Illinois P, 2008.

Wallace, Maurice O. *Constructing the Black Masculine: Identity and Ideality in African American Men's Literature and Culture, 1775–1995*. Durham and London: Duke UP, 2002.

————. and Shawn Michelle Smith. "Introduction." *Pictures and Progress: Early Photography and the Making of African American Identity*. Ed. Maurice O. Wallace. Durham and London: Duke UP, 2012. 1–17.

Wallace, Mike. "Nueva York: The Back Story. New York City and the Spanish-Speaking World from Dutch Days to the Second World War." *Nueva York, 1613–1945*. New York: New York Historical Society and Scala, 2010. 19–81.

Watkins-Owens, Irma. *Blood Relations: Caribbean Immigrants and the Harlem Community, 1900–1930*. Bloomington and Indianapolis: Indiana UP, 1996.

Weheliye, Alexander G. *Phonographies: Grooves in Sonic Afro-Modernity*. Durham and London: Duke UP, 2005.

Weiss, Nancy J. *The National Urban League 1910–1940*. New York: Oxford UP, 1974.

Wesley, Dorothy Porter, "Black Antiquarians and Bibliophiles Revisited, with a Glance at Today's Lovers of Books and Memorabilia." *Black Bibliophiles and Collectors: Preservers of Black History*. Ed. Elinor Des Verney Sinnette, W. Paul Coates, and Thomas C. Battle. Washington, DC: Howard UP, 1990. 3–20.

Wilkerson, Isabel. *The Warmth of Other Suns: The Epic Story of America's Great Migration*. New York: Random House, 2010.

Willis, Deborah, ed. *Picturing Us: African American Identity in Photography*. New York: New Press, 1994.

Willis-Brathwaite, Deborah. "They Knew Their Names." *Van Der Zee: Photographer, 1886–1983*. Ed. Roger Birt. New York: Harry N. Abrams, 1998. 8–25.

Winkiel, Laura A. "Nancy Cunard's *Negro* and the Transnational Politics of Race." *Modernism/modernity* 13: 3 (2006): 507–530.

Yochelson, Bonnie, and Daniel Czitrom, *Rediscovering Jacob Riis: Exposure Journalism and Photography in Turn-of-the-Century New York*. Chicago: U of Chicago P, 2014.

Yun, Lisa. *The Coolie Speaks: Chinese Indentured Labor and African Slaves in Cuba*. Philadelphia: Temple UP, 2008.

Zenón Cruz, Isabelo. *Narciso descubre su trasero*. 2 vols. Humacao, PR: Editorial Furidi, 1975.

INDEX

46. Whereas "afro" is wholly unsatisfying, the existence and successful usage of the prefix at least identifies that there was assimilation of these peoples—the indigenous remain without a linguistic marker in relation to *latinidad,* an indication that in the face of centuries-long campaigns in favor of *mestizaje,* we have not yet developed the language to adequately describe an assimilation that honors indigeneity and that does not result in whitening. Assimilation for the indigenous continues to be constructed of as "loss." All of these terms to some extent are unproductive because they all imply purity and authenticity, which is counterintuitive and counterproductive to how people actually live.

47. Flores and Jiménez Román 1.

48. Ibid 2.

49. Despite this assertion that "Afro-Latin@" is applicable on a hemispheric level, it is notable that the writings collected in this anthology focus solely on the United States, as López does in his study.

50. Flores and Román 2. These scholars use "@" as an attempt at inclusivity, however critics have argued that such a move reinscribes gender binaries, hence the decision of this author to use "x."

51. Ibid 3.

52. Hall 225.

53. López 4–5.

54. For an overview of the creation of this identity as well as a consideration of the impact of this new identity on Puerto Ricans in New York, see Flores (2000) 141–166. In his study of José Martí, Oscar Montero underscores that Martí used the term *latino* in the nineteenth century to mean "people from Latin America, wherever they might be: Mexico, New York, Tampa, or Key West" (2).

55. López 12.

56. Fleetwood 18.

57. Locke (1941).

58. McKay 142.

59. Johnson (2005) 449.

60. Neal 8.

61. Folder 4, Arthur Alfonso Schomburg Collection, Manuscripts, Archives and Rare Books Division, Schomburg Center of Research in Black Culture, The New York Public Library.

62. DeFrantz and Gonzalez 11.

63. Ibid.

64. Iton 195.

65. Ibid 200.

66. For two of the most popular theorizations about Caribbean identity, see Antonio Benítez-Rojo, *The Repeating Island: The Caribbean and the Postmodern Perspective* (1992) and Édouard Glissant, *Poetics of Relation* (1997).

67. Edwards (2007) 691.

68. Ibid. 690.

69. Hall 225.

70. Edwards (2003) 13.

71. Nwankwo 10.

72. Sánchez-Korrol (2014) n.p.

73. Sánchez González, "Transamerican Intellectual" 140–141.

74. Edwards (2003) 7.

75. Sinnette 35.

76. See Kutzinski 2.

77. Edwards (2003) 11–15; Kutzinski 3.

78. Lewis (1995) 783.

79. Ibid. 787.

CHAPTER 1. "PATRIA Y LIBERTAD"

All translations in this chapter are provided by the author of this project.

Sotero Figueroa closes a note, dated March 17, 1893, to Schomburg with the words *patria y libertad,* which mean "Homeland and Freedom"; Figueroa served as president of the Club Político Antillano "Borinquen." Sotero Figueroa, "Note." Reel 3 Frame 00953 Arthur A. Schomburg Papers, Jean Blackwell Hutson Research and Reference Division, Schomburg Center for Research in Black Culture, The New York Public Library. Figueroa (1851–1923) was a fellow Afro-Latino, a Puerto Rican of African descent who worked alongside Schomburg in this revolutionary club; see Edna Acosta Belén's profile of him.

1. In addition to Sinnette, Hoffnung-Garskof and Sanchez González have paid the greatest attention to this period in his life.

2. I use "creole" in accord with its Spanish definition, to mean children of Spanish immigrants born in the Americas. Schomburg himself comments on this when he writes in 1927: "The children of Spaniards who were born and reared in their possessions of Cuba, Santo Domingo, Jamaica, Mexico and Porto Rico are called to this day "criollo" to their respective countries and islands" (137).